Addison-Wesley Chemistry Laboratory Manual

Antony C. Wilbraham

Dennis D. Staley

Michael S. Matta

Addison-Wesley Publishing Company
Menlo Park, California • Reading, Massachusetts • New York
Don Mills, Ontario • Wokingham, England • Amsterdam
Bonn • Paris • Milan • Madrid • Sydney • Singapore
Tokyo • Seoul • Taipei • Mexico City • San Juan

Cover photograph: Joel Gordon

ISBN 0-201-86165- 8

6 7 8 9 10 - ML - 99 98

Contents

To the Student

Chemistry is exciting! Each day in the laboratory you are given the opportunity to confront the unknown, and to understand it. Each experiment holds many secrets. Look hard and you may see them. Work hard and you can solve them.

In this class, you are given the opportunity to do what scientists do. You can wonder how things work, ask why and how, and then try to think of ways to answer your own questions. You are given the chance to understand what is unknown to you and to many other people.

Safety

Chemistry is a laboratory science. As part of your laboratory experience, you will handle many chemical substances and manipulate specialized lab equipment. Many of these substances pose a health risk if handled improperly, while some of the laboratory equipment can cause severe injury if used improperly. This section is a guide to the safe laboratory practices you will use throughout this course.

Preparation and Safety

To get the most out of your laboratory experience, you must be well prepared for each experiment. This means that you must read the experiment thoroughly before coming to the laboratory. Make sure you have a clear idea of what the experiment is about. Be sure that you understand each step of the procedure. If you are unsure of any part of the experiment, ask your teacher for help before the laboratory begins.

Preparation is important not only to understanding, but also to safety. If you are well prepared for the laboratory, it is much less likely that an accident will occur. In the laboratory, you are responsible not only for your safety, but also for the safety of your classmates. This is all the more reason for you to take the time and make the effort to prepare for the laboratory.

Be sure to note the safety warnings listed in the Safety section of each experiment. Note that these warnings are emphasized by symbols appearing in the margins. The symbols identify those parts of the procedure that may be hazardous. In addition, be sure to observe the general safety precautions described in the safety section at the beginning of the manual. Finally, remember the most important safety advice of all: **Always wear safety goggles in the chemistry laboratory!**

Safety in the Chemistry Laboratory

Everyone who works in a chemistry laboratory should follow these safety precautions:

1. Wear safety goggles and a laboratory apron at all times.

2. Shoes must be worn in the laboratory. Avoid wearing overly bulky or loose fitting clothing. Remove any dangling jewelry.

3. Conduct only assigned experiments, and do them only when your teacher is present.

4. Know the locations of safety equipment such as eyewash fountains, fire extinguishers, emergency shower, and fire blanket. Be sure you know how to use the equipment.

5. Do not chew gum, eat, or drink in the laboratory. Never taste any chemicals. Keep your hands away from your face when working with chemicals.

6. Wash your hands with soap and water at the end of each laboratory.

7. Read all of the directions for a laboratory procedure before proceeding with the first part. Reread each instruction before you do it.

8. Notify your teacher immediately if any chemicals, such as concentrated acid or base, are spilled.

9. Report all accidents to the teacher immediately.

10. Pin back long hair and roll up loose sleeves if working with flames.

11. Do not leave a lighted burner unattended.

12. Use a hot plate, not a flame, if a flammable liquid is present.

13. Read the label on a reagent bottle carefully *before* using the chemical. After removing the chemical from the bottle, check to make sure that it is the correct chemical for that procedure.

14. To avoid contamination, do not return unused chemicals to a reagent bottle. Similarly, never put a pipet, spatula, or dropper into a reagent bottle. Instead, pour some of the reagent into a small clean beaker and use that as your supply.

15. Do not use chipped or cracked glassware.

16. When diluting an acid, *always* pour the acid slowly into water with stirring to dissipate the heat generated. **CAUTION:** *Never pour water into a concentrated acid.*

17. When heating a liquid in a test tube, turn the mouth of the test tube away from yourself and others.

18. Clean up spills and broken glass immediately. Leave your work area clean at the end of the laboratory period.

Laboratory Hazards

You should be aware of possible hazards in the laboratory and take the appropriate safety precautions. By doing so, the risks of doing chemistry can be minimized. This safety section is intended to acquaint you with the hazards that exist in the laboratory and to indicate how you can avoid these hazards. In addition, information is provided on what to do if an accident should occur.

Thermal Burns

A thermal burn can occur if you touch hot equipment or come too close to an open flame. You can prevent thermal burns by being aware that hot and cold equipment look the same. If a gas burner or hot plate has been used, some of the equipment nearby may be hot. Hold your hand near an item to feel for heat before touching it. Treat a thermal burn by *immediately* running cold water over the burned area. Continue applying the cold water until the pain is reduced. This usually takes several minutes. In addition to reducing pain, cooling the burned area also serves to speed the healing process. Greases and oils should not be used to treat burns because they tend to trap heat. Medical assistance should be sought for any serious burn. **Notify your teacher immediately if you are burned.**

Chemical Burns

A chemical burn occurs when the skin or a mucous membrane is damaged by contact with a substance. The Materials section of each exercise indicates which substances can cause chemical burns. [C] **stands for corrosive**. It indicates that the chemical can cause severe burns. [I] **stands for irritant**. It indicates that the chemical can irritate the skin and the membranes of the eye, nose, throat, and lungs. Chemicals that are marked [C] or [I] should be treated with special care. Chemical burns can be severe. Permanent damage to mucous membranes can occur despite the best efforts to rinse a chemical from the affected area.

The best defense against chemical burns is *prevention.* **Without exception, wear safety goggles during all phases of the laboratory period—even during clean-up.** Should any chemical splash in your eye, immediately use a continuous flow of running water to flush your eye for a period of 20 minutes. Call for help. If you wear contact lenses, remove them immediately. This is especially crucial if the chemical involved is an acid or base. It can concentrate under the lens and cause extensive damage. Wear a laboratory apron and close-toed shoes (no sandals) to protect other areas of your body. If corrosive chemicals should contact your exposed skin, wash the affected area with water for several minutes.

An additional burn hazard exists when concentrated acids or bases are mixed with water. The heat released in mixing these chemicals with water can cause the mixture to boil, spattering corrosive chemical. The heat can also cause nonpyrex containers to break.

To avoid these hazards, follow these instructions: Always add acid or base to water, very slowly and with stirring; never the reverse. One way to remember this critical advice is to think of the phrase, "pouring acid into water is doing what you ought-er."

Cuts from Glass

Cuts occur most often when thermometers or pieces of glass tubing are forced into rubber stoppers. Prevent cuts by using the correct technique for this procedure. The hole should be lubricated with glycerol or water to facilitate the movement of the glass tubing. The glass should not be gripped directly with the hands, but rather, by means of paper towels. The towels will protect your hands if the glass should break. Use a gentle twisting motion to move the tube smoothly into the stopper.

Avoid cuts from other sources by discarding chipped and cracked glassware according to your teacher's instructions. If you should receive a minor cut, allow it to bleed for a short time. Wash the injured area under cold running water, and notify your teacher. Serious cuts and deep puncture wounds require immediate medical help. Notify your teacher immediately. While waiting for assistance, control the bleeding by applying pressure with the finger tips or by firmly pressing with a clean towel.

Fire

A fire may occur if chemicals are mixed improperly or if flammable materials come too close to a burner flame or hot plate. When using this equipment, prevent fires by tying back long hair and loose fitting clothing. Do not use a burner when flammable chemicals are present. **Flammable chemicals are designated with the symbol** [F] in the materials section for each exercise. Use a hot plate as a heat source instead of a burner when flammable chemicals are present.

If hair or clothing should catch fire, DO NOT run, because running fans a fire. Drop to the floor and roll slowly to smother the flames. Shout for help. If another person is the victim, get a fire blanket to smother the flames. If a shower is nearby, help the victim to use it.

In case of a fire on a laboratory bench, turn off all accessible gas outlets and unplug all accessible appliances. A fire in a container may be put out by covering the container with a nonflammable object. It could also be smothered by covering the burning object with a damp cloth. If not, call for a fire extinguisher. Spray the base of the fire with foam from the extinguisher. **CAUTION:** *Never direct the jet of a fire extinguisher into a* *person's face.* Use a fire blanket instead. If a fire is not extinguished quickly, leave the laboratory. Crawl to the door if necessary to avoid the smoke. Do not return to the laboratory.

Poisoning

Many of the chemicals used in the experiments in this manual are toxic. **Toxic chemicals are identified in the materials sections with the symbol** [T].

You should do several things to prevent poisoning. Never eat, chew gum or drink in the laboratory. Do not touch chemicals. Clean up spills. Keep your hands away from your face. In this way you will prevent chemicals from reaching your hands, mouth, nose, or eyes.

In some cases, the detection of an odor is used to indicate that a chemical reaction has taken place. It is important to note, however, that many gases are toxic when inhaled. If you must detect an odor, use your hand to waft some of the gas toward your nose. Sniff the gas instead of taking a deep breath. This will minimize the amount of gas sampled.

Safety Symbols

Take appropriate precautions whenever any of the following safety symbols appear in an experiment.

Eye Hazard
- Wear safety goggles.

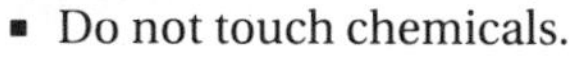

Corrosive Substance Hazard
- Do not touch chemicals.

Fire Hazard
- Tie back hair and loose clothing.
- Do not use a burner near flammable materials.

Poison Hazard
- Do not chew gum, drink, or eat in the laboratory.
- Keep your hands away from your face.

Electrical Hazard
- Use care when using electrical equipment.

Inhalation Hazard
- Avoid inhaling this substance.

Thermal Burn Hazard
- Do not touch hot equipment.

Breakage Hazard
- Do not use chipped or cracked glassware.
- Do not heat the bottom of a test tube.

Disposal Hazard
- Dispose of this chemical only as directed.

Radiation Hazard
- Use only calibrated and sealed sources.

Emergency Procedures

Report any injury, accident, or spill to your teacher immediately. Know the location of the closest eye wash fountain, fire blanket, fire extinguisher, and shower.

Situation	Safe Response
Burns	Immediately flush with cool water until the burning sensation subsides.
Fainting	Provide fresh air (for instance, open a window). Move the person so that the head is lower than the rest of the body. If breathing stops, use artificial resuscitation.
Fire	Turn off all gas outlets. Unplug all appliances. Use a fire blanket or fire extinguisher to smother the fire. **CAUTION:** Do not cut off a person's air supply.
Eye Injury	Immediately flush the eye with running water. Remove contact lenses. Do not allow the eye to be rubbed if a foreign object is present in the eye.
Minor Cuts	Allow to bleed briefly. Wash with soap and water.
Poisoning	Note what substance was responsible. Alert teacher immediately.
Spills on Skin	Flush with water.

Equipment

Working in the chemistry laboratory requires the use of a wide variety of specialized laboratory equipment. This section provides an illustrated listing of the equipment required in this course. Also provided is a brief description of each piece of equipment and an inventory list so you can keep track of the equipment assigned to you.

Student Equipment

At the beginning of the year, prepare a table similar to the one shown on the following page and copy it into your laboratory notebook. As the year progresses, record any changes in your equipment inventory in this table in your notebook.

Item	**Quantity Checked In**	**Quantity Checked Out**	**Breakage**
beaker, 100 mL			
beaker, 250 mL			
beaker, 400 mL			
ceramic plate			
crucible, with cover			
crucible tongs			
dropper pipet (eye dropper)			
evaporating dish			
flask, Erlenmeyer, 125 mL			
flask, Erlenmeyer, 250 mL			
forceps			
funnel			
graduated cylinder, 10 mL			
graduated cylinder, 25 mL			
graduated cylinder, 100 mL			
laboratory apron			
mortar and pestle			
safety goggles			
screw clamp or pinch clamp			
spatula, scoopula			
stirring rod and policeman			
test tube, 13 × 100 mm (small)			
test tube, 20 × 150 mm (medium)			
test tube holder			
thermometer (–10°C to 110°C)			
triangle			
watch glass			
wire gauze			

Laboratory Equipment

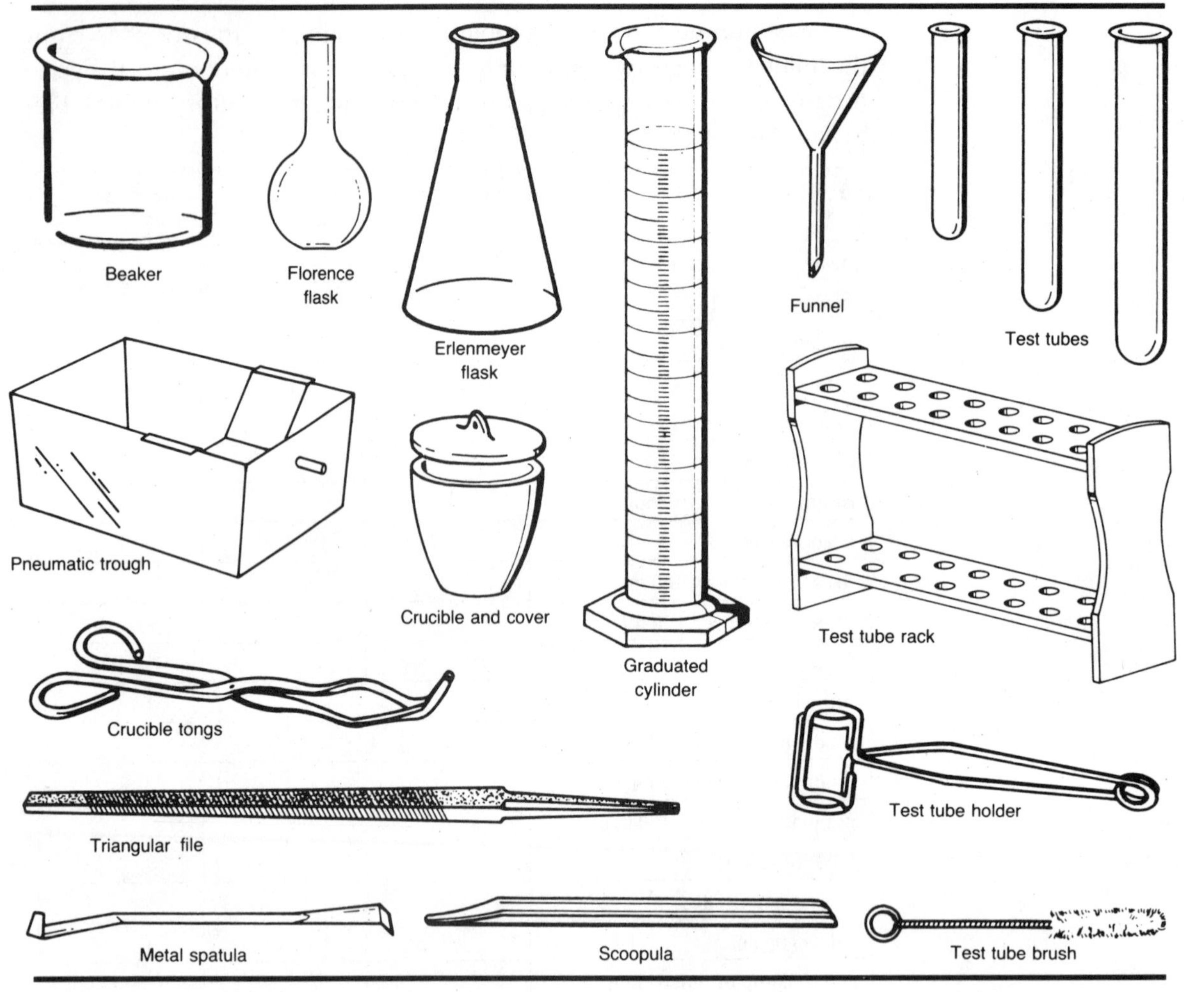

Beaker: glass or plastic; common sizes are 50 mL, 100 mL, 250 mL, 400 mL; glass beakers may be heated.
Florence flask: glass, common sizes are 125 mL, 250 mL, 500 mL, may be heated, used in making and for storing solutions.
Erlenmeyer flask: glass, common sizes are 100 mL, 250 mL; may be heated, used in titrations.
Graduated cylinder: glass or plastic, common sizes are 10 mL, 50 mL, 100 mL, used to measure approximate volumes; must not be heated.
Funnel: glass or plastic, common size holds 12.5-cm diameter filter paper.
Test tubes: glass, common sizes small (13 mm × 100 mm), medium (20 mm × 150 mm), large (25 mm × 200 mm), may be heated.
Pneumatic trough: galvanized container with shelf, used in experiments where a gas is collected.
Crucible and cover: porcelain, used to heat small amounts of solid substances at high temperatures.
Test tube rack: wood or plastic, holds test tubes in a vertical position.
Crucible tongs: iron or nickel, used to pick up and hold small items.
Triangular file: metal, used to scratch glass tubing prior to breaking to desired length.
Test tube holder: spring metal, used to hold test tubes or glass tubing.
Spatula, scoopula: metal or porcelain; used to transfer solid chemicals; the scoopula has a larger capacity.
Test tube brush: bristles with wire handle, used to scrub small diameter glassware.

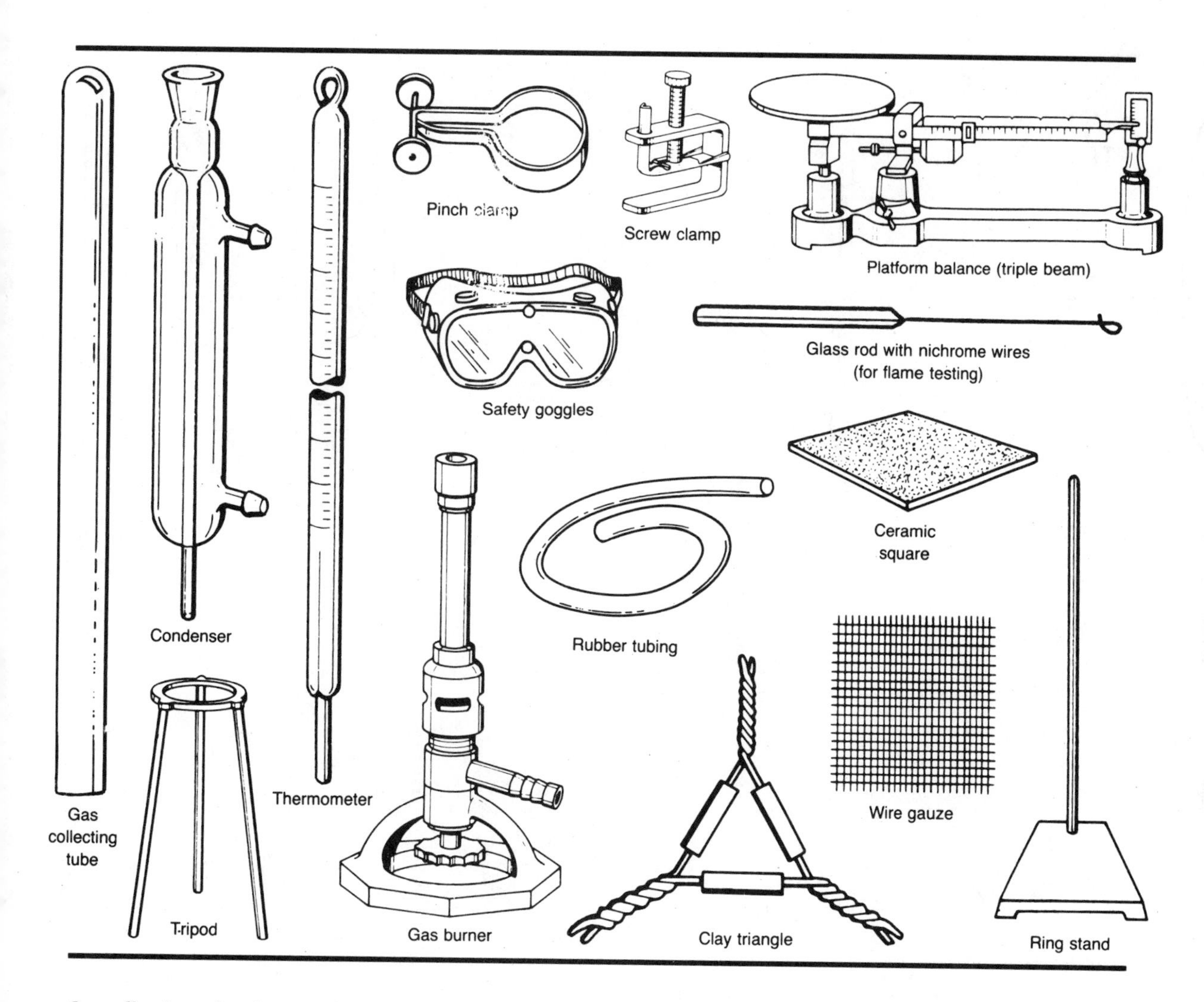

Gas collecting tube: glass; marked in mL intervals; used to measure gas volumes.
Condenser: glass; used in distillation procedures.
Thermometer: mercury in glass, common range –10°C to 110°C.
Screw clamp, pinch clamp: metal, used to block off rubber tubing.
Platform balance: also known as a triple beam balance.
Safety goggles: plastic; must be worn at all times while working in the laboratory.
Glass rod with nichrome wire: used in flame tests.
Tripod: iron, used to support containers of chemicals above the flame of a burner.

Gas burner: constructed of metal; connected to a gas supply with rubber tubing; used to heat chemicals (dry or in solution) in beakers, test tubes, and crucibles.
Rubber tubing: used to connect apparatus so as to transfer liquids or gases.
Ceramic square: used under hot apparatus or glassware.
Clay triangle: wire frame with porcelain supports, used to support a crucible.
Wire gauze: used to spread the heat of a burner flame.
Ringstand: metal rod fixed upright in a heavy metal base; has many uses as a support.
Plastic wash bottle: flexible plastic, squeeze sides to dispense water.

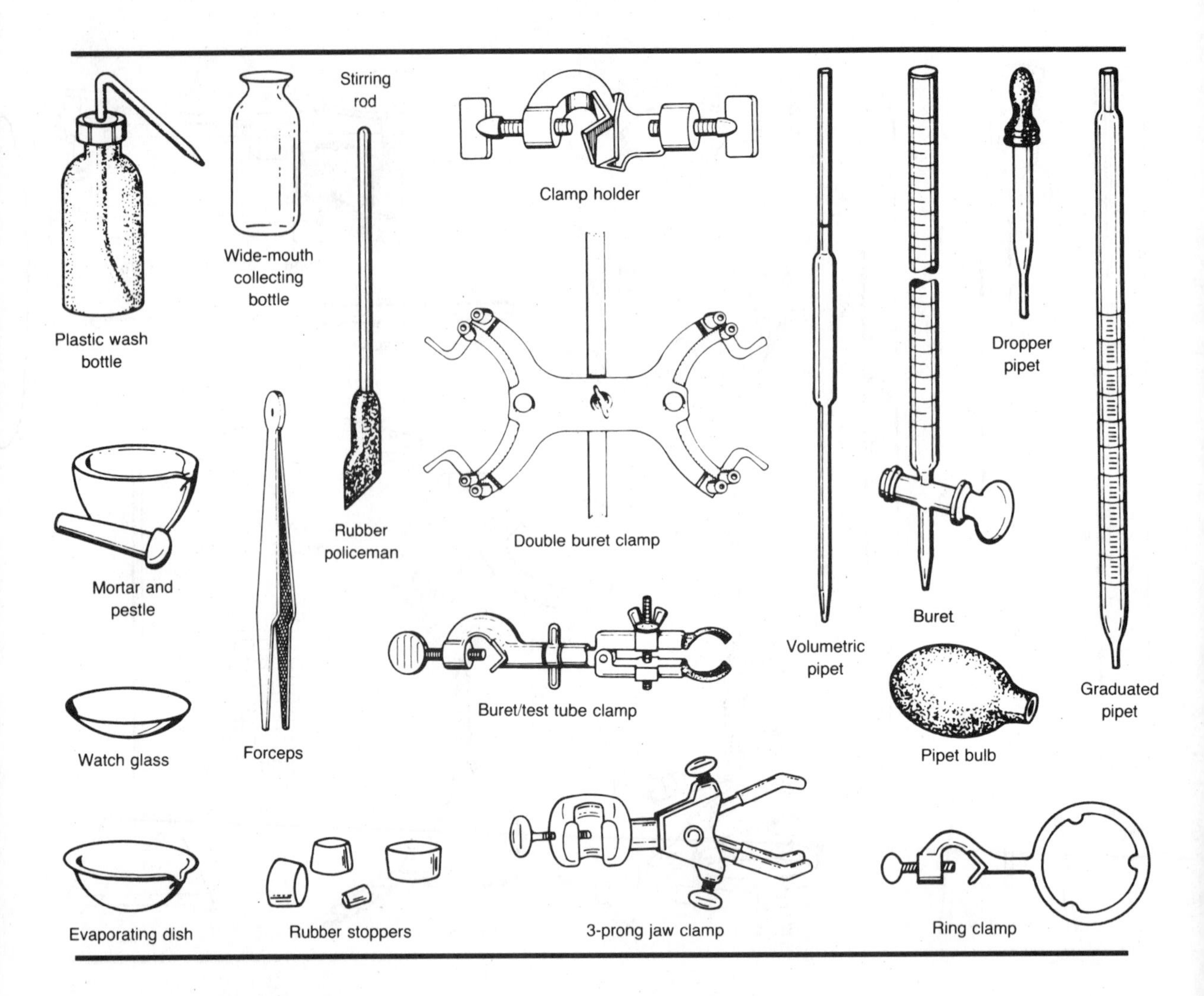

Wide-mouth bottle: glass, used with pneumatic trough.
Stirring rod and rubber policeman: glass with rubber sleeve; used to stir, assist in pouring liquids, and for removing precipitates from a container.
Clamps: the following types of clamps may be fastened to support apparatus: buret/test-tube clamp, clamp holder, double buret clamp, ring clamp, 3-pronged jaw clamp.
Volumetric pipet: glass, common sizes are 10 mL, 25 mL, used to measure solution volumes accurately, must not be heated.
Buret: glass; common sizes are 25 mL, and 50 mL; used to measure volumes of solutions in titrations.
Dropper pipet: glass tip with rubber bulb; used to transfer small volumes of liquid.
Graduated pipet: glass, common sizes are 10 mL, 25 mL; used to measure solution volumes; less accurate than a volumetric pipet.
Mortar and pestle: porcelain, may be used to grind crystals and lumpy chemicals to a powder.
Watch glass: glass, used to cover an evaporating dish or beaker.
Forceps: metal, used to hold or pick up small objects.
Pipet bulb: rubber, used in filling a pipet with a solution, a pipet must never be filled by mouth.
Evaporating dish: porcelain, used to contain small volumes of liquid being evaporated.
Rubber stoppers: several sizes.

Laboratory Techniques

Working in the chemistry laboratory, you will be handling potentially dangerous substances and performing unfamiliar tasks. This section provides you with a guide to the safe laboratory techniques needed in this course. While performing experiments throughout the year, refer back to this section any time you are unsure of proper laboratory techniques.

Pouring Liquids

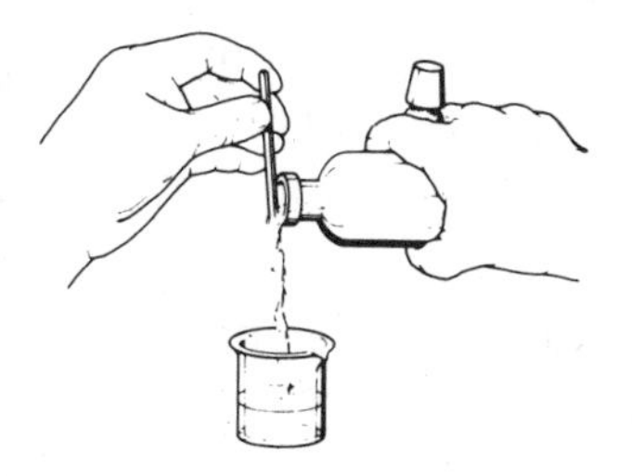

Figure 1 *Pouring from a reagent bottle into a beaker.*

- Always read the label on a reagent bottle before using its contents.
- Always wear safety goggles when handling chemicals.
- Never touch chemicals with your hands.
- Never return unused chemicals to their original containers. To avoid waste, do not take excessive amounts of reagents.

Follow this procedure when pouring liquids:

1. Use the back of your fingers to remove the stopper from a reagent bottle. Hold the stopper between your fingers until the transfer of liquid is complete. Do not place the stopper on your workbench.

2. Grasp the container from which you are pouring with the palm of your hand covering the label.

3a. When you are transferring a liquid to a test tube or measuring cylinder, the container should be held at eye level. Pour the liquid slowly until the correct volume has been transferred.

3b. When you are pouring a liquid from a reagent bottle into a beaker, the reagent should be poured slowly down a glass stirring rod (Figure 1). When you are transferring a liquid from one beaker to another, you can hold the stirring rod and beaker in one hand.

Filtering a Mixture

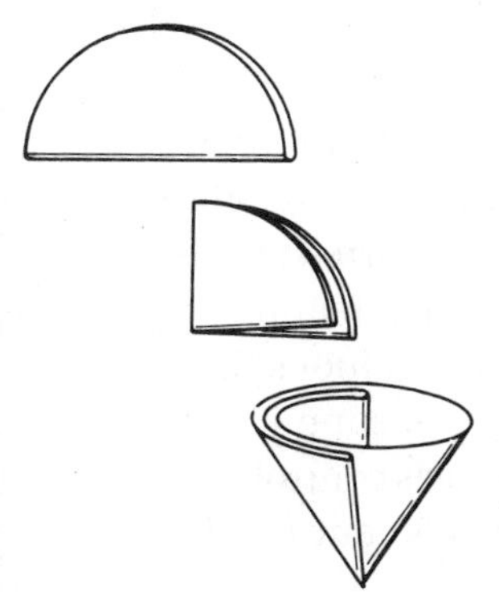

Figure 2 *Folding the filter paper.*

Sometimes it is necessary to separate a solid (for example, a precipitate) from a liquid. The most common method of separating such a mixture is filtration.

1. Fold a filter paper circle in half and then quarters. Open the folded paper to form a cone with one thickness of paper on one side and three thicknesses on the other (Figure 2).

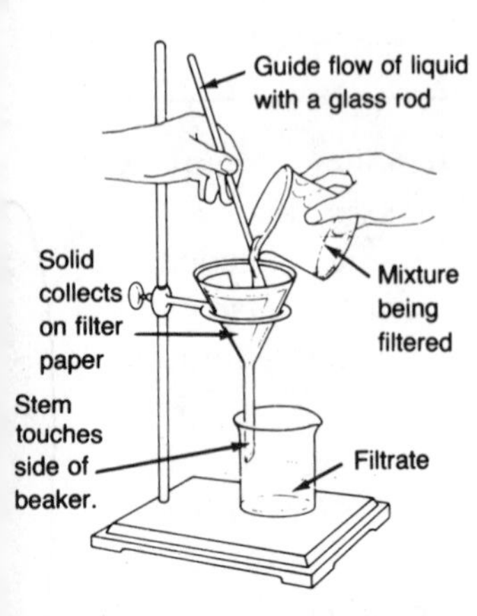

Figure 3 *Filtration assembly.*

2. Put the paper cone in a filter funnel. Place the funnel in an iron ring clamped to a ring stand. Moisten the filter paper with a small volume of distilled water, and gently press the paper against the sides of the funnel to give a good fit. (If the correct size of filter paper has been used, the top edge of the cone will be just below the rim of the filter funnel.)

3. Place a beaker beneath the funnel to collect the filtrate. The tip of the funnel should touch the inside surface of the beaker and extend about one inch below the rim (Figure 3).

4. Decant the liquid from the solid (precipitate) by pouring it down a glass stirring rod into the funnel. Be careful to keep the liquid below the top edge of the cone of filter paper at all times; the liquid must not overflow. Finally, use a jet of distilled water from a wash bottle to wash the solid (precipitate) into the filter.

5. When the filtration is complete, wash the solid residue on the filter paper with distilled water to remove traces of solvent. Dry the solid.

6. If the filtrate contains a dissolved salt it may be recovered by evaporation if desired.

Using a Gas Burner

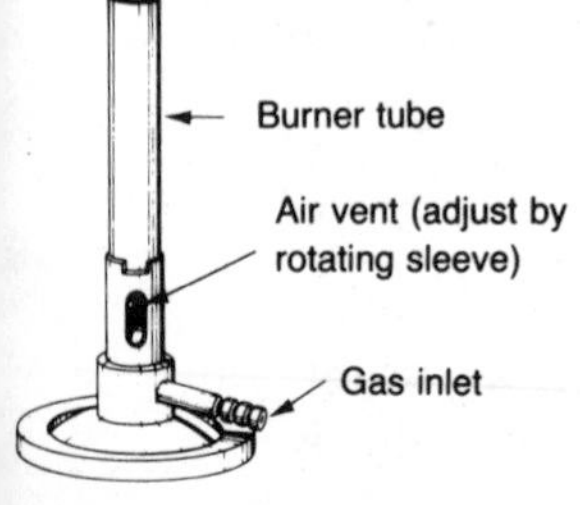

Bunsen burner

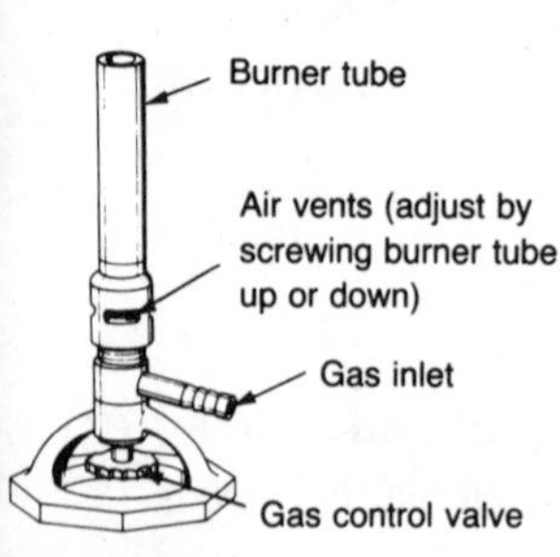

Tirrell burner

Figure 4 *Gas burners.*

Laboratory gas burners produce various kinds of flames when different mixtures of gas and air are burned. The two most common models are the Bunsen burner and the Tirrell burner. Both have adjustable air vents; the Tirrell burner also has a gas control valve in its base (Figure 4).

1. Examine your laboratory burner. Determine which model you have.

2. Connect the burner to the gas supply with rubber tubing.

3. Close the air vents. (If your model is a Tirrell burner, also close the gas control valve at the base of the burner.)

4. Hold a lighted match at the top of the burner tube and turn on the gas supply by opening the main gas supply valve located on top of the nozzle to which you attached the hose. (If your model is a Tirrell burner, open the gas control valve at the base approximately $\frac{1}{2}$ turn after opening the main gas supply valve.) You should get a yellow or luminous flame (Figure 5). When a Tirrell burner is used, the main gas supply valve should be opened fully and the gas flow regulated by the gas control valve at the base of the burner. Gas supply to a Bunsen burner is controlled by the main gas valve.

5. Open the air vents slowly, to admit more air into the flame, to produce a light blue (nonluminous) cone-shaped flame. If the flame "blows out" after lighting, the gas supply should be reduced.

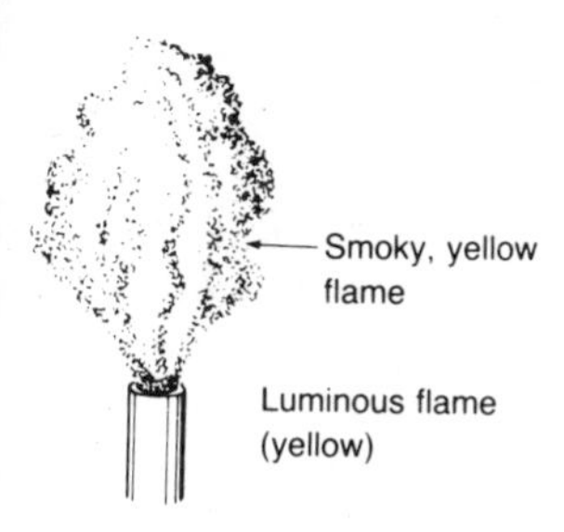

a. air vents closed

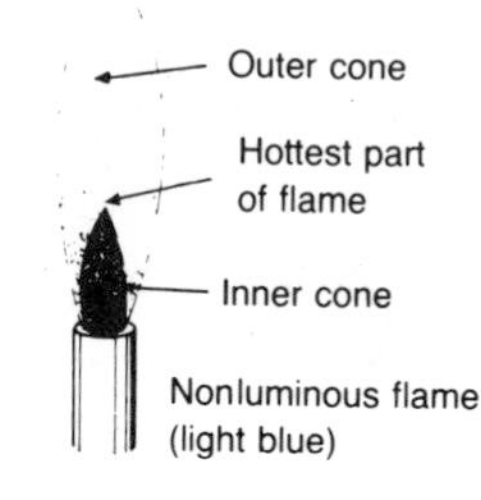

b. air vents open

Figure 5 *Flame characteristics.*

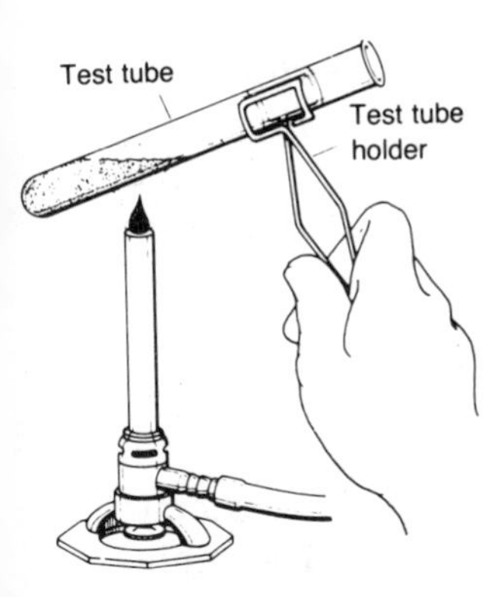

Figure 6 *Heating a liquid in a test tube.*

6. Adjust the air vents and gas supply to produce the desired size of flame. For most laboratory work, the blue inner cone of the flame should be about one inch high and free of yellow color. If you want a smaller flame, close the air vent slightly and reduce the gas supply. You will learn how to control the burner flame by trial and error.

7. Turn the burner off at the main gas supply valve as soon as you have finished.

CAUTION: *Confine long hair and loose clothing when using a gas burner. Do not reach over a burner. Ensure that flammables are not being used when a burner is lit. Never leave a lit burner unattended. Know the location of fire extinguishers, the fire blanket, and safety shower.*

Heating Liquids

Heating a Liquid in a Test Tube

The correct procedure for heating liquids in the laboratory is important to laboratory safety.

1. Adjust your gas burner to give a gentle blue flame.

2. Fill a test tube one-third full with the liquid to be heated.

3. Grasp the test tube with a test-tube holder near the upper end of the tube.

4. Hold the test tube in a slanting position in the flame, and gently heat the tube a short distance below the surface of the liquid (Figure 6).

5. Shake the tube gently as it is being heated until the liquid boils or reaches the desired temperature.

CAUTION: *Never point the open end of a test tube you are heating either toward yourself or anyone working nearby. Never heat the bottom of the test tube.*

Heating a Liquid in a Beaker

Many laboratory experiments require the use of a hot-water or boiling-water bath. This procedure describes how to assemble a water bath.

1. Fasten an iron ring securely to a ring stand so that it is about two to four centimeters above the top of a gas burner placed on the ring stand base.

2. Place a 250-mL beaker one-half filled with water on a wire gauze resting on the iron ring (Figure 7).

3. Light your gas burner and adjust it to give a hot flame.

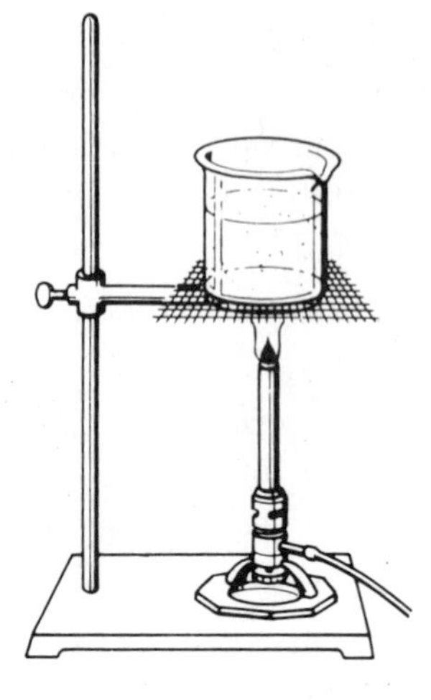

Figure 7 *Heating a liquid in a beaker.*

4. Place the burner beneath the wire gauze. For a slower rate of heating, reduce the intensity of the burner flame.

CAUTION: *Never heat plastic beakers or graduated glassware in a burner flame. Never let a boiling water bath boil dry; add water to it as necessary.*

Inserting Glass Tubing

In many experimental procedures you are required to insert a thermometer or a length of glass tubing into a hole in a rubber stopper. It is essential that you know the correct way to do this. Otherwise, serious injury may result.

1. Lubricate the end of the glass tubing with a few drops of water, washing-up liquid, glycerol, or vegetable oil.

2. Hold the glass tubing close to where it enters the hole in the rubber stopper. Protect your hands with work gloves or pieces of cloth.

3. Ease the tubing into the hole with a gentle twisting motion. Push the tubing through the hole as far as is required. Do not use force!

4. Wipe excess lubricating material from the tubing before continuing with the experiment.

5. If the glass tubing is to be removed from the stopper, it should be done immediately after the experiment is completed.

CAUTION: *The end of the glass tubing should be fire-polished or smoothed with emery cloth before being inserted into a rubber stopper. Do not try to bend the glass tubing—it will break. Ensure that the palm of the hand holding the rubber stopper is not in line with the emerging glass tube.*

Measuring Mass

In many experiments you are required to determine the mass of a chemical used or produced in a reaction. An object's mass is determined by measuring it on a balance. When we determine the mass of an object, we are comparing its mass with a known mass. In the SI the base unit of mass is the kilogram.

There are many types of laboratory balances. The one used most frequently in schools is the centigram balance (Figure 8). The following general rules apply to the use of all balances:

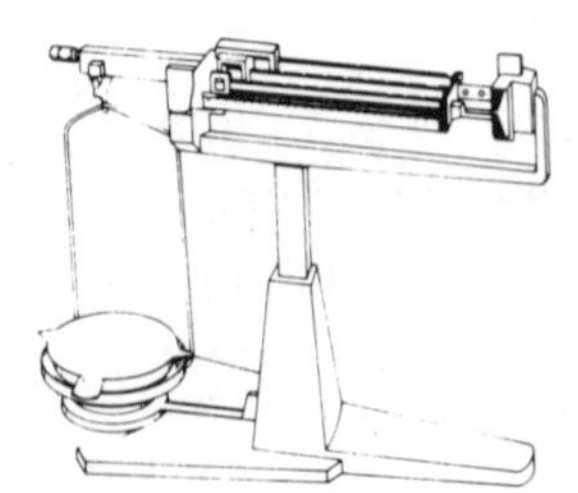

Figure 8 *The centigram balance.*

- Check the balance before you start weighing. The balance pan should be empty and clean, and all masses (or dials) should be set on zero. The balance must be level. Check the bubble level on the base. See your teacher if you need assistance with checking your balance.

- Objects to be weighed directly on the balance pan must be clean, dry, and at room temperature. Solid chemicals and liquids must never be put directly on the balance pan. Liquid samples should be placed in beakers or sealed containers. Solid chemicals can be conveniently placed in beakers, disposable plastic weighing boats, or on 10-cm squares made of glossy paper.
- The balance is a precision instrument that must be handled with care. To avoid damaging it, always be sure that the balance is in an arrested position when objects are placed on or removed from the pan. Always turn all dials slowly.
- Never move or jar either a balance or the balance table.
- If you spill a chemical on or near the balance, clean it up immediately. If in doubt, inform your teacher. A camel-hair brush is usually provided to wipe minute traces of solid from the balance pan before you use it.
- Never attempt to weigh an object with a mass greater than the maximum capacity of the balance.
- When you finish weighing, return all the masses to zero, and make sure the balance pan is clean.

Do not attempt to use a balance until your teacher has demonstrated the proper technique.

Using a Centigram Balance

1. Examine a centigram balance. The maximum capacity for this balance is 300 g and the sensitivity (limit of detection) is 0.01 g. The balance has four beams and four riders.

2. Move all the riders to their zero points (to the left side of their respective beams). Ensure that the riders rest in the notches on the beams.

3. Check to see that the beam is balanced. The pointer should move the same distance above and below the zero line on the scale or come to rest at the zero line. Use the zero adjustment screw if necessary. Always zero the balance before you begin any weighing. When the balance has been checked and adjusted, you are ready to begin weighing.

4. Place the object whose mass is to be determined on the pan. (It must be dry and at room temperature [see the general rules].)

5. Slide the riders gently along the beams, one at a time, beginning with the largest. If a beam is notched, be sure that the rider is in a notch. Note that all the beams have notches except the one carrying the smallest rider. When the added masses (the positions of the riders) is equal to the mass of the object on the pan, then the pointer will be on the zero line. It may also swing equal distances above and below the zero line.

6. To record the mass of the object, sum the masses indicated by the positions of the riders on their respective beams.

7. Return all riders to zero and remove your sample. Make sure that the balance pan is left clean.

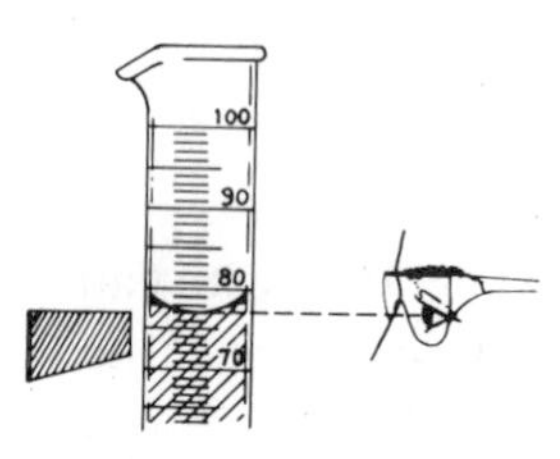

Figure 9 *Reading volume in a graduated cylinder.*

Measuring Volume

Volume measurements are important in many experimental procedures. Sometimes volume measurements must be accurate; other times they can be approximate. Most volume measures in the laboratory are made using equipment calibrated in milliliters. Although some beakers have graduation marks, these marks are designed only for quick, rough estimates of volume. Accurate volumes must be measured with pipets, burets, or volumetric flasks.

Using a Graduated Cylinder

Half-fill a 100-mL graduated cylinder with water, and set the cylinder on your laboratory bench. Examine the surface of the water. Notice how the surface curves upwards where the water contacts the cylinder walls. This curved surface is called a meniscus.

A volume measurement is always read at the bottom of the meniscus, with your eye at the same level as the liquid surface. To make the meniscus more visible, you can place your finger or a dark piece of paper behind and just below the meniscus while making the reading (Figure 9).

Graduated cylinders are available in many capacities. The 100-mL cylinder is marked in 1-mL divisions, and volumes can be estimated to the nearest 0.1 mL. The last digit in these measurements is therefore significant but uncertain.

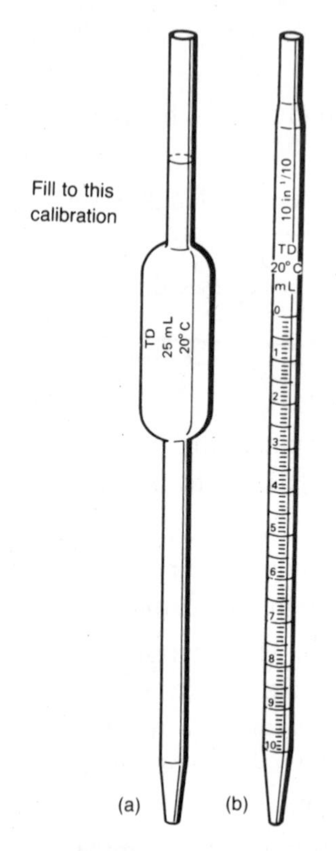

Figure 10 *The volumetric pipet (a) and the measuring or graduated pipet (b).*

Using a Pipet

A pipet is used to accurately measure and deliver volumes of liquids. Two types are in common use: volumetric pipets and graduated or measuring pipets (Figure 10). The use of a volumetric pipet will be described. A volumetric pipet has a single calibration mark and delivers the volume printed on the bulb of the pipet at the temperature specified. (A graduated pipet has calibrations along the length of the pipet.) Volumes can be measured more accurately with a volumetric pipet than with a graduated pipet.

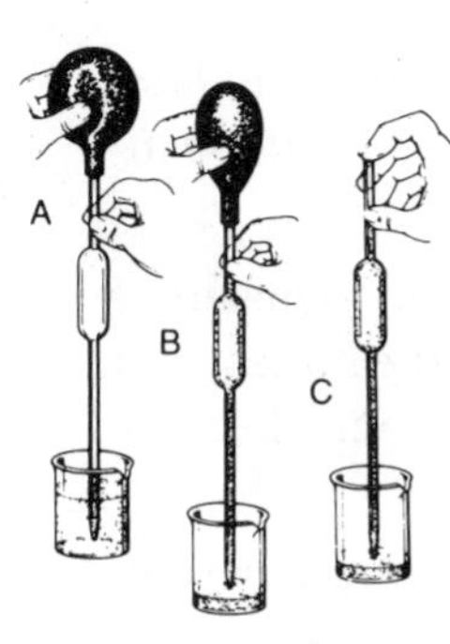

1. Place the tip of the pipet below the surface of the liquid to be dispensed.

2. Compress a pipet bulb and press the hole in the bulb against the upper end of the pipet. **CAUTION:** *Never fill a pipet by applying suction with your mouth.* Never push the pipet bulb over the end of the pipet.

3. Slowly release pressure on the bulb so that liquid is drawn into the pipet to a level about 2 cm above the calibration mark.

4. Remove the bulb and simultaneously place your index finger over the end of the pipet. If you are right-handed, you should hold the pipet in your right hand and the pipet bulb in your left (Figure 11).

5. Keep your index finger pressed firmly against the end. Withdraw the pipet from the liquid, and carefully wipe the outside of the stem with a paper towel.

6. Slowly reduce the pressure on your finger to allow the excess liquid to drain into a waste receiver, until the bottom of the meniscus is at the calibration mark.

7. Now, deliver the remaining liquid in the pipet into the designated receiver. When releasing liquid from a volumetric pipet, let it drain completely. Wait 20 seconds, then touch the pipet tip to the side of the flask or surface of the liquid. This action will remove some, but not all, of the liquid in the tip. The pipet delivers the stated volume when this procedure is followed. A small amount of liquid remains in the tip. Do not blow this out into your receiver.

Figure 11 *Filling and emptying a pipet.*

Glassworking

Cutting and Fire Polishing

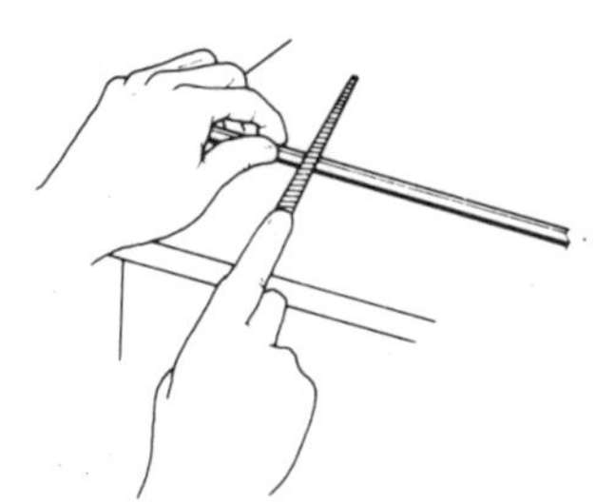

Figure 12

1. Place the glass tubing or glass rod on a flat surface (such as the laboratory bench).

2. Hold the glass tightly with one hand close to the area to be cut.

3. Using a firm stroke, make a *single* deep scratch with a triangular file (Figure 12).

CAUTION: *Do not use a sawing motion or repeated scratching.*

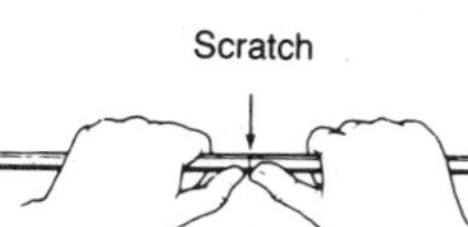

Figure 13

4. Grasp the glass in both hands, with the scratch facing away from you and both thumbs directly behind the scratch (Figure 13).

5. Push firmly with the thumbs and pull with your fingers. The glass should snap with a clean break.

Correctly fire polished

Tube closed up (heated too much)

Figure 14

Wing top on burner

Figure 15

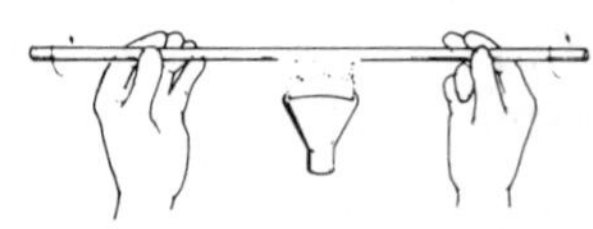

Heating glass tubing over a wing top prior to bending

Figure 16

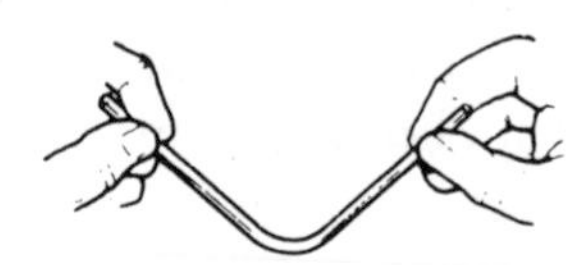

Bend and hold at desired angle

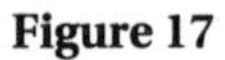

Figure 17

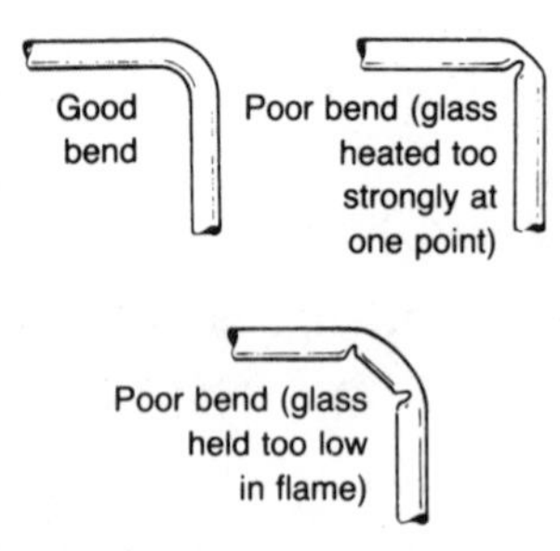

Figure 18

CAUTION: *Be careful with the cut ends of the glass. They may be sharp and jagged. Do not attempt to break glass tubing having an outside diameter greater than 6 mm.*

6. The cut ends of the glass tubing should be fire-polished to make the tubing safe to handle. Rotate one end of the glass tube in the hottest part of a burner flame until the sharp edges have softened and become rounded (Figure 14).

CAUTION: *Do not hold the tubing in the flame too long. If you do, the hole in the tube will close.*

7. Place the hot glass on a wire gauze square to cool.

CAUTION: *Hot glass and cold glass look alike. Make sure one end of a piece of glass has cooled before you attempt to fire-polish the other end.*

Bending Glass Tubing

1. Put a wing top or flame spreader on your gas burner.

2. Light the burner and adjust the flame to give an even blue (hot) flame across the wing top (Figure 15).

3. Grasp a length of glass tubing that has been fire-polished at both ends. Hold the center of it lengthwise in the flame just at the top of the blue region. This is the hottest part of the flame (Figure 16).

4. Rotate the tubing in the flame to heat approximately a 5-cm section uniformly until it becomes soft and just begins to sag.

5. Remove the tubing from the flame and bend it to the desired shape in one movement (Figure 17). Examples of good and bad bends are shown in Figure 18.

6. When it has hardened, put the glass tubing on a wire gauze to cool.

CAUTION: *Hot and cold glass look alike.*

Experiment

1 Observing and Inferring

Text reference:
Section 1.2

Background

Throughout the day you continually use your senses to observe the world. You hear your alarm clock go off in the morning, you smell lunch as you approach the school cafeteria, and you see your friend walking down the hall toward you.

You can make inferences based upon your observations. If your car won't start and you also observe that the radio, horn, and lights do not work, you might infer (or hypothesize) that your car battery is dead.

Observation, followed by the development of a hypothesis, are the first steps in the scientific method. Experiments (tests) are then designed and carried out to test the hypothesis under controlled conditions. If the results of the initial experiment support the hypothesis, additional testing is done to further check the hypothesis. If, however, the experimental results do not support the original hypothesis, then the hypothesis must be changed or modified. When the results of many, many experiments support the hypothesis, it can be called a theory. A theory is a hypothesis that is supported by the results of repeated experiments.

In this experiment you will observe a series of chemical phenomena demonstrated by your teacher. You will then formulate hypotheses to explain your observations.

Goals

- **Observe** several chemical phenomena.
- **Hypothesize** explanations for each phenomena.

Equipment

safety goggles
3 100-mL beakers
3 250-mL beakers
3 watch glasses
4 glass stirring rods
1 plastic wash bottle

1 2-L graduated cylinder
1 crucible tongs
2 insulated gloves

Materials

saturated calcium ethanoate, $Ca(C_2H_3O_2)_2$
0.05*M* silver nitrate, $AgNO_3$ [C] [T]
0.1*M* sodium hydroxide, NaOH [C] [T]
3% hydrogen peroxide, H_2O_2
cornstarch, $(C_6H_{10}O_5)_n$
copper wire, Cu
95% ethanol, C_2H_5OH [F]
ice, $H_2O(s)$
dry ice, $CO_2(s)$ [C]
manganese(IV) oxide, MnO_2 [T]
wood splints
matches
universal indicator solution
distilled water

Safety

- Note the Safety Symbols used here and in the Procedure section. Review safety information on pages 7–10.
- Always wear safety goggles when working in the lab.
- Only handle chemicals when instructed to do so by the teacher.
- Always use insulated gloves or tongs when handling dry ice.

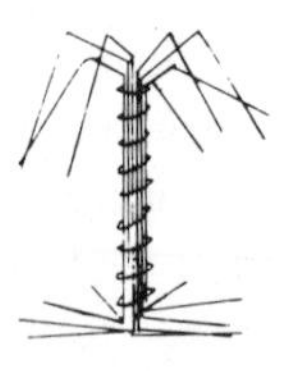

Figure 1.1

Procedure

Copy Table 1.1 into your laboratory notebook. As your teacher performs the demonstrations, record your observations in this table.

1. Place a piece of ice and a piece of dry ice on separate watch glasses. Observe what happens with time. **CAUTION:** *Do not touch the dry ice. It can cause frostbite.*

2. Add 30 g of cornstarch to three 100-mL beakers containing 10 mL, 15 mL, and 20 mL of water, respectively. Observe what happens when each mixture is stirred with its own glass stirring rod and when some of each mixture is picked up with the rod.

3. Twist ten strands of clean copper to form a "tree" as shown in Figure 1.1. **CAUTION:** *Avoid contact with silver nitrate solution. It can cause temporary skin discoloration and skin burns.* Place the tree in a 250-mL beaker containing 200 mL of the silver nitrate solution. Observe this system at intervals during the class period.

4. Place several small pieces of dry ice in a plastic wash bottle half-filled

with distilled water. Observe what happens when the jet assembly of the wash bottle is replaced and tightened.

5. Add a small amount of manganese(IV) oxide powder to 50 mL of hydrogen peroxide solution in a 250-mL beaker. Cover the beaker with a watch glass for 15 seconds. Observe what happens when a *glowing* wood splint is inserted into the upper part of the beaker.

6. CAUTION: *Ethanol is flammable.* Observe what happens when 50 mL of saturated calcium ethanoate is poured into a 250-mL beaker containing 50 mL of ethanol.

7. Add about 20 drops of universal indicator solution to 1500 mL of water in a 2-L graduated cylinder. Record what happens when 150 mL of sodium hydroxide solution is added and the mixture is stirred. Observe what occurs when several small pieces of dry ice are added.

8. Your teacher will properly dispose of the materials.

Data Record

Table 1.1 Table of Observations

System	Observations
ice	
dry ice	
cornstarch 10 mL H_2O cornstarch 15 mL H_2O cornstarch 20 mL H_2O	
$Cu(s)$ $AgNO_3(aq)$	
dry ice wash bottle	
$MnO_2(s)$ 3% $H_2O_2(aq)$	

Table 1.1 (cont.) Table of Observations

System	Observations
$Ca(C_2H_3O_2)_2(aq)$ $C_2H_5OH(aq)$	
H_2O universal indicator $NaOH(aq)$	

Data Analysis

For each demonstration, write two hypotheses that could explain the behavior that you observed. Indicate which of the two you believe to be the better hypothesis, and give reasons for your choice.

1. ice
2. dry ice
3. cornstarch and water
4. copper and silver nitrate
5. dry ice in water-filled wash bottle
6. manganese(IV) oxide, hydrogen peroxide, and wood splint
7. calcium ethanoate and ethanol
8. sodium hydroxide, dry ice, and water with an indicator

Experiment

2 Physical and Chemical Change

Text reference:
Sections 1.3, 1.9

Background

Have you ever thought of your eyes as powerful tools for studying chemistry? Many of the properties of matter and the changes it undergoes can easily be determined through careful observation. *Physical properties* include color, odor, density, solubility, and the state of the matter. *Chemical properties* describe the changes that take place when new substances are formed during a chemical reaction.

When matter undergoes a change, it is classified as either a physical change or a chemical change. During a *physical change*, only the size, temperature, or physical state of the substance changes. Melting, dissolving, grinding, and evaporating are all physical changes. No new substances are produced during a physical change. However, *chemical changes* always result in the formation of one or more new substances. The rusting of iron, during which the new substance iron(III) oxide forms from iron (Fe) and oxygen (O_2), is an example of a chemical change.

In this experiment you will observe a variety of materials and describe their physical properties. You will then cause some of the substances to undergo changes. Based upon your observations, you will determine whether the changes are physical changes or chemical changes.

Goals

- **Observe** the physical and chemical properties of several substances.
- **Classify** observed changes as physical or chemical.
- **Demonstrate** that mass is conserved in a chemical reaction.

Equipment

safety goggles
13 small test tubes
1 test-tube rack
1 test-tube holder
2 100-mL beakers
1 funnel
1 watch glass
1 plastic wash bottle
1 glass stirring rod
1 evaporating dish
1 magnifying glass
1 crucible tongs
1 magnet
1 spatula
4 centigram balances/class
1 gas burner
1 ring stand
1 ring support
1 wire gauze
1 forceps
1 cleanup sponge
2 pieces of exposed film
Fume hood

Materials

sulfur, powdered, S [F] [T]
iron filings, Fe
sodium hydrogen carbonate, $NaHCO_3$
sodium chloride, NaCl
sucrose, $C_{12}H_{22}O_{11}$
sand
magnesium ribbon, Mg [F]
6*M* hydrochloric acid, HCl [C] [T]
coarse filter paper
9 pieces paper, 10 cm × 10 cm
distilled water

Safety

- Note the Safety Symbols used here and in the Procedure section. Review safety information on pages 7–10.
- Always wear safety goggles when working in the lab.
- Hydrochloric acid is very corrosive and can cause severe burns.
- Do not look directly at burning magnesium. The intense light may damage your eyes. View the magnesium reaction through the exposed pieces of film. Do not inhale the smoke that is produced when magnesium burns.
- Powdered sulfur is irritating to the moist membranes of the eyes, nose, and throat. Avoid getting the dust into the air.

Procedure

Copy Tables 2.1 and 2.2 into your laboratory notebook.

Part A. The Physical Properties of Matter

Record your observations for Part A in Table 2.1.

1. CAUTION: *Do not taste any of the substances or touch them with your hands.* Label a separate piece of paper for each of the first seven substances in the Materials list. Place two pieces of magnesium ribbon, one 5 cm long and one 1 cm long, on the paper labeled "magnesium." Using a clean spatula, transfer a pea-sized sample of the other substances to their correctly labeled papers.

2. Examine each substance with a magnifying glass. Record your observations in Table 2.1.

3. Test the effect of a magnet on each substance by passing the magnet under the sheet of paper.

4. In separate small test tubes, test the solubility of each substance by mixing a small amount of each sample with 3 mL of distilled water. "Flick" each test tube to mix the contents.

5. Return the strip of magnesium ribbon in the test tube to its paper. Follow your teacher's instructions for proper disposal of the other materials.

Part B. Causing a Physical or Chemical Change

Record your observations for Part B in Table 2.2.

6. Mix the iron filings and sulfur on a clean piece of paper. Examine the mixture with a magnifying glass. Test the effect of a magnet by passing the magnet under the paper. Give this mixture to your teacher for use in Part C.

7. Mix the sodium chloride and sand on a clean piece of paper. Examine the mixture with a magnifying glass, and test the effect of a magnet.

8. Transfer the salt-sand mixture to a clean 100-mL beaker. Add 30 mL of tap water and stir. Record observations. Prepare a filtration setup as shown in Figures 2.1 and 2.2. Filter the mixture and record your observations. Pour 10 mL of the filtrate into an evaporating dish. Prepare a setup to heat the liquid in the evaporating dish. Heat the dish gently until the

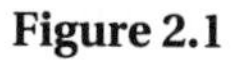

Figure 2.1

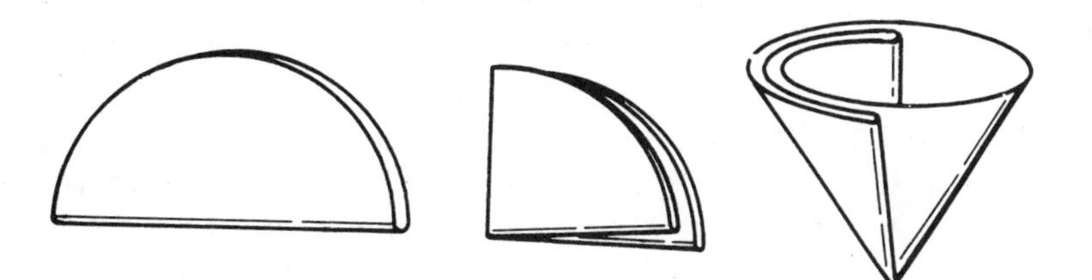

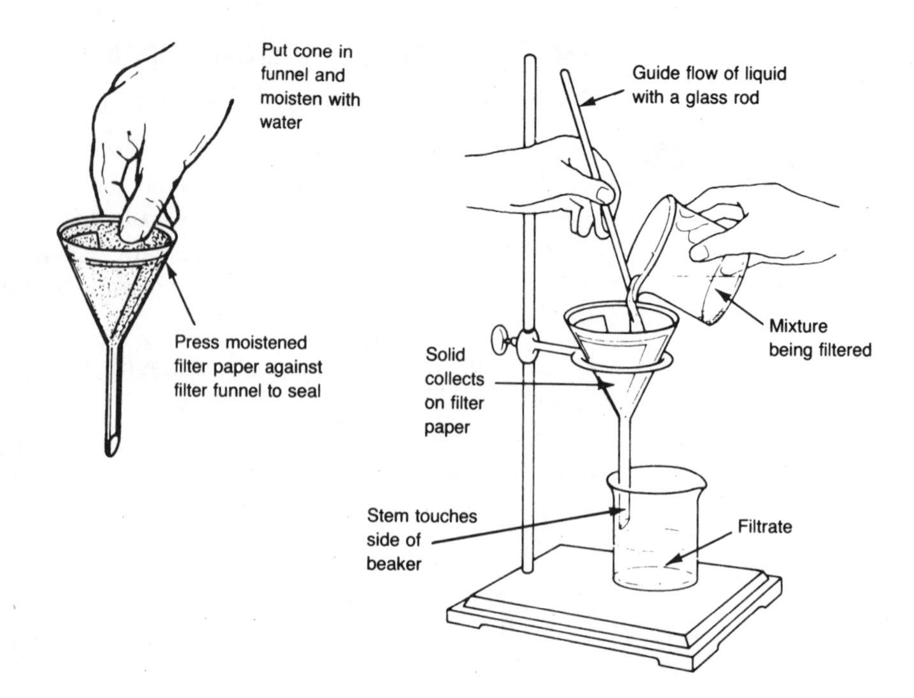

Figure 2.2

filtrate has completely evaporated. Examine both the dry residue in the evaporating dish and the wet residue on the filter paper.

9. CAUTION: *Do not look directly at burning magnesium; look through the exposed film.* Position a watch glass near the gas burner. Using crucible tongs, grasp one end of the 5-cm strip of magnesium ribbon and hold it in the burner flame until the magnesium ignites. Quickly position the burning magnesium so that the combustion products fall on the watch glass. Compare the appearance of this product with that of the original magnesium ribbon.

10. Place the unburned 1-cm strip of magnesium and the combustion product from the watch glass into separate test tubes. **CAUTION:** *Hydrochloric acid is corrosive.* Add 10 drops of 6*M* hydrochloric acid to each tube. Feel the bottom of each test tube. Record your observations.

Figure 2.3

11. Put half of your sucrose sample into a test tube. **CAUTION:** *When heating a test tube, never point the mouth of it at yourself or anyone else.* Heat the tube gently in a burner flame and watch carefully for changes. Periodically remove the tube from the flame and check for odors by fanning the fumes toward your nose, as shown in Figure 2.3.

Now heat the residue in the test tube more vigorously for 1–2 minutes. **CAUTION:** *Hot glass looks just like cool glass. Be sure the tube is cool before handling it.* After cooling the tube, use a spatula to scrape some of the residue into a clean test tube. Examine the residue and test its solubility in water.

12. Transfer the sodium hydrogen carbonate sample to a test tube. **CAUTION:** *Hydrochloric acid is corrosive.* Carefully add 5 drops of 6*M* hydrochloric acid. Touch the bottom of the test tube with your hand. Record your observations.

13. Follow your teacher's instructions for proper disposal of the materials.

Part C. Conservation of Mass (Teacher Demonstration)

Record your observations for Part C in Table 2.2.

14. Several samples of the iron-sulfur mixture from Part B will be combined in a clean, dry test tube. The mass of the test tube and its contents will be determined and recorded. The test tube is heated gently, then vigorously, for several minutes. **CAUTION:** *This heating must be done in a fume hood.* After heating is complete, the mass is remeasured and recorded. Examine the reaction product. The effect of a magnet on the reaction product will be tested.

15. Your teacher will properly dispose of the materials.

Data Record

Table 2.1 Data Table for Part A

Substance	Physical State	Color	Odor	Solubility in Water	Effect of Magnet
S					
Fe					
$NaHCO_3$					
NaCl					
$C_{12}H_{22}O_{11}$					
sand					
Mg					

Table 2.2 Data Table for Parts B and C	
System	**Observations**
Fe and S mixture —tested with magnet	
NaCl and sand mixture —mixed with water —filtered —filtrate allowed to evaporate	
Mg —burned in air	
Mg —reacted with 6*M* HCl	
combustion product —reacted with 6*M* HCl	
$C_{12}H_{22}O_{11}$ —heated	
$NaHCO_3$ —reacted with 6*M* HCl	
Fe and S mixture —heated initial mass final mass	

Data Analysis

1. Following is a list of changes you observed in Parts B and C. Indicate whether each change was a physical change or a chemical change and give reasons for your answer.

- **a.** Mixing iron and sulfur. (Part B, step 6)
- **b.** Mixing salt, sand, and water. (Part B, step 8)
- **c.** Burning magnesium. (Part B, step 9)

d. Mixing magnesium and the combustion product with hydrochloric acid. (Part B, step 10)

e. Heating sucrose. (Part B, step 11)

f. Mixing sodium hydrogen carbonate and hydrochloric acid. (Part B, step 12)

g. Heating iron and sulfur. (Part C, step 14)

2. Was mass conserved in the reaction of iron and sulfur? Explain.

3. Except for the reaction between iron and sulfur, none of the reactions in this experiment can be used to demonstrate the law of conservation of mass. Explain why.

Conclusions

1. How do you decide whether an observed property of matter is a physical or chemical property?

2. What criteria are used to distinguish between a chemical change and a physical change?

3. State in your own words the law of conservation of mass.

Extensions

1. Design an experiment that would demonstrate that mass is conserved when magnesium is burned in air.

2. The black residue left in step 11 weighs less than the original sucrose sample. Propose a hypothesis to explain this loss of mass and an experiment to test your hypothesis.

Experiment

3 Observing a Chemical Reaction

Text reference:
Section 1.9

Background

You and your friend's feelings about a movie you've just seen may be very different. You may disagree about whether you liked the movie, or about the movie's intended meaning. Although you both have *observed* the same movie, your *interpretations* of the movie may differ. Distinguishing between observation and interpretation is very important in chemistry. An *observation* is a statement of fact, based on what you detect by your senses. An *interpretation* is your judgment or opinion about what you have observed. A statement such as "The liquid is clear and colorless" is an observation. It would be an interpretation to say, without further testing, that the clear and colorless liquid is water.

The purpose of this experiment is to help you distinguish observation from interpretation while examining a chemical reaction. Try to make as many observations of the reaction as possible. Remember that there are two types of observations: A *quantitative observation* is an observation that involves a measurement; a *qualitative observation* is a general description and does not involve a measurement. "The liquid is hot" is a qualitative observation. "The temperature of the liquid is 95.0°C" is a quantitative observation.

Goals

- **Observe** several chemical reactions.
- **Distinguish** between observations and interpretations.
- **Classify** observations as qualitative or quantitative.

Equipment

safety goggles
1 100-mL beaker
1 thermometer
1 glass stirring rod
1 plastic spoon
1 magnifying glass

Materials

copper(II) chloride dihydrate, $CuCl_2 \cdot 2H_2O$ [T] [I]

aluminum foil, 8 cm × 8 cm

Safety

- Note the Safety Symbols used here and in the Procedure section. Review safety information on pages 7–10.
- Always wear safety goggles when working in the lab.
- Check for odors by waving a hand across the top of the container, toward your nose, as shown in Figure 2.3.
- Mercury is extremely toxic. If you break a mercury thermometer, report it immediately to the teacher.
- Copper(II) chloride is an irritant. Avoid skin contact with this chemical.

Procedure

Copy Table 3.1 into your laboratory notebook. As you perform the experiment, record your observations in this table.

1. Obtain and describe a sample of copper(II) chloride dihydrate, $CuCl_2 \cdot 2H_2O$ crystals.

2. Fill the 100-mL beaker about one-fourth full of water. Without stirring, add 1 level teaspoonful of crystals to the water. Record your observations of both the crystals and the water.

3. Use the glass stirring rod to stir the mixture until the crystals are completely dissolved. Record your observations of the solution.

4. Place the thermometer in the copper(II) chloride solution and record the temperature. **CAUTION:** *Observe the mixture from the side: do not look directly down into the beaker.* Place a loosely crumpled ball of aluminum in the solution and record your observations. Stir the mixture occasionally and observe for at least 10 minutes. Record any change in temperature.

5. Follow your teacher's instructions for proper disposal of the materials.

Data Record

Table 3.1 Table of Observations

System	Observations
dry copper(II) chloride dihydrate	
copper(II) chloride in water	
stirred solution of copper(II) chloride in water	
copper(II) chloride solution plus aluminum foil	
initial temperature: final temperature:	

Data Analysis

1. Check your observations. Cross out any that are interpretations rather than observations.

2. List each of your observations in one of the four following sections. Number your observations consecutively. Circle the number of any observation that is quantitative.

a. observations of the dry crystals

b. observations of the wet crystals before stirring

c. observations of the solution before addition of aluminum

d. observations of the reaction that occurs when the aluminum is added to the solution

Conclusions

1. Would you expect your observations or your interpretations to most closely match those of your classmates? Explain.

Extensions

1. What is your interpretation of what happened in this reaction? Which of the observations led to your hypothesis?

2. Describe any additional experiment you would do to support your hypothesis.

Experiment

4 Mass, Volume, and Density

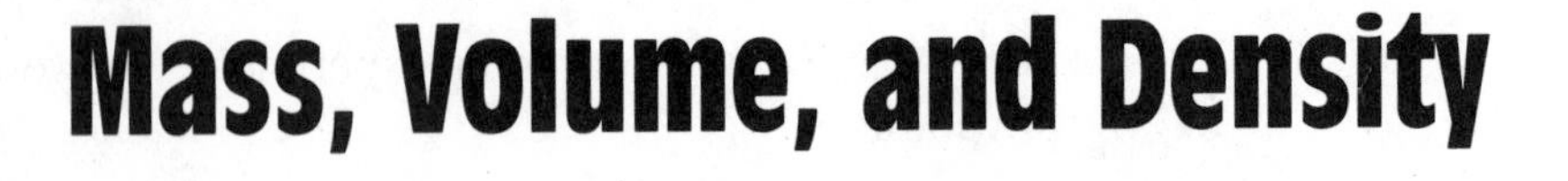

Text reference:
Sections 2.7–2.10

Background

An old riddle asks "Which is heavier, a pound of feathers or a pound of lead?" The question is nonsensical, of course, since a pound of feathers and a pound of lead both weigh the same, one pound. Nevertheless, there is clearly something different about a small lead brick and a large bag of feathers, even though they weigh the same. The key to answering the riddle is understanding the relationship that exists between a substance's mass and the volume it occupies. This relationship is expressed by the physical property called density. *Density* is defined as the ratio of a substance's mass to the volume it occupies.

$$\text{Density} = \text{mass of substance (g)} / \text{volume of substance (mL)}$$

In this experiment, you will measure the mass and volume of several unknown materials. You will then use your data to explore the relationship between the mass and volume of the materials and to calculate their density.

After performing this lab, if someone asks you the riddle about feathers and lead, you can explain to them the difference between weight and density.

Goals

- **Measure** the mass and volume of several samples of matter, using the centigram balance and the method of water displacement.
- **Infer** whether there is a constant relationship between mass and volume for each unknown substance.
- **Compute** the density of a solid object from its mass and volume.

Equipment

safety goggles
1 25-mL graduated cylinder
8 centigram balances/class
1 ruler

Materials

metal samples

paper towels

Safety

- Note the Safety Symbol used here. Review safety information on pages 7–10.
- Always wear safety goggles when working in the lab.

Procedure

Copy Tables 4.1, 4.2, and 4.3 into your laboratory notebook. As you perform the experiment, record your data in Tables 4.1 and 4.2.

1. Determine the mass of two different unknown metal samples to the nearest 0.01 gram, using a centigram balance. Record masses in Tables 4.1 and 4.2.

2. Find the volume of each metal sample by water displacement. Fill a 25-mL graduated cylinder about half-full with water, measure the volume, and record as "volume of water alone" in Table 4.1. Tilt the graduated cylinder and carefully slide one of the metal samples down the side. Make sure the metal sample is completely submerged in the water. Measure the volume and record the measurement as "volume of water + metal" in Table 4.1.

3. Repeat step 2, using the other metal sample. Dry both samples and return them to your teacher.

Data Record

Table 4.1 Individual Data and Calculations

	Metal A	Metal B
mass (g)	6.96	6.85
volume of water alone (mL)	50 ml	50 ml
volume of water + metal (mL)	51.5 ml	53 ml
volume of metal (mL)	1.5 ml	3 ml
density of metal (g/mL) =	4.64	2.283

Table 4.2 Class Data: Mass and Volume of Metal Samples				
	Metal A		Metal B	
Lab Pair	mass (g)	volume (mL)	mass (g)	volume (mL)
1	18.37	2	18.8	7 ml
2	10.63	1	3.888	0.4
3	6.96	1.5	6.85	3
4	10.518	1	5.95	2
5	13.1	1	10.34	3.5
6	12.658	1	15.86	4.
7	4.786	.7	7.0268	7 ml
8				
9				
10				
11				
12				
13				
14				
15				

Data Analysis

Note, **one page of graph paper** is required for your laboratory report.

1. Compute the volume of each metal sample, using data from Table 4.1. Compute the density of each metal sample, showing your work (including units), in Table 4.1. Remember, density = mass (g)/volume (mL).

2. Complete Table 4.2 by recording the mass and volume data collected by you and your classmates.

3. Using the class data, plot a graph of mass versus volume. Represent the plotted points for each metal with a different symbol. Draw a "best fit" straight line through each group of plotted points.

4. Determine the slope of each of the lines on your graph. Record the slope of each line and your method of calculation in Table 4.3. **Hint:** The general equation for a line is $y = mx + b$ where m is the value for the slope and b is the value for the y-intercept. Pay special attention to the units of the slope.

Table 4.3 Density Calculations from Class Data (slopes)	
Metal A	**Metal B**
$y/x = \frac{30 \text{ g}}{6 \text{ mL}} =$ 5 g/mL	$y/x = \frac{2 \text{ g}}{1 \text{ mL}} =$ 2 g/mL

Conclusions

1. What does the slope of the line for each metal represent? **Hint:** Look back at Table 4.1.

2. Looking at your graph, what does this experiment demonstrate about the density of a substance? What does it demonstrate about the densities of different substances?

3. Calculate the percent error in the density calculations for the two samples. (See Data Analysis, step 1.) Your teacher will provide the accepted value for the density of each metal.

$$\text{percent error} = \frac{|\text{accepted value} - \text{experimental value}|}{\text{accepted value}} \times 100 \text{ percent}$$

4. Calculate the percent error in the values of density obtained from the slopes of the lines in your graph.

5. Look back at the percent errors calculated in steps 3 and 4. Generally, the slope of the line will give a more accurate value for density than a single sample. Explain why this is usually true.

6. Can you identify a substance if you know its density? Explain your answer. Try to identify the metals used in this experiment by referring to tables of density.

Extensions

1. Do you think that determining the volumes of your metal samples by measuring their dimensions and calculating would be more or less accurate than determining these volumes by water displacement? Explain. Would measuring the dimensions of a solid always be possible? Explain.

2. How would you modify this experiment to determine the density of table sugar, wood chips, and milk?

Experiment

5 Atomic Structure: Rutherford's Experiment

Text reference: Section 4.3

Background

As you have done experiments, you have learned to make useful observations and to draw reasonable conclusions from data. But imagine how little you would be able to accomplish if the room in which you worked were so dark that you could not see the materials you were working with. Imagine how limited your observations would be if the object of your scrutiny were so small that it could not be seen, even with a microscope. When you think of how difficult experimentation would be under such adverse conditions, you will gain some appreciation for the enormous technical problems confronting early atomic scientists.

These scientists had as their target the atom—a bit of matter so small that there was no hope of seeing it directly. Nevertheless, these ingenious experimenters were able to infer that the atom had a nucleus.

It is impractical to reproduce the classic experiments that led to the discovery of the nucleus in a high school laboratory. You can get some idea of the challenge that these researchers faced, however, by playing the game described in this experiment. In playing, you will infer the size and shape of an object that you cannot see or touch.

Goal

- **Predict** the size and shape of an object by indirect means.

Equipment

safety goggles
1 marble
1 sheet of heavy cardboard or thin plywood sheet, 60 cm × 60 cm
1 sheet construction paper
1 sheet notebook paper

Materials

1 plastic foam shape

Safety 

- Always wear safety goggles when working in the lab.

Procedure

Record your observations of this experiment in your laboratory notebook.

1. At your lab station, you will find a sheet of cardboard resting on top of a hidden object. *Do not look under the cardboard!* Roll a marble under the cardboard from various directions and observe where it comes out. (Have your teacher retrieve the marble if it stays under the board; no peeking!)

2. Place a large sheet of construction paper on top of the board and trace the entry and exit path of each roll of the marble.

3. Continue rolling the marble and recording its path until you think you know the size and shape of the object. Draw a full-sized sketch of the object on a piece of paper. Check your results with the teacher. Do not look under the board until the teacher confirms your results.

4. Ask the teacher for a second mystery object if you have time to repeat the game.

Conclusions

1. How does this game simulate early efforts to determine the structure of the atom? In what ways is it different?

2. You eventually had the satisfaction of seeing the shape under the board. Did the early atomic scientists have this same opportunity? Do scientists today have this opportunity?

Extension

1. Design another simulation that illustrates the problem of identifying something that cannot be observed directly.

Experiment

6 Identification of Anions and Cations in Solution

Text reference:
Sections 5.6–5.11

Background

Detectives in mystery novels often rush evidence from the crime scene to the lab for analysis. In this experiment you will become a chemical detective. You will conduct laboratory analyses to determine the ionic composition of an unknown solution. The process of determining the composition of a sample of matter by conducting chemical tests is called *qualitative analysis.* Solutions of unknown ions can be subjected to chemical tests and the results can be compared to the results given by known ions, in the same tests. By conducting the appropriate tests and applying logic, the identities of the ions present in an unknown solution can be determined.

The analyses you perform are based upon the idea that no two ions produce the same set of chemical reactions. Each ion reacts in its own characteristic way. In this experiment, you will observe several types of chemical reactions commonly used as tests in qualitative analysis. These reactions include a color change, the evolution of a gas, and the formation of a precipitate—a solid product. As you do this experiment, remember that careful observation and logical reasoning are the keys to being a good detective. Who knows what ions lurk in your unknown solution?

Goals

- **Observe** the reactions of common anions and cations in solution to simple chemical tests.
- **Predict** the ions present in an unknown solution based on the logical application of chemical tests.

Equipment

safety goggles
9 small test tubes
1 test-tube rack
1 cobalt-blue glass
1 test-tube holder
1 ring stand

1 25-mL graduated cylinder
1 250-mL beaker
1 gas burner
1 dropper pipet
1 nichrome wire (10-cm length)
1 ring support
1 wire gauze
1 crucible tongs
1 plastic wash bottle
1 forceps

Materials

Part A. Anions

0.1*M* silver nitrate, $AgNO_3$ T I
0.1*M* sodium sulfate, Na_2SO_4
0.1*M* barium chloride, $BaCl_2$ T
0.1*M* sodium hydrogen carbonate, $NaHCO_3$
0.1*M* ammonium molybdate, $(NH_4)_2MoO_4$
0.1*M* sodium chloride, NaCl
0.05*M* sodium phosphate, Na_3PO_4 I
6*M* nitric acid, HNO_3 C
6*M* hydrochloric acid, HCl C T
distilled water
unknown solutions (anions) T

Part B. Cations

0.1*M* iron(III) sulfate, $Fe_2(SO_4)_3$
0.1*M* sodium chloride, NaCl
0.1*M* potassium thiocyanate, KSCN T
0.1*M* potassium chloride, KCl
0.1*M* calcium nitrate, $Ca(NO_3)_2$
0.1*M* sodium oxalate, $Na_2C_2O_4$ T
0.1*M* ammonium nitrate, NH_4NO_3
3*M* sulfuric acid, H_2SO_4 C T
6*M* sodium hydroxide, NaOH C
6*M* hydrochloric acid, HCl C T
distilled water
red litmus paper, 1 cm × 10 cm
unknown solutions (cations)

Safety

- Note the Safety Symbols used here and in the Procedure section. Review safety information on pages 7–10.
- Always wear safety goggles when working in the lab.
- Nitric acid, hydrochloric acid, sulfuric acid, and sodium hydroxide are corrosive and can cause severe injury.
- Silver, barium, and oxalate compounds are poisonous. Avoid contact with these chemicals.
- Silver nitrate will stain skin and clothing.

- Never pick up a dropper bottle by its cap. Always hold a dropper with the tip lower than the rubber bulb, so that liquid does not run into the bulb.
- Never cover the opening of a test tube with your finger when mixing chemicals in the tube. To mix the contents, "flick" the tube as demonstrated by your teacher.

Procedure

Copy Table 6.1 into your laboratory notebook. As you perform the experiment, record your observations in this table.

Procedure note: In testing for different ions in steps 3–13 you will always begin with two test tubes. For each step you must add 2 mL of the known solution to one test tube, and 2 mL of your unknown solution to a second test tube. The name of the known solution to be used is given in each step.

Note that 1 mL is approximately 20 drops. Count out 40 drops of water in a test tube and make note of the level of water in the tube. Throughout the experiment, fill a test tube to this same level whenever a 2-mL sample is called for. This practice will save you considerable time. Always clean the medicine dropper after each use.

Part A. Testing for Anions (Day 1)

1. Set up a boiling water bath for use in step 6.

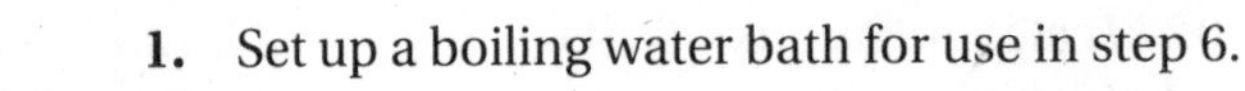

2. Thoroughly clean all the test tubes used in this experiment, rinsing them well with distilled water. Record the number of the unknown solution you will be testing.

3. Test for chloride ion, Cl^-. Known solution is sodium chloride. **CAUTION:** *Nitric acid is corrosive. Do not put your finger over the top of the tube to cover it.* Add 2 mL of 6*M* nitric acid to each tube and gently flick the tubes to mix. Add 10 drops of silver nitrate to each tube, and flick to mix. Record observations.

4. Test for sulfate ion, SO_4^{2-}. Known solution is sodium sulfate. **CAUTION:** *Hydrochloric acid is corrosive.* Add 2 mL of 6*M* hydrochloric acid to each tube and mix. Add 10 drops of barium chloride solution to each tube and mix. Record observations.

5. Test for hydrogen carbonate ion, HCO_3^-. Known solution is sodium hydrogen carbonate. Carefully observe the test tubes as you add 2 mL of 6*M* hydrochloric acid to each tube. Record observations.

Turned yellow

unknown did nothing

6. Test for phosphate ion, PO_4^{3-}. Known solution is sodium phosphate. Add 1 mL of $6M$ nitric acid and 10 drops of ammonium molybdate solution to each tube and mix. Place the tubes in a boiling water bath and heat for 5 minutes. Allow tubes to cool in a test-tube rack for 10 minutes. Record observations. (Retain the water bath for Part B, step 12.)

7. Follow your teacher's instructions for proper disposal of the materials.

Part B. Testing for Cations (Day 2)

8. Review the general directions at the beginning of the Procedure section. Prepare your test tubes as in Part A, step 2.

D.

9. Test for iron(III) ion, Fe^{3+}. Known solution is iron(III) sulfate. **CAUTION:** *Sulfuric acid is corrosive.* Add 5 drops of $3M$ sulfuric acid and 5 drops of potassium thiocyanate solution to each tube. Flick gently to mix. Record observations.

10. Flame-test for sodium ion, Na^+. Known solution is sodium chloride. Add 3 drops of $6M$ hydrochloric acid to each tube. Flick gently to mix.

Add 3–4 mL of $6M$ hydrochloric acid to a small test tube in a test-tube rack. Heat the end of a 10-cm length of nichrome wire in a hot burner flame, as shown in Figure 6.1. While it is still hot, dip the end of the wire into the hydrochloric acid in the test tube. Remove the wire from the acid and immediately reheat it in the burner flame. Repeat this acid cleaning of the wire until the flame remains unchanged when the wire is heated.

Dip the acid-cleaned wire into the sodium chloride solution. Immediately hold it in the hot burner flame. Observe the color of the flame. Acid-clean the wire and then test the unknown solution. Record the color of the flame. (A faintly colored flame is not considered a positive test for sodium.) Save the prepared unknown solution for the next test.

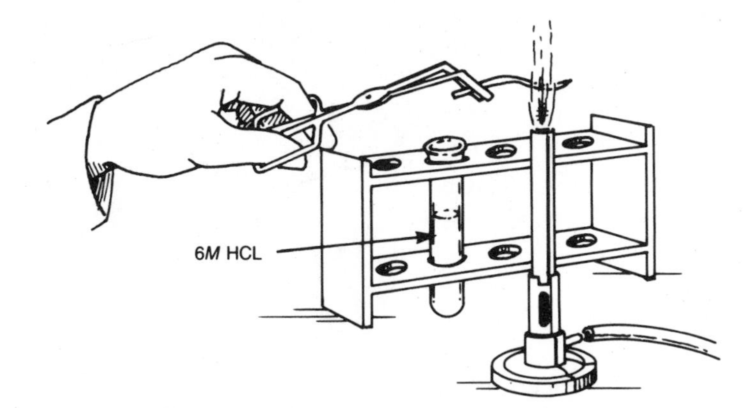

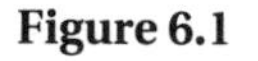

Figure 6.1

11. Flame-test for potassium ion, K^+. Known solution is potassium chloride. Add 3 drops of 6*M* hydrochloric acid to each tube and flick gently to mix. Acid-clean the nichrome wire. Flame-test the potassium chloride solution. Acid-clean the wire and test your unknown. If your unknown contains sodium, the color of the sodium flame will mask the color that is characteristic of potassium. You will be able to see the potassium color, if it is there, by looking at the flame through a piece of cobalt-blue glass. Record your results.

12. Test for calcium ion, Ca^{2+}. Known solution is calcium nitrate. To each tube, add 10 drops of sodium oxalate solution. Warm the tubes in the boiling water bath for a few minutes. Record your observations.

turns white

(Optional) You can also perform a flame test for calcium. Add 3 drops of 6*M* hydrochloric acid to fresh 2-mL samples of the calcium nitrate solution and the unknown solution. Perform flame tests as in step 10. Record the color of the calcium flame and the results for your unknown.

nothing.

13. Test for ammonium ion, NH_4^+. Known solution is ammonium nitrate. **CAUTION:** *Sodium hydroxide can cause burns.* To each tube, add 3 drops of 6*M* sodium hydroxide. Hold the tube containing the ammonium nitrate solution in a test-tube holder. *Gently* warm the tube along its sides using a back-and-forth motion through a burner flame. Do not allow the solution to boil. **CAUTION:** *At all times make sure that the opening of the tube is pointed away from other people.* Hold a moistened piece of red litmus paper near the mouth of the test tube, as shown in Figure 6.2. The test will be spoiled if the solution contacts the litmus paper. Record the changes you observe. Fan the vapors coming out of the tube toward your nose with your hand. Cautiously sniff the vapors. Record your observations. Repeat the procedure for your unknown solution.

litmus paper turned blue.

there was a powdery substance in the test tube. No change in litmus paper

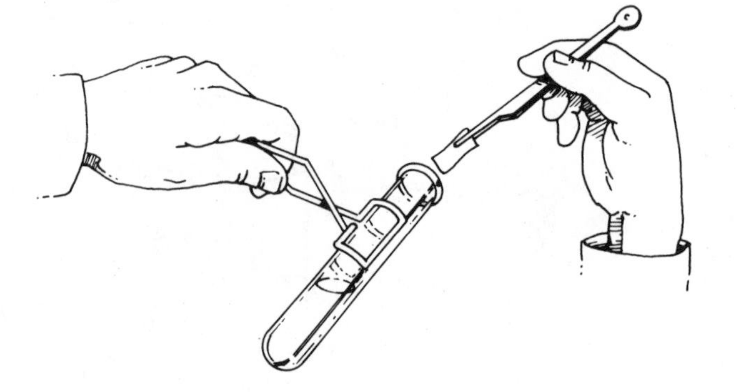

Figure 6.2

14. Follow your teacher's instructions for proper disposal of the materials.

Data Record

Table 6.1 Tests for Common Ions

Ion	Test Reagents/ Test Procedure	Test Results for Solution with Ion	Test Results for Unknown Solution No. ___	Is Ion Present in Unknown?
Cl^-		turned white	No reaction	N
SO_4^{2-}		turned white	no reaction	N
HCO_3^-		bubbles created	bubbles created	Y
PO_4^{3-}		turned yellow	no change	N
Fe^{3+}		turned brown	turned brown	yes.
Na^+		turned red	no change	N
K^+		turned pink	turned pink	Y
Ca^{2+}		turned white	nothing	N
NH_4^+		litmus turned blue.	rust color substance in tube. no litmus change.	N

Conclusions

1. List the anions present in your unknown.
2. List the cations present in your unknown.
3. It is possible to get a false-positive or a false-negative result when testing for ions. Propose a situation that could lead to a false positive for a particular ion. Choose a different ion and show how a false negative could result. Which do you think is more likely to happen, a false-positive or a false-negative result? Explain your reasoning.

Extensions

1. In the test for the sulfate ion (step 4), hydrochloric acid was added before the barium chloride solution was added. Hypothesize why the hydrochloric acid is needed, then design an experiment to test your hypothesis.

2. The combination of a solution of chloride ions and a solution of silver nitrate resulted in a precipitate of silver chloride (step 3). The combination of a solution of sulfate ions and a solution of barium chloride produced the insoluble product, barium sulfate (step 4). Look up the solubilities of silver chloride and barium sulfate in the *Handbook of Chemistry and Physics.* Are there other common anions that might also produce insoluble compounds of silver or barium?

Experiment

7 Precipitation Reactions

Text reference: Section 5.6

Background

Two colorless solutions, cadmium chloride ($Cd(NO_2)_2$) and potassium sulfide (K_2S), are poured together. As the solutions mix, a bright yellow solid forms. This insoluble compound, cadmium sulfide (CdS), was once used as a yellow pigment for oil paint. The paint was called cadmium yellow.

An insoluble substance that "falls out" of a solution is called a *precipitate.* The formation of precipitates other than cadmium sulfide is often less dramatic. For example, the scum that forms a ring around the bathtub is, in part, a precipitate formed by the reaction of calcium ions in the bathwater with soap ions. Whenever you mix solutions containing ions, you may obtain new combinations of ions. If one or more of these new ion combinations happens to be insoluble in water, it falls out of the solution as a precipitate.

In this experiment, you will mix pairs of six different ionic solutions in all possible combinations to determine which pairs result in precipitate formation. Based upon your results, you will infer what reactions have occurred and write complete and net ionic equations for each reaction that has taken place.

Goals

- **Observe** which combinations of ionic solutions form precipitates.
- **Identify** the precipitate formed in each reaction.
- **Write** complete and net ionic equations for chemical reactions.

Equipment

safety goggles
1 glass stirring rod
1 plastic wash bottle
1 spot plate or 5–15 small test tubes

Materials

Set 1

0.1*M* barium nitrate, $Ba(NO_3)_2$ T
0.1*M* sodium sulfate, Na_2SO_4
0.1*M* aluminum sulfate, $Al_2(SO_4)_3$ T I
0.1*M* magnesium nitrate, $Mg(NO_3)_2$
0.1*M* magnesium chloride, $MgCl_2$ T
0.1*M* aluminum chloride, $AlCl_3$ T I
distilled water
paper towels

Set 2

0.1*M* potassium chloride, KCl
0.1*M* magnesium chloride, $MgCl_2$
0.1*M* sodium sulfate, Na_2SO_4
0.2*M* sodium hydroxide, NaOH T C
0.1*M* barium chloride, $BaCl_2$ T
0.1*M* magnesium sulfate, $MgSO_4$
distilled water
paper towels

Set 3

0.1*M* barium chloride, $BaCl_2$ T
0.1*M* magnesium nitrate, $Mg(NO_3)_2$
0.2*M* sodium chromate, Na_2CrO_4 C T
0.2*M* aluminum sulfate, $Al_2(SO_4)_3$ T I
0.2*M* potassium chromate, K_2CrO_4 C T
0.2*M* silver nitrate, $AgNO_3$ C T
distilled water
paper towels

Safety

- Note the Safety Symbols used here and in the Procedure section. Review safety information on pages 7–10.
- Always wear safety goggles in the lab.
- Potassium chromate, sodium chromate, and sodium hydroxide are toxic, corrosive substances that can cause severe skin and eye injury.
- Aluminum chloride is an irritant. Avoid skin contact with this chemical.
- Silver and barium compounds are poisonous. Avoid contact with these chemicals and wash your hands thoroughly after use.
- Silver nitrate will stain skin and clothing.

Procedure

Copy Tables 7.1 and 7.2 into your laboratory notebook. As you perform this experiment, record your observations in Table 7.1.

1. Obtain a spot plate and a set of chemicals in dropper bottles. (If spot plates are not available, the tests may be done in small test tubes.)

2. Using Table 7.1 as a guide, mix every possible pair of solutions in a set in a separate spot plate depression or test tube. Use two drops of each solution. Do not contaminate the individual droppers with different solutions. Mix the solutions with a stirring rod. Rinse the rod with distilled water after each mixing. Observe each mixture carefully for signs of a precipitate. (Some precipitates are light in color and hard to see.) Note the color of any precipitate formed. Record the results in Table 7.1.

3. Follow your teacher's instructions for proper disposal of the materials.

Data Record

Table 7.1 Tests for Precipitate Formation

Solution A	Solution B	Results of Mixing A and B
Set 1:		
1 $Ba(NO_3)_2$	2 Na_2SO_4	white
1 $Ba(NO_3)_2$	3 $Al_2(SO_4)_3$	white.
1 $Ba(NO_3)_2$	4 $Mg(NO_3)_2$	nothing
1 $Ba(NO_3)_2$	5 $MgCl_2$	nothing
1 $Ba(NO_3)_2$	6 $AlCl_3$	nothing
2 Na_2SO_4	3 $Al_2(SO_4)_3$	nothing
2 Na_2SO_4	4 $Mg(NO_3)_2$	nothg
2 Na_2SO_4	5 $MgCl_2$	nothing
2 Na_2SO_4	6 $AlCl_3$	nothing.
3 $Al_2(SO_4)_3$	4 $Mg(NO_3)_2$	nothing
3 $Al_2(SO_4)_3$	5 $MgCl_2$	nothing
3 $Al_2(SO_4)_3$	6 $AlCl_3$	nothing
4 $Mg(NO_3)_2$	5 $MgCl_2$	nothing
4 $Mg(NO_3)_2$	6 $AlCl_3$	nothing.
5 $MgCl_2$	6 $AlCl_3$	nothing.

Table 7.1 (cont.) Tests for Precipitate Formation		
Solution A	**Solution B**	**Results of Mixing A and B**
Set 2:		
1 KCl	2 $MgCl_2$	nothing
1 KCl	3 Na_2SO_4	nothing
1 KCl	4 NaOH	nothing
1 KCl	5 $BaCl_2$	nothing
1 KCl	6 $MgSO_4$	nothing
2 $MgCl_2$	3 Na_2SO_4	nothing
2 $MgCl_2$	4 NaOH	formed white-clear gelatin
2 $MgCl_2$	5 $BaCl_2$	nothing
2 $MgCl_2$	6 $MgSO_4$	nothing
3 Na_2SO_4	4 NaOH	nothing
3 Na_2SO_4	5 $BaCl_2$	turned white
3 Na_2SO_4	6 $MgSO_4$	nothing
4 NaOH	5 $BaCl_2$	nothing
4 NaOH	6 $MgSO_4$	white-clear gelatin
5 $BaCl_2$	$MgSO_4$	milky white
Set 3:		
1 $BaCl_2$	2 $Mg(NO_3)_2$	nothing
1 $BaCl_2$	3 Na_2CrO_4	yellow
1 $BaCl_2$	4 $Al_2(SO_4)_3$	white
1 $BaCl_2$	5 K_2CrO_4	yellow
1 $BaCl_2$	6 $AgNO_3$	white
2 $Mg(NO_3)_2$	3 Na_2CrO_4	nothing
2 $Mg(NO_3)_2$	4 $Al_2(SO_4)_3$	nothing
2 $Mg(NO_3)_2$	5 K_2CrO_4	nothing
2 $Mg(NO_3)_2$	6 $AgNO_3$	nothing
3 Na_2CrO_4	4 $Al_2(SO_4)_3$	cloudy orange
3 Na_2CrO_4	5 K_2CrO_4	nothing
3 Na_2CrO_4	6 $AgNO_3$	Brown-red
4 $Al_2(SO_4)_3$	5 K_2CrO_4	nothing
4 $Al_2(SO_4)_3$	6 $AgNO_3$	nothing
5 K_2CrO_4	6 $AgNO_3$	Brown-red

Data Analysis

1. For each combination of solutions that gave a precipitate, write correct formulas for the two new compounds that could form from the ions present. (Remember to balance the ionic charges!) Enter these formulas in Table 7.2.

Chap 6.

171-171

41-43, 45-52

Read 207-222

Pg. 231-232

(25-29)

cab6

Table 7.2 Precipitation Results and Analysis		
Solution Pairs Yielding Precipitates	**Formulas of Possible Precipitates (Circle Choice)**	**Reason for Choice**
Set 1:		
$Ba(NO_3)_2 + Na_2SO_4 \rightarrow BaSO_4 + Na_2NO_3$		
$3Ba(NO_3)_2 + Al_2(SO_4)_3 \rightarrow 3BaSO_4 + 2Al(NO_3)_3$		
Set 2:		
$Mg^{+2}Cl_2^{-1} + Na^{+1}OH^{-1} \rightarrow$		
$Na_2^{+1}(SO_4)^{-2} + Ba^{+2}Cl_2^{-1} \rightarrow$		
$Na^{+1}OH^{-1} + Mg^{+2}SO_4^{-2} \rightarrow$		
$Ba^{+2}Cl_2^{-1} + Mg^{+2}SO_4^{-2} \rightarrow$		
Set 3:		
$Ba^{+2}Cl_2^{-1} + Na_2^{+1}CrO_4^{-2} \rightarrow$		
$Ba^{+2}Cl_2^{-1} + Al_2^{+3}(SO_4)_3^{-2} \rightarrow$		
$Ba^{+2}Cl_2^{-1} + K_2^{+1}CrO_4^{-2} \rightarrow$		
$Ba^{+2}Cl_2^{-1} + Ag^{+1}NO_3^{-1} \rightarrow$		
$Na_2^{+1}CrO_4^{-2} + Al_2^{+3}(SO_4)_3^{-2} \rightarrow$		

$Na_2^{+1}CrO_4^{-2} + Ag^{+1}NO_3^{-1} \rightarrow$

$K_2^{+1}CrO_4^{-2} + Ag^{+1}NO_3^{-1} \rightarrow$

2. For those combinations that produced a precipitate, decide which of the two new compounds is the precipitate by eliminating the other. Remember that all compounds in your sets are soluble, so they cannot be precipitates in any of the reactions. Also, a combination of ions will either always form a precipitate or never form one. Circle the formula of each compound you believe to be a precipitate, and record the reasons for your choices in Table 7.2.

3. Write complete ionic equations for the precipitation reactions that you observed. Show the reactants as ions, the precipitate as a solid, and the spectator ions as unchanged. Balance each equation for mass and charge. The total charge should be zero on each side of the equation.

4. Write net ionic equations for each reaction in the preceding question above.

Conclusions

1. What is the function of spectator ions in a precipitation reaction?

2. Explain in your own words why a precipitate forms.

3. How does a complete ionic equation differ from a net ionic equation?

Extensions

1. Think of a reaction between two soluble ionic compounds in which the net ionic equation is identical to the complete ionic equation. Write the equation.

2. Assuming that silver sulfate is relatively insoluble, identify four compounds that, when mixed according to the grid that follows, would form precipitates in every case. Write the names of the precipitates formed. What are the spectator ions in each reaction?

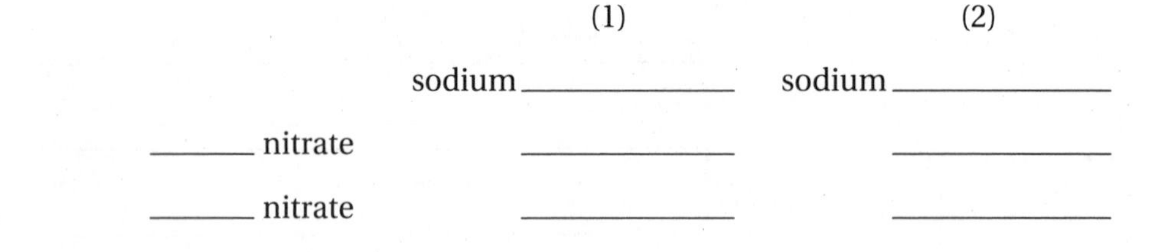

Experiment

8 The Masses of Equal Volumes of Gases

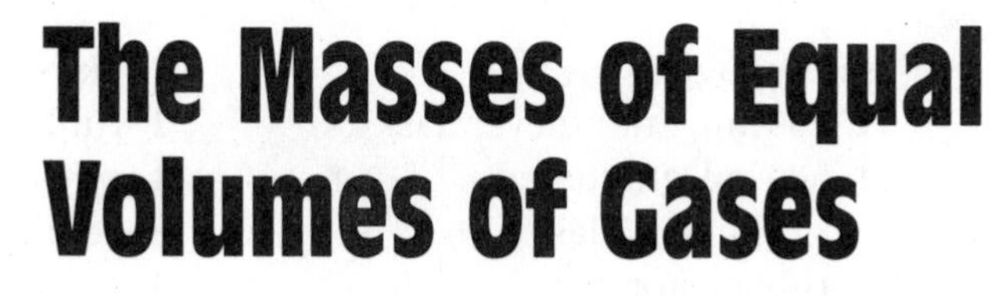

Text reference:
Sections 6.4–6.6

Background

Because many gases are colorless, odorless, and have low densities, you might think they would be difficult to work with in the laboratory. For example, you cannot place an unconfined gas on a balance and find its mass. However, surprisingly, many experiments involving gases are quite easy to perform. In fact, you can easily find the mass of a volume of a contained gas using a simple laboratory balance.

Molecules of different gases have different masses. A molecule of oxygen, O_2, has a mass of 32 atomic mass units (amu); a molecule of nitrogen, N_2, has a mass of 28 amu. Thus, the mass ratio of oxygen molecules to nitrogen molecules is 32/28. As a result of Avogadro's hypothesis, if equal volumes of oxygen and nitrogen are compared at the same temperature and pressure, the mass ratio between the molecules will always be 32/28. This fact forms the basis of the investigation in this experiment.

In this experiment, you will determine the masses of equal volumes of two different gases, argon and carbon dioxide. The volumes you will work with will contain only about 0.01 mol of gas molecules. You will calculate the ratio between these masses and compare this ratio with the established value for the ratio between the molar masses of these gases.

Goals

- **Measure** the masses of equal volumes of two different gases.
- **Compute** the ratio between the molar masses of these gases.

Materials

argon, Ar	carbon dioxide, CO_2

Equipment

safety goggles	1 glass delivery tube
1 250-mL Erlenmeyer flask	1 rubber connecting tube
4 500-mL graduated cylinders/class	1 pinch clamp
	8 centigram balances/class
1 rubber stopper	4 glass-marking pencils/class

Safety 

- Note the Safety Symbol used here. Review safety information on pages 7–10.
- Always wear safety goggles when working in the lab.

Procedure

Copy Table 8.1 into your laboratory notebook. As you perform this experiment, record your data in this table.

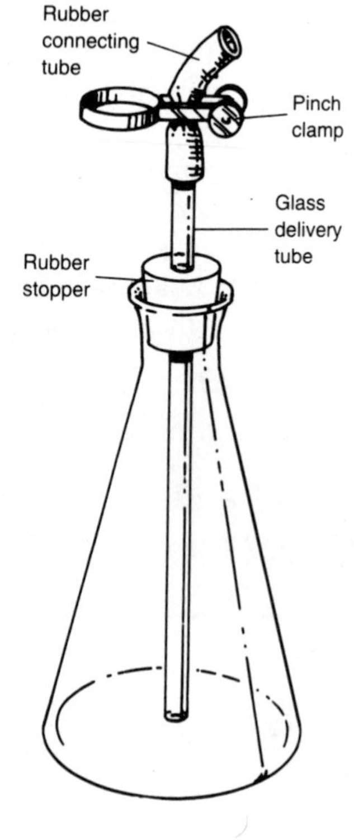

Figure 8.1

1. Obtain a 250-mL Erlenmeyer flask and set it up as shown in Figure 8.1. Keep the assembly dry throughout the experiment. Do not allow the glass delivery tube to touch the bottom of the flask when the stopper is pushed firmly into the neck.

2. Determine the mass of the "empty" flask assembly to the nearest 0.01 g and record.

3. Attach the rubber tube to the delivery jet on the argon tank. Loosen the rubber stopper in the flask and loosen the pinch clamp on the rubber tube so the tube is open. Allow argon gas to flow into the flask for 20–30 seconds—this flushes out all the air in the flask. Quickly push the stopper firmly into neck of the flask and close the pinch clamp on the rubber tube. Shut off the argon gas and disconnect the rubber tube from the delivery jet. Remeasure the mass of the flask, now full of argon, to the nearest 0.01 g.

4. Repeat step 3 until you obtain a constant measurement for the mass of the argon-filled flask. Measurements that agree within 0.01 g can be considered constant.

5. Repeat steps 3 and 4, using carbon dioxide gas.

6. Draw a line on the neck of the flask, at the bottom of the rubber stopper, using a glass-marking pencil. Set the stopper assembly aside to keep it dry.

7. Fill the Erlenmeyer flask with water to the height of the pencil mark. Carefully pour the water into a 500-mL graduated cylinder. Measure and record the volume.

8. Measure and record the room temperature and pressure.

Data Record

Table 8.1 Data	
mass of flask asssembly with air	
mass of flask assembly with Ar	(1) (2)
mass of flask assembly with CO_2	(1) (2)
volume of flask	
room temperature	
room pressure	

Data Analysis

1. Calculate the mass of air in the "empty" flask. To do this, use the density relationship between mass and volume.

$$\text{density} = \text{mass}/\text{volume}$$

Solve this equation for mass. In your calculation, use Table 8.2 to find the density of air at the conditions recorded in Table 8.1, and use the volume determined in step 7.

2. Calculate the mass of the flask when it is actually empty, by subtracting the mass of the air in the flask from the mass of the flask when it was full of air.

3. Use the mass of the empty flask to calculate the mass of argon and carbon dioxide contained in the flask.

4. Determine the ratio of the mass of carbon dioxide contained in the flask to the mass of argon gas contained in the flask.

5. Using data from the periodic table, calculate the actual ratio of the molar masses of carbon dioxide and argon.

Table 8.2 Density of Dry Air (g/cm^3)

Temperature (°C)	Pressure (mm Hg) 720	730	740	750	760	770
20	0.001141	0.001157	0.001173	0.001189	0.001205	0.001221
21	0.001137	0.001153	0.001169	0.001185	0.001201	0.001216
22	0.001134	0.001149	0.001165	0.001181	0.001197	0.001212
23	0.001130	0.001145	0.001161	0.001177	0.001193	0.001208
24	0.001126	0.001142	0.001157	0.001173	0.001189	0.001204
25	0.001122	0.001138	0.001153	0.001169	0.001185	0.001200
26	0.001118	0.001134	0.001149	0.001165	0.001181	0.001196
27	0.001115	0.001130	0.001146	0.001161	0.001177	0.001192

Conclusions

1. Avogadro's hypothesis states that equal volumes of different gases, at the same temperature and pressure, contain equal numbers of particles (or moles) of gases. Explain why similiarity between the ratios calculated in questions 4 and 5 in the Data Analysis section would support Avogadro's hypothesis.

2. Calculate the percent error in the experimentally determined mass ratio of equal volumes of argon and carbon dioxide. Use the ratio of the actual molar masses as the accepted value.

$$\text{Percent error} = \frac{|\text{accepted value} - \text{experimental value}|}{\text{accepted value}} \times 100 \text{ percent}$$

3. Why must the flask assembly be kept absolutely dry during this experiment? How would your results be affected if the flask became wet any time after step 2 in the procedure?

4. Is it still accurate to call Avogadro's hypothesis a *hypothesis*? Explain.

Extensions

1. Could you find the relative mass of helium by using the procedure in this experiment? Propose a modified experimental procedure for helium and other "light" gases.

2. Demonstrate with calculations how this procedure could be used to identify an unknown gaseous element.

Experiment

9 Empirical Formula Determination

Text reference: Section 6.10.

Background

Carbon dioxide (CO_2), water (H_2O), and ammonia (NH_3) are just a few of many chemical compounds that you are familiar with. Have you ever seen a compound with a formula such as $Na_{.23}Cl_{3.9}$? In fact, such a formula is impossible. Only whole atoms, not fractions of atoms, react with each other to form products. Also, although elements may react in different proportions to form more than one compound, the proportions of atoms in those compounds will always be a ratio of small whole numbers.

An empirical formula gives the simplest whole-number ratio of the different atoms in a compound. For example, while the molecular formula for hydrogen peroxide is H_2O_2, the simplest whole-number ratio of hydrogen and oxygen atoms can be expressed as HO. Thus, the empirical formula of hydrogen peroxide is HO.

In this lab you will experimentally determine the empirical formula of magnesium oxide, the compound formed when magnesium metal reacts with oxygen.

Goal

- **Compute** the empirical formula of magnesium oxide.

Equipment

safety goggles
1 crucible
1 crucible lid
1 crucible tongs
1 clay triangle
1 ring stand
1 ring support
8 centigram balances/class
1 gas burner
2 pieces of exposed film

Materials

magnesium ribbon, Mg [F]

Safety

- Note the Safety Symbols used here and in the Procedure section. Review safety information on pages 7–10.
- Always wear safety goggles when working in the lab.
- Always handle the crucible and crucible lid with crucible tongs, as shown in Figure 9.1.
- Do not look directly at burning magnesium.
- Do not inhale the smoke produced when the magnesium is burned.

Procedure

Copy Table 10.1 into your laboratory notebook. As you perform the experiment, record your data in this table.

1. Set up the equipment as shown in Figure 9.2. Clean a crucible and its cover with water. Dry them by heating in the hottest part of the flame for

Figure 9.1

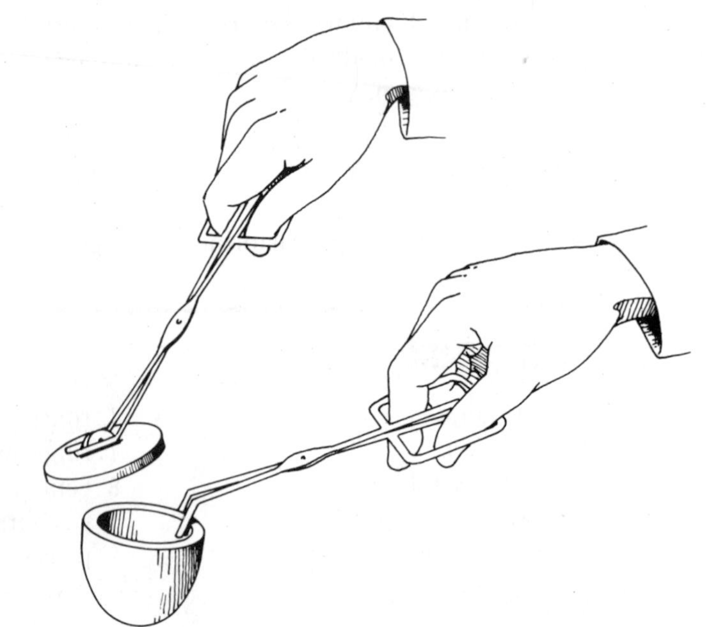

5 minutes. Allow them to cool for at least 10 minutes. Measure the combined mass of the crucible and lid to the nearest 0.01 g and record.

2. Place a coiled 25-cm length of magnesium ribbon in the crucible. Measure and record the combined mass of the crucible, lid, and magnesium.

3. **CAUTION:** *Do not look directly at the burning magnesium. View the reaction through the pieces of the film provided by your teacher.* Over a high flame, heat the uncovered crucible on the triangle, until the magnesium ignites. **CAUTION:** *Do not inhale the smoke produced.* When the magnesium begins to burn, immediately cover the crucible (using tongs) and remove the burner.

4. After smoke production has ceased, replace the burner and continue heating the crucible. **CAUTION:** *Do not lean over the crucible.* Remove the burner and carefully lift the lid and check the reaction every 2 or 3 minutes. After heating for a total of 10 minutes, check to see if the reaction is complete. The magnesium should be wholly converted to a light gray powder, magnesium oxide. If ribbonlike material remains in the crucible, replace burner and continue heating.

5. Turn off and remove the burner. Allow the crucible to cool completely (at least 10 minutes).

6. Measure and record the combined mass of the crucible, crucible lid, and magnesium oxide.

7. Follow your teacher's instructions for proper disposal of the materials.

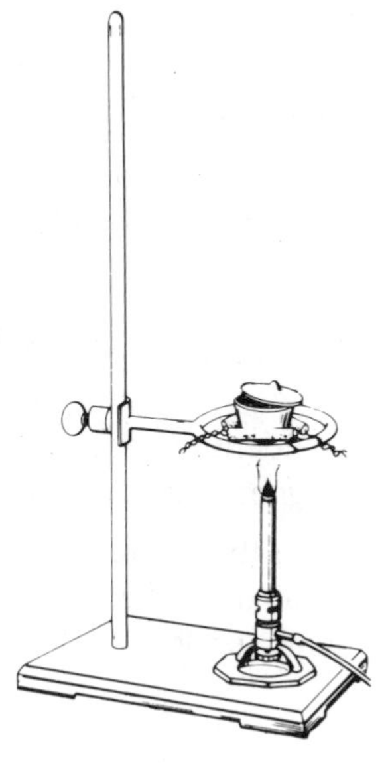

Figure 9.2

Data Record

Table 9.1 Data	
Item	**Mass**
empty crucible and lid	
crucible, lid, and Mg (before heating)	
crucible, lid, and combustion product (Mg_xO_y)	

Data Analysis

1. Determine the mass of magnesium used.

2. Determine the number of moles of magnesium used.
Hint: mol Mg = (mass Mg/molar mass Mg).

3. Determine the mass of magnesium oxide formed.

4. Determine the mass of oxygen that combined with the magnesium.

5. Calculate the number of moles of oxygen atoms that were used.

6. Calculate the ratio between moles of magnesium used and moles of oxygen used. Express this ratio in simplest whole-number form.

7. Based on your experimental data, write the empirical formula for magnesium oxide.

Conclusions

1. Calculate the percent error in your determination of the magnesium:oxygen mole ratio, using the accepted value provided by your teacher.

$$\text{Percent error} = \frac{|\text{accepted value} - \text{experimental value}|}{\text{accepted value}} \times 100 \text{ percent}$$

2. Identify major sources of error in this experiment. Explain how the magnesium:oxygen ratio would be affected by each error you identify.

3. Is there agreement among the results obtained by others in the class? What does the class data tell you about the empirical formula of a compound?

4. Interpret, in terms of atoms and in terms of moles, the subscripts in a chemical formula such as C_2H_6.

Extension

1. Hydrogen and oxygen gases combine explosively to form water. Design an experiment to determine the empirical formula of water. It might be useful here to recall what you learned in Experiment 8.

Experiment

10 Qualitative Analysis

Text reference: Section 7.5

Background

In Experiment 6, you learned how to identify the presence of common ions by conducting chemical tests, a process called qualitative analysis. But how do you test a solution containing mixtures of ions with similar chemical behavior? For example, both calcium and barium ions react with oxalate ions ($C_2O_4^{2-}$) to form white precipitates. If you add oxalate ions to an unknown solution and a white precipitate forms, you cannot say conclusively whether the solution contains only calcium ions, only barium ions, or a combination of both. Additional tests are required to identify the unknown solution.

In this experiment you will observe the reactions that occur when four solutions are mixed with each of three different reagents. Using these reactions as a reference, you will develop a systematic set of tests to identify an unknown solution. The solutions and reagents are deliberately unlabeled; knowledge of the chemicals used is not important. Instead, focus your attention on making careful observations and developing a logical, systematic approach for identifying the unknown solution.

Goals

- **Observe** reactions between a set of solutions and a set of reagents.
- **Design** an analytical scheme to identify an unknown solution.
- **Identify** an unknown solution.

Equipment

safety goggles
1 spot plate or 3–12 small test tubes
1 plastic wash bottle

Materials

set of solutions: 1, 2, 3, 4 [T] [I]
set of reagents: A, B, C [T] [I]
unknown solutions
paper towels
distilled water

Safety

- Note the Safety Symbols used here and in the Procedure section. Review safety information on pages 7–10.
- Always wear safety goggles when working in the lab.
- Some of the chemicals used in this experiment are poisonous. Treat all chemicals with care. Do not mix any chemicals except as directed in the Procedure section.

Procedure

Copy Table 10.1 into your laboratory notebook. As you perform the experiment, record your observations in this table.

1. Clean the spot plate or test tubes with distilled water. In separate depressions on the spot plate or in separate test tubes, mix solutions 1 through 4, one at a time with each of the reagents. Use 1–2 drops of each solution. Record results.

2. Study your results and plan how to identify your unknown using the fewest number of tests.

3. Obtain an unknown and identify it as solution 1, 2, 3, or 4 by testing it with the reagents. Record the tests done and the results obtained.

4. Repeat step 3 with a second unknown solution. Record the tests done and the results obtained.

5. Follow your teacher's instructions for proper disposal of the materials.

Data Record

Table 10.1 Results of Mixing Solutions and Reagents			
	Reagent A	Reagent B	Reagent C
Solution 1			
Solution 2			
Solution 3			
Solution 4			
Unknown			
Unknown			

Conclusions

1. Without knowing the identity of the chemicals in the experiment, you identified an unknown solution. Explain how.

2. Based on your experimental results, how would you distinguish between solutions 1 and 3? Between solutions 2 and 3?

Extension

1. Suppose someone has randomly relabeled the solutions used in this experiment as I, II, III, and IV and the reagents as X, Y, and Z. Using the facts that follow, consult Table 10.1 and correctly identify the solutions and reagents by their original designations (1, 2, 3, 4, A, B, C).

When mixed:

I and Y produce a red precipitate.
II and Y produce no precipitate.
II and X produce a yellow precipitate.
III and Z produce a white precipitate.

Experiment

11 Types of Chemical Reactions

Text reference:
Sections 7.6–7.10

Background

Although countless chemical reactions exist, nearly all of them can be classified into a few specific categories. In this experiment, you will learn to differentiate five general types of chemical reactions. Some of the reactions you will perform; others will be demonstrated by your teacher. From observations, you will identify the products of each reaction and determine the type of reaction that has taken place. You will consider the following reaction types: *combination reactions, decomposition reactions, single-replacement reactions, double-replacement reactions,* and *combustion reactions.* The majority of common chemical reactions can be classified as belonging to one of these categories.

Goals

- **Observe** chemical reactions of different reaction types.
- **Classify** chemical reactions according to type.
- **Write** balanced chemical equations for each reaction.

Equipment

(Student Experiment)
safety goggles
2 small test tubes
2 medium test tubes
1 test-tube rack
1 gas burner
1 ring stand
1 utility clamp
1 dropper pipet
1 crucible tongs

(Teacher Demonstration)
1 electrolysis apparatus
1 rubber stopper, one-holed
1 large test tube
1 glass tube, 25-cm length, bent at 90° angle in center

Materials

(Student Experiment)

iron filings, Fe
magnesium turnings, Mg [F]
$0.1M$ copper(II) sulfate, $CuSO_4$ [T]
$0.1M$ lead(II) nitrate, $Pb(NO_3)_2$ [T]
$0.1M$ potassium iodide, KI [T]
3% hydrogen peroxide, H_2O_2
$6M$ hydrochloric acid, HCl [C] [T]
wood splints
matches

(Teacher Demonstration)

sodium hydrogen carbonate, $NaHCO_3$
limewater, saturated solution of calcium oxide, CaO [I]
wood splints
matches

Safety

- Note the safety symbols used here and in the Procedure section. Review safety information on pages 7–10.
- Always wear safety goggles when working in the lab.
- Hydrochloric acid is corrosive and can cause severe burns.
- Lead and copper compounds are toxic. Use as little of these compounds as practical.

Procedure

Copy Table 11.1 into your laboratory notebook. As you perform the experiment, record your observations in this table.

Part A. Student Experiments

1. **Iron metal and copper(II) sulfate solution.** Half-fill a small test tube with copper(II) sulfate solution. Add about 2 g of iron filings to the solution. After 5 minutes record your observations.

2. **Lead(II) nitrate and potassium iodide solutions.** Put 2 mL of lead(II) nitrate solution into a small test tube. Add 5–10 drops of potassium iodide solution. Record your observations.

3. **Magnesium metal and hydrochloric acid. CAUTION:** *Hydrochloric acid is corrosive.* Half-fill a medium-sized test tube with $6M$ hydrochloric acid. Place the test tube in a test-tube rack and add several magnesium

turnings. Identify any gas that forms by using crucible tongs to hold a *burning* wood splint at the mouth of the test tube. Record your observations.

4. Action of heat on hydrogen peroxide. Add 2 mL of the 3% hydrogen peroxide solution to a medium-sized test tube. Clamp the test tube to a ring stand as shown in Figure 11.1. **CAUTION:** *Make sure that the mouth of the tube is pointed away from you and away from everyone else.* Heat the solution *very gently.* Identify any gas that forms by using crucible tongs to insert a *glowing* wood splint into the mouth of the test tube. Record your observations.

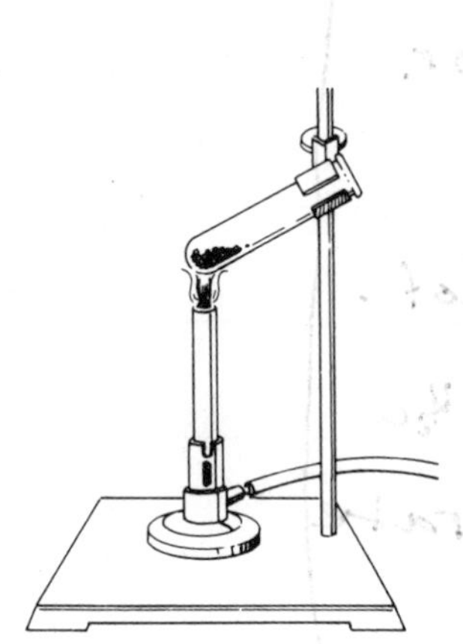

Figure 11.1

Part B. Teacher Demonstrations

5. Action of electricity on water (electrolysis). Water can be broken down to its component elements by passing electricity through it. This process is called *electrolysis.* Your teacher will explain the apparatus shown in Figure 11.2. Make observations of the reaction during a 10-minute period.

6. Action of heat on sodium hydrogen carbonate. Solid sodium hydrogen carbonate will be heated strongly in a large test tube for 2 minutes. The gas that is given off will be tested by exposing it to a burning splint and by bubbling it through limewater. Record your observations of these tests.

7. Follow your teacher's instructions for proper disposal of the materials.

Figure 11.2

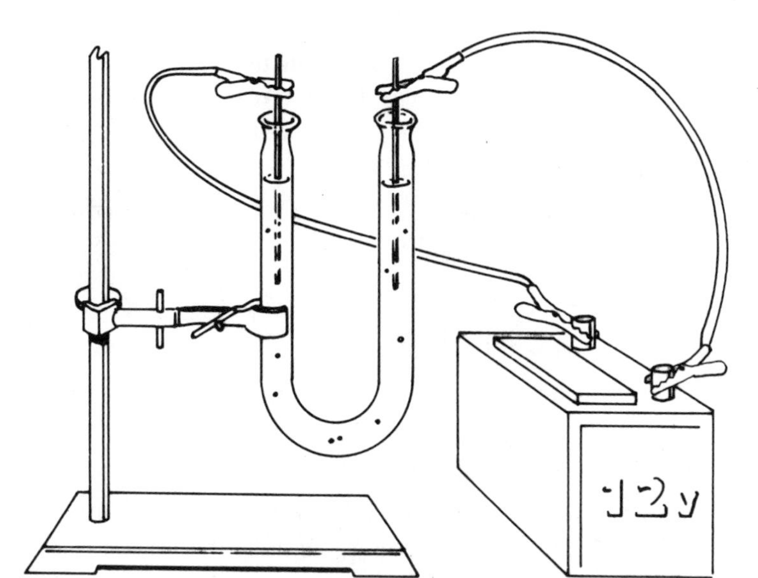

Data Record

Table 11.1 Observations

Reaction	Observations	Reaction Type
Fe and $CuSO_4$	loses blue color.	
$Pb(NO_3)_2$ and KI	turned yellow	
Mg and HCl	Bubbled and turned hot.	
H_2O_2 and heat	produced bubbles of H_2O	
electrolysis of H_2O	H, O_2 seperate	
$NaHCO_3$ and heat	explosion	

produced Hydrogen

Data Analysis

1. Classify each of the reactions you observed as one of the five reaction types discussed in the Background section. Record your answers in Table 11.1.

2. Write an equation for each reaction observed. Indicate the state (*s, l, g, aq*) for each reactant and product, then balance each equation.

3. Although no combustion reactions were described in the Procedure section, two combustion reactions did occur in the course of this experiment. The reactants were H_2 and CH_4 (natural gas), respectively. Write a balanced equation for the combustion of each of these substances.

4. Identify the combustion reaction in the previous question that is also a combination reaction.

Conclusions

1. Describe in your own words the five types of chemical reactions listed in the Background section. Explain how to distinguish each of these types of reactions.

2. List the tests that were used to identify the three gases produced in this experiment.

3. Which type(s) of reactions are characterized by:

   a. two products
   b. a single reactant
   c. two reactants
   d. a single product

Extensions

1. Make a list of the reactions observed in Experiments 1–10. Identify the type of reaction in as many cases as possible.

Experiment

12 Quantitative Analysis

Text reference:
Sections 8.1–8.4

Background

By now you are familiar with seeing and working with balanced chemical equations. But how do you know the coefficients in these equations are correct? Do the coefficients reflect how the chemical substances actually combine? In this experiment, you will determine the values for the coefficients used in a balanced chemical equation. The coefficients you are trying to determine are for the reaction of iron metal with a copper(II) chloride solution, which produces copper metal and an iron compound.

You will use the fact that the coefficients of the substances in a chemical equation represent the relative number of moles of each substance involved in the reaction. You will determine the relative numbers of moles of each reactant and product in the reaction you observe. From the mole ratios, you will derive the appropriate coefficients to be used in the chemical equation. If your experiment is successful, you should be able to determine the mole ratio of the *iron used* to the *copper produced.*

Goals

- **Measure** the number of moles of iron consumed and copper produced in the reaction of iron with aqueous copper(II) chloride.
- **Write** a balanced chemical equation for the reaction.

Equipment

safety goggles
1 50-mL graduated cylinder
2 250-mL beakers
1 plastic wash bottle
1 glass stirring rod
2 drying ovens/class or
2 heat lamps/class
1 crucible tongs
8 centigram balances/class
1 glass-marking pencil/class

Materials

iron nails, Fe
1*M* copper(II) chloride
dihydrate, $CuCl_2 \cdot 2H_2O$ T
steel wool
paper towel
distilled water

Safety

- Note the Safety Symbols used here and in the Procedure section. Review the safety information on pages 7–10.
- Always wear safety goggles when working in the lab.
- Copper(II) chloride solution is toxic. Avoid skin contact with this material.

Procedure

Copy Tables 12.1 and 12.2 into your laboratory notebook. As you perform the experiment, record your data in Table 12.1 and your observations in Table 12.2.

Day 1

1. Using a glass-marking pencil, label a clean, dry 250-mL beaker with your name. Determine the mass of the beaker to the nearest 0.01 g, and record the measurement in Table 12.1.

2. Add 50 mL of copper(II) chloride solution to the beaker.

3. Clean two iron nails with steel wool to remove any rust or protective coating. Determine the combined mass of the nails to the nearest 0.01 g and record.

4. Slide the nails carefully into the solution of copper(II) chloride. Let the beaker stand undisturbed for at least 20 minutes. Record any evidence of a chemical reaction in Table 12.2.

5. Using crucible tongs, remove one of the nails from the reaction solution. Hold the nail over the reaction beaker. Rinse the adherent reaction product off the nail and into the beaker, using a jet of distilled water from a wash bottle, as shown in Figure 12.1. Repeat this procedure for the second nail.

6. Allow the nails to dry on a paper towel in a safe place. (You will remeasure their mass later.)

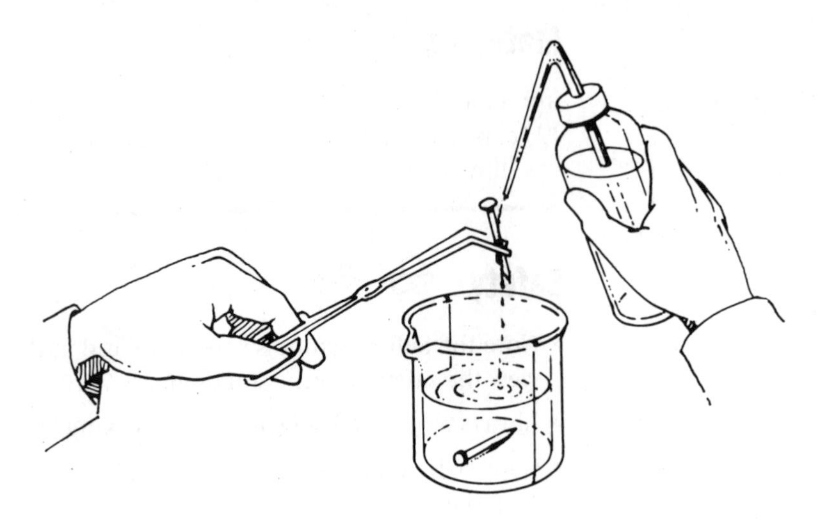

Figure 12.1

7. Carefully decant the liquid portion of the reaction solution into another 250-mL beaker, as shown in Figure 12.2. Leave the solid reaction product in the original beaker. Dispose of the decanted solution by pouring it into the sink.

8. Use 25 mL of distilled water to wash the reaction product contained in the beaker. Decant the wash water into the collection container. Repeat the washing and decanting procedures two more times, being

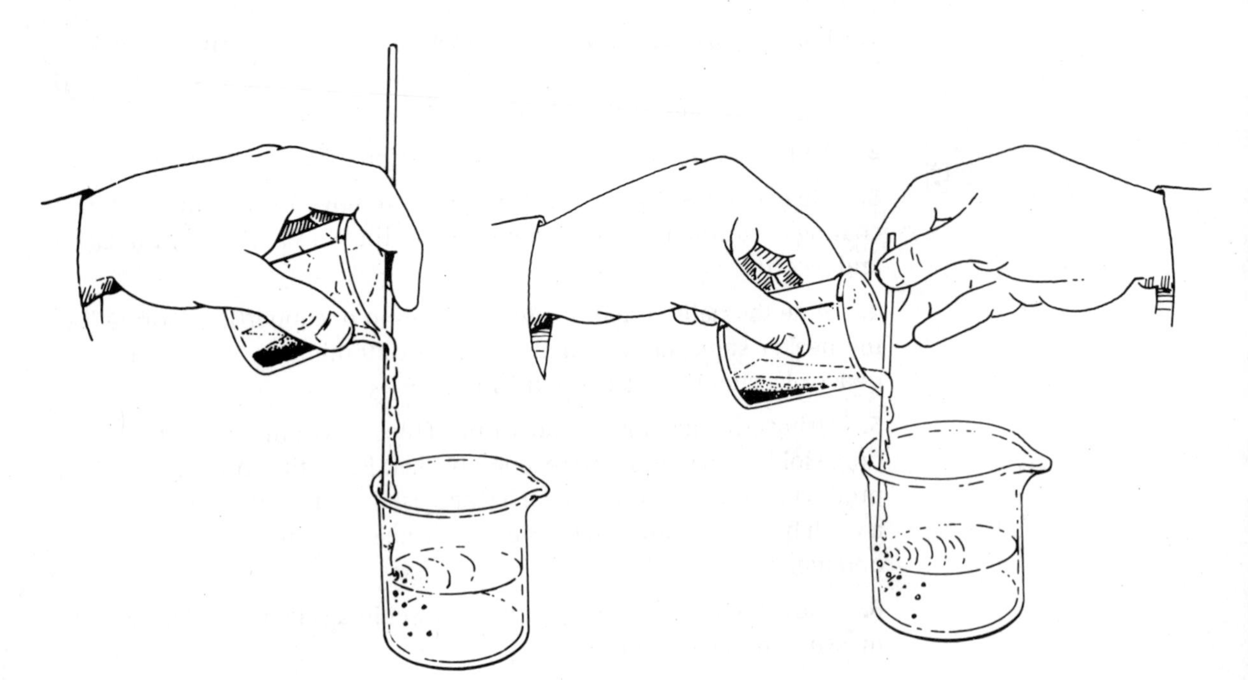

Figure 12.2

careful to avoid losing any reaction product. Pour the contents of the collection container into the sink.

9. Give the reaction beaker containing the solid product to your teacher to be dried.

Day 2

10. Determine the combined mass of the dry nails to the nearest 0.01 g and record the measurement.

11. Determine the mass of the beaker and the dry reaction product to the nearest 0.01 g and record the measurement. When you are finished, dispose of the nails and the solid product in a waste container.

Data Record

Table 12.1 Mass Determinations

Items	Mass (g)
empty dry beaker	
iron nails (before reaction)	
iron nails (after reaction)	
beaker and dry product	

Table 12.2 Observations

Step	Observations

Data Analysis

1. Determine the mass of iron lost by the nails.
2. Calculate the number of moles of iron used.
3. Determine the mass of the product produced.
4. Assuming that one of the products is copper metal, calculate the number of moles of copper produced.
5. Calculate the mole ratio of iron used to copper produced. Express this ratio as a simple whole-number ratio.

Conclusions

1. Calculate the percent error in your value for the mole ratio. Your teacher will give you the accepted value.

$$\text{Percent error} = \frac{|\text{accepted value} - \text{experimental value}|}{\text{accepted value}} \times 100 \text{ percent}$$

2. Assuming that one product is iron(II) chloride, write a balanced equation for the reaction. What type of reaction is this?
3. Copper could be lost in this experiment during the steps of washing and decanting. How would this effect the iron:copper mole ratio? Explain.
4. What other factors might account for any error in your mole ratio?
5. Examine the data collected by other members of the class. Were the masses of iron and copper the same in all experiments? Were the mole ratios the same? Does the mole ratio of a substance in a chemical equation depend on the amounts of reactants used?

Extensions

1. What test could you do to prove that the product is copper?
2. There was evidence that not all the copper chloride was consumed in this reaction. Describe the evidence. Design an experiment that would measure the amount of iron and copper chloride used. Show how you would calculate the mole ratio of copper chloride used to copper produced.
3. Identify two other cations besides the copper(II) ion that could be used in this experiment. For one of your choices, design and carry out an experiment to find the mole ratio of iron used to metal produced.

Experiment

13 Balanced Chemical Equations

Text reference:
Section 8.6

Background

Like a gymnast on a beam, the amounts of material involved in a chemical reaction must be properly balanced. An unbalanced gymnast will fall off the beam; an unbalanced equation will waste chemical reactants. In this experiment, you will examine the stoichiometry—the relationship between amounts of materials—of the reaction between lead nitrate and sodium iodide. The balanced equation is:

$$Pb(NO_3)_2(aq) + 2NaI(aq) \rightarrow PbI_2(s) + 2NaNO_3(aq)$$

You will also explore the concepts of limiting and excess reactants. A *limiting reactant* is completely used up in a reaction. The amount of product that can be formed depends on the quantity of limiting reactant present. An *excess reactant* is so called because after the reaction is complete, there is still an amount left unreacted. Finally, you will estimate the actual yield of one product, lead iodide, and compare it with the theoretical yield predicted from the balanced equation.

Goals

- **Compute** the mole ratio required for lead nitrate and sodium iodide to be completely converted into reaction products.
- **Observe** what happens when either lead nitrate or sodium iodide is present in excess.
- **Classify** reactants as either excess or limiting reactants.
- **Make graphs** comparing the actual and theoretical yields of lead iodide.

Materials

0.5*M* lead(II) nitrate, $Pb(NO_3)_2$ T   0.5*M* sodium iodide, NaI T

Equipment

safety goggles
2 250-mL beakers
6 large test tubes
1 test-tube rack
2 50-mL burets
1 twin buret clamp
1 ring stand
6 rubber stoppers
1 spot plate
1 dropper pipet
1 centimeter ruler

Safety

- Note the Safety Symbols used here and in the Procedure section. Review safety information on pages 7–10.
- Always wear safety goggles when working in the lab.
- Lead nitrate is toxic. Wash your hands thoroughly after use.

Procedure

Copy Tables 13.1 and 13.2 into your laboratory notebook. As you perform the experiment, record your results in these tables.

Part A

1. Number with the numerals 1–6, six large, clean, and dry test tubes.

2. Mount two 50-mL burets on a ring stand, using a twin buret clamp. Label one buret "NaI"; label the other "$Pb(NO_3)_2$".

3. Obtain, in separate labeled 250-mL beakers, about 50 mL of 0.5*M* $Pb(NO_3)_2$ and 75 mL of 0.5*M* NaI. Fill the labeled burets with these solutions.

4. Using the filled burets, add the solutions to the six test tubes according to the following table. Place each tube in a test-tube rack.

	Tube 1	Tube 2	Tube 3	Tube 4	Tube 5	Tube 6
0.5*M* $Pb(NO_3)_2$ (mL)	2.0	4.0	6.0	8.0	10.0	12.0
0.5*M* NaI (mL)	16.0	14.0	12.0	10.0	8.0	6.0

Keep the remaining solutions in the burets for later use.

5. Seal each tube with a rubber stopper. Mix the contents by inverting each tube *three times.* Do not shake.

6. Leave the tubes undisturbed in the test-tube rack for at least 10 minutes.

7. Measure the height of the yellow precipitate (lead iodide) in each tube to the nearest 0.1 cm and record the measurement.

Part B

8. **Testing the supernatant for excess reagent.** The liquid above a settled precipitate is called the *supernatant.* With a dropper pipet, remove a sample of supernatant from tube 1. Add *one* drop of supernatant to each of two adjacent depressions on a spot plate. Rinse the dropper with distilled water and repeat this procedure for tubes 2–6.

9. Add a drop of 0.5*M* $Pb(NO_3)_2$ to one set of samples from tubes 1–6.

10. Add a drop of 0.5*M* NaI to the other set of samples.

11. Record the results of these spot-plate tests in Table 13.2.

12. Follow your teacher's instructions for proper disposal of the materials.

Data Record

Table 13.1 Data for Reaction Mixtures

Tube Number	$Pb(NO_3)_2$ (mL)	$Pb(NO_3)_2$ (mol)	NaI (mL)	NaI (mol)	Height Ppt. (cm)	Maximum Theoretical Yield Ppt. (mol)
1	2	.001 moles	16	.008 moles	1.5	.001
2	4	.002 moles	14	.007 moles	2.	.002
3	6	.003 moles	12	.006 moles	4.0	.003
4	8	.004 moles	10	.005 moles	4.2	.004
5	10	.005 moles	8	.004 moles	2.6	.004
6	12	.006 moles	6	.003 moles	2.3	.003

Table 13.2 Spot Tests of Supernatant Samples from Reaction Tubes						
Substance Added	Tube 1 Ppt.?	Tube 2 Ppt.?	Tube 3 Ppt.?	Tube 4 Ppt.?	Tube 5 Ppt.?	Tube 6 Ppt.?
$Pb(NO_3)_2$	Y	Y	n	n	n	n
NaI	n	n	Y	Y	Y	Y
reagent present in excess:	NaI	NaI	$Pb(NO_3)_2$	$Pb(NO_3)_2$	$Pb(NO_3)_2$	$Pb(NO_3)_2$

Data Analysis

Note, **one page of graph paper** is required for your report.

1. Calculate the number of moles of $Pb(NO_3)_2$ and NaI added to each tube. (**Hint:** Calculate how many moles would be in 1 mL and then multiply by the number of milliliters in the sample.) Enter your result in Table 13.1.

2. For the tube with the greatest amount of precipitate, calculate the mole ratio between $Pb(NO_3)_2$ and NaI.

3. Plot two *separate* bar graphs showing the height of lead iodide (cm) versus tube number. One graph should show the height of lead iodide actually obtained in each tube, and the other should show the maximum theoretical number of moles of lead iodide in each tube. Number the tubes 1–6 from left to right.

Conclusions

1. Which tube had little or no reaction of the supernatant with either $Pb(NO_3)_2$ or NaI? What is the mole ratio of the reactants in this tube?

2. How are your two graphs similar?

3. **a.** Write a complete ionic equation for the reaction observed in this experiment.

b. Indicate which ions are spectator ions in this reaction.

c. Write a net ionic equation for this reaction.

4. Examine the class data, especially for tube 3. Explain any inconsistency you observe in the results.

Extensions

1. The height of the precipitate formed was used as a measure of the amount of product formed in this experiment. Design a similar experiment for the reaction between calcium carbonate and hydrochloric acid, where the product to be measured is a gas.

2. Explain how this experiment would have to be redesigned if 6 moles of NaI were required for each mole of $Pb(NO_3)_2$ in the balanced equation.

Experiment

14 Changes of Physical State

Text reference: Section 9.7

Background

If you have ever cooled a glass of water with ice cubes and watched water vapor condense on the outside of the glass, you know water can exist in distinct physical states—the solid state (ice), the liquid state (water), and the gaseous state (water vapor). In any pure substance, changes of physical state occur at constant, discrete temperatures that are uniquely characteristic of the substance. Changes in physical state include solids melting, liquids freezing and boiling, and gases condensing.

In this experiment, you will closely examine what happens when a pure substance undergoes a change in physical state. Specifically, you will investigate the melting and freezing behavior of a sample of an organic compound called lauric acid, $CH_3(CH_2)_{10}COOH$. You are chiefly concerned with two questions. First, does liquid lauric acid begin to freeze at the same temperature that solid lauric acid begins to melt? Second, what happens to the temperature of the lauric acid between the time freezing or melting begins and the time it is complete? You will also consider what happens to the energy that is put into or removed from the lauric acid system during melting or freezing.

Goals

- **Observe** the behavior of lauric acid during melting and freezing.
- **Make a graph** of the heating and cooling curves for lauric acid.
- **Interpret** the graph to find the freezing point and melting point of lauric acid.
- **Hypothesize** what happens to the energy that is put into or removed from lauric acid during melting and freezing.

Materials

lauric acid, $CH_3(CH_2)_{10}COOH$

copper wire, Cu

Equipment

safety goggles
2 400-mL beakers
2 thermometers
1 large test tube
2 wire gauzes
2 utility clamps
2 gas burners
2 ring stands
2 ring supports
1 timer with second hand/class
beaker tongs or 1 insulated glove
2 pliers/class
copper wire stirrer
rubber stopper

Safety

- Note the Safety Symbols used here and in the Procedure section. Review the safety information on pages 7–10.
- Always wear safety goggles when working in the lab.
- Mercury is extremely toxic, and mercury spills are very difficult to clean up. If you should break a mercury thermometer, immediately report the incident to your teacher.

Procedure

Copy Table 14.1 into your laboratory notebook. As you perform the experiment, record your data in this table.

Part A. The Change from Liquid to Solid

1. Heat about 250 mL of water in a 400-mL beaker to 30°C. Separately, heat 250 mL of water in another 400-mL beaker to 60°C.

2. Use a utility clamp to support a large test tube containing approximately 20 g of lauric acid in the hot (60°C) water. Make sure the lauric acid is totally beneath the water in the beaker and that the test tube does not touch the bottom of the beaker.

3. While the sample is heating, use the pliers to construct a stirrer from a piece of stiff copper wire as shown in Figure 14.1. When the crystals have melted, slip the loop of the wire stirrer around a thermometer fitted with a rubber stopper. Referring to Figure 14.2, place the stirrer-thermometer assembly in the test tube so that the thermometer bulb is at the center of the molten lauric acid and the stirrer moves easily up and down. The bulb of the thermometer should not touch the bottom of the test tube. Make certain that the markings on the thermometer can be easily read.

Figure 14.1

4. Carefully replace the beaker containing the 60°C water with the beaker containing the 30°C water. Do this by removing the gas burner and lowering the ring stand while holding the beaker with tongs or insulated gloves. Return the ring stand to its previous position.

5. Gently stir the lauric acid. When its temperature has fallen to about 55°C, take a temperature reading every 30 seconds. Record the temperatures to the nearest 0.1°C. Continue stirring the lauric acid and recording temperature readings until the temperature of the material has fallen to 40°C or lower. (Note: When most of the lauric acid has solidified, you will no longer be able to stir the contents. Continue taking temperature readings during this period.)

Part B. The Change from Solid to Liquid

6. Replace the beaker containing 30°C water with one that contains water at approximately 55°C. Begin to collect temperature data immediately. Record temperature measurements of the test-tube contents every 30 seconds, until the lauric acid is completely melted. Begin stirring as soon as you are able to move the copper stirrer freely. **CAUTION:** *Do not force the stirrer.*

7. Carefully disassemble the apparatus and dispose of the lauric acid as directed by your teacher.

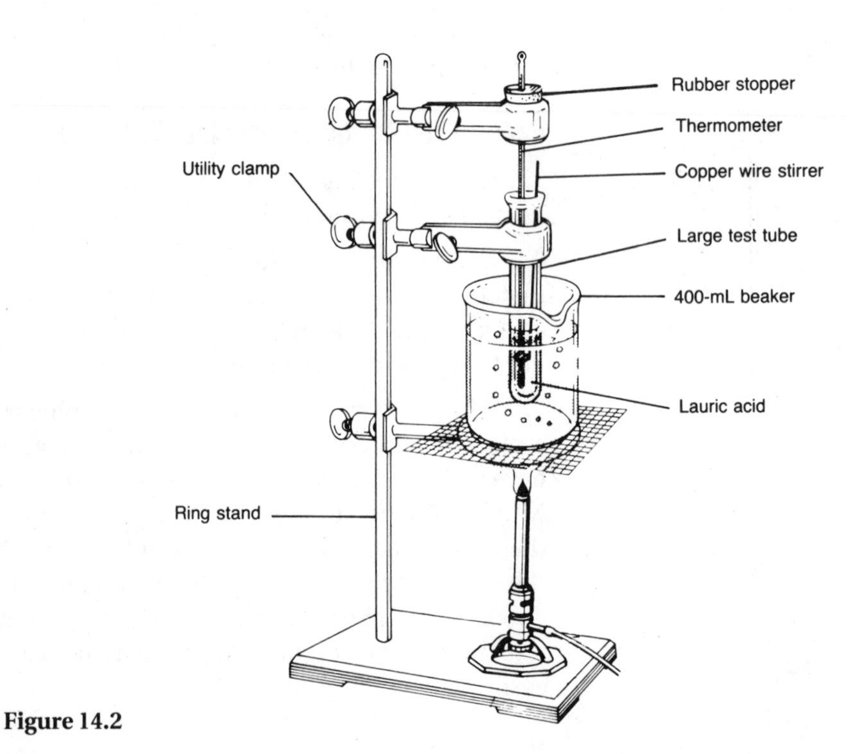

Figure 14.2

Data Record

Table 14.1 Heating and Cooling Data

Part A		Part B	
Time (min)	Temperature (°C)	Time (min)	Temperature (°C)

Data Analysis

Note, **one page of graph paper** is required for your report.

1. Construct a graph of your data from Part A. Plot temperature versus time. Choose a scale that uses the full sheet of graph paper. Draw a smooth curve through the points.

2. Plot the data from Part B on the same graph and draw a smooth curve.

3. Does the temperature of a substance vary while it is melting or freezing? Explain.

4. Using data from Part A, determine the freezing point of lauric acid.

5. Using data from Part B, determine the melting point of lauric acid.

6. Does lauric acid melt and freeze at the same temperature?

Conclusions

1. Explain the shape of the curves in terms of the energy changes that are occurring in the sample as it heats up and melts and as it cools down and freezes.

2. Explain how an increase in the amount of lauric acid used would affect the shape of the curves.

3. Explain in your own words what is going on at the molecular level as liquid lauric acid cools and freezes.

Extension

1. Construct a model that illustrates the energy effects and the structural changes that occur during a change of state.

Experiment

15 The Specific Heat of a Metal

Text reference:
Sections 10.2, 10.3

Background

On a sunny day, the water in a swimming pool may warm up a degree or two while the concrete around the pool may become too hot to walk on in your bare feet. This may seem strange because both the concrete and the water are being heated by the same source—the sun. This evidence suggests it takes more heat to raise the temperature of some substances than others. This, in fact, is true: the amount of heat required to equally raise the temperature of equal masses of different substances depends on what the substances are. The amount of heat that is required to raise the temperature of 1 g of a substance by 1° Celsius is called the *specific heat capacity*, or simply the *specific heat*, of that substance. Water, for instance, has a specific heat of 1.0 cal/(g × °C). This value is high in comparison with the specific heats for other materials, such as concrete. In this experiment, you will use a simple calorimeter and your knowledge of the specific heat of water to determine the specific heat of lead.

Goals

- **Measure** the specific heat of lead.
- **Identify** an unknown metal from its specific heat (optional).

Equipment

safety goggles
1 50-mL beaker
1 250-mL beaker
1 400-mL beaker
1 100-mL graduated cylinder
1 large test tube
1 glass stirring rod
1 utility clamp
1 ring stand
1 ring support
1 wire gauze
1 gas burner
8 centigram balances/class
1 plastic-foam cup
1 thermometer

Materials

lead shot, Pb [T]
unknown metal [T]
distilled water

Safety

- Note the Safety Symbols used here and in the Procedure section. Review safety information on pages 7–10.
- Always wear safety goggles when working in the lab.
- Lead is a toxic metal. Wash your hands thoroughly after use.
- Mercury is extremely toxic, and mercury spills are very difficult to clean up. If you should break a mercury thermometer, immediately report the incident to your teacher.

Procedure

Copy Table 15.1 into your laboratory notebook. As you perform the experiment, record your data in this table.

1. Heat 250 mL of water in a 400-mL beaker, until it is boiling gently.

2. While the water is heating, determine the mass of a clean, dry 50-mL beaker to the nearest 0.01 g and record. Add between 80 g and 120 g of lead shot to the beaker. Measure the combined mass of the beaker and lead to the nearest 0.01 g and record the measurement.

3. Transfer the lead shot to a large, dry test tube. Use the utility clamp to suspend the test tube in the boiling water as shown in Figure 15.1. The lead shot should be below the level of the water in the beaker. Leave the test tube in the boiling water bath for at least 10 minutes.

4. While the lead shot is heating, measure 100 mL of distilled water in a graduated cylinder. Pour the water into a plastic-foam cup, and place the cup in a 250-mL beaker for support, as shown in Figure 15.2.

5. Measure and record the temperature of the water in the plastic-foam cup and of the water in the boiling bath.

6. Remove the test tube from the boiling water and quickly pour the lead shot into the water-filled plastic-foam cup. Place a thermometer and a glass stirring rod into the cup. Use the stirring rod to gently stir the lead shot. Do not stir the shot with the thermometer. Note the temperature frequently, and record the maximum temperature reached.

7. Pour the water off, and return the lead shot to your teacher.

8. (Optional) Follow the same procedure to determine the specific heat of an unknown metal.

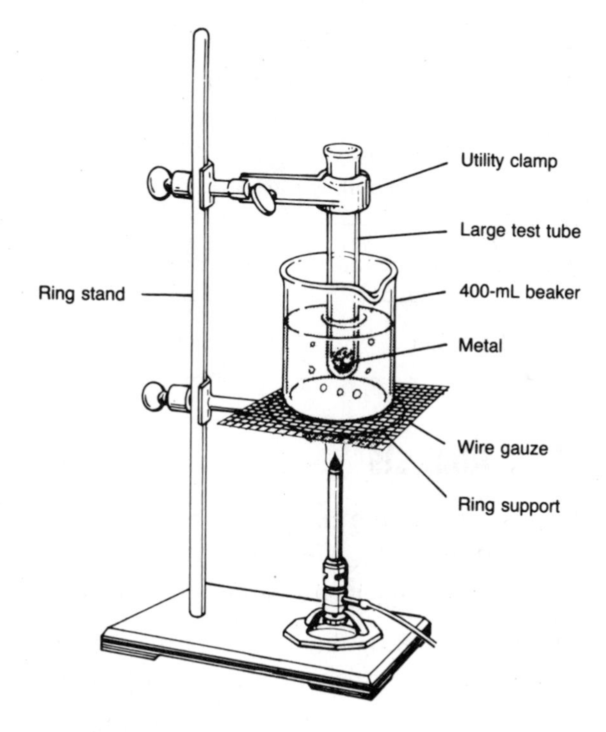

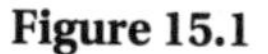

Figure 15.1

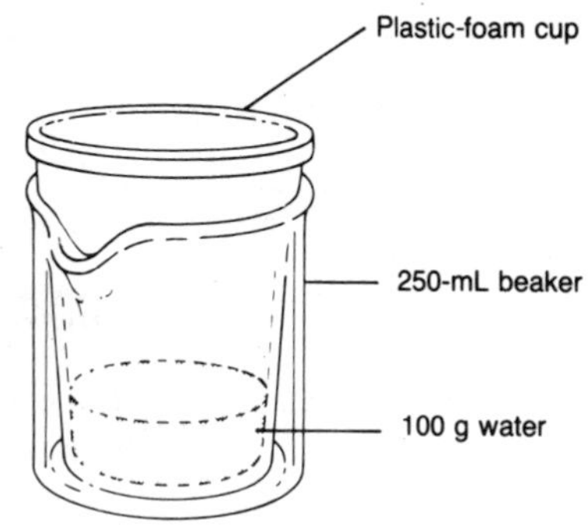

Figure 15.2

Data Record

Table 15.1 Data		
	Trial 1	**Trial 2**
mass of 50-mL beaker		
mass of 50-mL beaker + lead shot		
mass of lead shot		
initial temperature of water in cup		
initial temperature of lead shot (temperature of boiling water)		
maximum temperature of lead + water		
mass of water		

Data Analysis

1. Determine the changes in temperature of the water (ΔT_{water}) and of the lead shot (ΔT_{lead}) for each trial.

2. Calculate the heat gained by the water in each trial.

3. Remembering that the heat gained by the water is equal to the heat lost by the lead, calculate the specific heat of lead for each trial.

4. Calculate the average value for the specific heat of lead in your experiment.

5. If you tested an unknown, repeat these calculations to determine the specific heat of the unknown metal.

Conclusions

1. Calculate the percent error in the specific heat value that you determined experimentally. Use the accepted value given by your teacher.

$$\text{percent error} = \frac{|\text{accepted value} - \text{experimental value}|}{\text{accepted value}} \times 100 \text{ percent}$$

2. You assumed that the initial temperature of the lead shot was the same as that of the boiling water. If the lead shot was actually at a lower temperature than the water, how would your value for the specific heat be affected?

3. Identify other possible sources of error in this experiment.

4. Compare your value for the specific heat of lead to the values obtained by your classmates. Can specific heat be used to identify substances?

Extension

1. Design experiments to determine the specific heats of ethyl alcohol, methyl alcohol, and oil.

Experiment

16 Heats of Reaction

Text reference: Sections 10.4–10.6

Background

Energy changes occur in all chemical reactions; energy is either absorbed or released. If energy is released in the form of heat, the reaction is called *exothermic*. If energy is absorbed, the reaction is called *endothermic*. In this experiment, you will measure the amounts of heat released in these three related exothermic reactions:

(1) $NaOH(s) \rightarrow Na^+(aq) + OH^-(aq) + x_1$ kcal

(2) $NaOH(s) + H^+(aq) + Cl^-(aq) \rightarrow H_2O + Na^+(aq) + Cl^-(aq) + x_2$ kcal

(3) $Na^+(aq) + OH^-(aq) + H^+(aq) + Cl^-(aq) \rightarrow H_2O + Na^+(aq) + Cl^-(aq) + x_3$ kcal

After determining the heats of reaction, you will analyze your data and verify the additive nature of heats of reaction.

Goals

- **Measure** the heat released in three different exothermic reactions.
- **Demonstrate** that heats of reaction are additive.

Equipment

safety goggles
1 plastic-foam cup
1 100-mL graduated cylinder
1 400-mL beaker
1 50-mL beaker
1 thermometer
8 centigram balances/class
1 spatula

Materials

sodium hydroxide pellets, NaOH [C] [T]
1.0*M* sodium hydroxide, NaOH [C] [T]
0.5*M* hydrochloric acid, HCl [T] [I]
1.0*M* hydrochloric acid, HCl [T] [I]
distilled water

Safety

- Note the Safety Symbols used here and in the Procedure section. Review safety information on pages 7–10.
- Always wear safety goggles when working in the lab.
- $0.5M$ and $1.0M$ hydrochloric acid are eye and skin irritants.
- Sodium hydroxide is a very corrosive material that can cause severe skin burns and permanent eye damage. Under no circumstances should you handle solid sodium hydroxide with your fingers.
- Sodium hydroxide pellets absorb water from the air and can eventually be mistaken for a puddle of water. Never leave the sodium hydroxide pellets on the balance or on the laboratory bench.
- Mercury is extremely toxic, and a mercury spill is very difficult to clean up. If you should break a mercury thermometer, immediately report the incident to your teacher.

Procedure

Copy Tables 16.1 and 16.2 into your laboratory notebook. As you perform the experiment, record your data in Table 16.1.

Procedure note: After each reaction, dispose of the solution as directed by your teacher and rinse the cup and thermometer with water.

Reaction 1

1. Measure 100 mL of distilled water into a plastic-foam cup. Place the cup inside a 400-mL beaker for support. This assembly, together with a thermometer, will serve as your calorimeter.

2. Measure and record the mass of a 50-mL beaker to the nearest 0.01 g. **CAUTION:** *NaOH is extremely corrosive.* Using a spatula, add as close to 2.0 g as possible of sodium hydroxide pellets to the beaker. Measure and record the combined mass of the beaker and sodium hydroxide to the nearest 0.01 g. (Do this operation as quickly as possible to avoid error due to absorption of water by the NaOH.)

3. Measure and record the temperature of the water in the foam cup to the nearest 0.5°C. Add the weighed NaOH pellets to the water in the calorimeter. Stir the mixture *gently* with the thermometer, until all the solid has dissolved. **CAUTION:** *Hold the thermometer with your hand at all times.* Record the highest temperature reached during the reaction.

Reaction 2

4. Measure 100 mL of 0.50*M* HCl into the plastic-foam cup and place the cup inside a 400-mL beaker. **CAUTION:** *Low concentration hydrochloric acid can irritate your skin.*

5. Using a spatula, measure out 2.00 g of solid NaOH pellets using a spatula. **CAUTION:** *NaOH is extremely corrosive.*

6. Measure and record the temperature of the HCl solution in the foam cup. Add the NaOH pellets to the acid solution and stir *gently* until the solid is dissolved. Measure and record the highest temperature reached by the solution during the reaction.

Reaction 3

7. Place the plastic-foam cup inside a 400-mL beaker. Measure 50 mL of 1.0*M* HCl into the cup. Rinse the graduated cylinder and fill with 50 mL of 1.0*M* NaOH.

8. Measure and record the temperature of the HCl solution (in the cup) and the NaOH solution (in the cylinder) to the nearest 0.5°C. Rinse the thermometer between measurements.

9. Pour the NaOH solution into the foam cup. Stirring the mixture *gently*, measure and record the highest temperature reached.

Data Record

Table 16.1 Data

	Reaction 1	Reaction 2		Reaction 3
mass (beaker)			initial temperature (HCl solution)	
mass (beaker + NaOH)			initial temperature (NaOH solution)	
mass (NaOH)			average initial temperature	
initial temperature			final temperature	
final temperature				

Data Analysis

1. Determine the change in temperature, ΔT, for each reaction. Record your results in Table 16.2.

2. Calculate the mass of the reaction mixture in each reaction. (To do this, first determine the total volume of the solution. Then calculate the mass of the solution, based on the assumption that the density of the solution is the same as that of pure water, 1.0 g/mL.) Record your results in Table 16.2.

3. Calculate the total heat released in each reaction, assuming that the specific heat of the solution is the same as that of pure water, 1.0 cal/(g × °C). Remember:

$$\text{heat of reaction} = \text{specific heat} \times \Delta T \times \text{mass}$$

Record your results in Table 16.2.

4. Calculate the number of moles of NaOH used in reactions 1 and 2, and record the results in Table 16.2.

5. In reaction 3, the number of moles of NaOH can be calculated from the concentration of the solution (1.0*M*, or 1.0 mole of NaOH per liter of solution) and the volume used. The calculation is:

$$50 \text{ mL NaOH} \times \frac{1 \text{ mol NaOH}}{1000 \text{ mL NaOH}} = 0.050 \text{ mol NaOH}$$

Enter this result in Table 16.2.

6. Calculate the energy released per mole of NaOH for each reaction and enter your results in Table 16.2.

Table 16.2 Results of Calculations

Rxn Number	Mass of Rxn Mixture	ΔT	Total Heat Released	mol NaOH Consumed	Heat Released per mol NaOH
1					
2					
3					

Conclusions

1. Show that the equations for reactions 1 and 3, which are given in the Background section, add up to give the equation for reaction 2. Include the energy released per mole of NaOH in each equation.

2. Examine all the class data. Does the sum of the energy released per mole of NaOH for Reactions 1 and 3 equal the energy released per mole of NaOH in reaction 2? What factors might account for any difference?

3. Calculate the percent difference between the heat given off in reaction 2 and the sum of the heats given off in reactions 1 and 3. Assume that the heat given off in reaction 2 is correct.

$$\begin{array}{l}\text{percent difference} \\ \text{(in evolved heat)}\end{array} = \frac{|\text{heat}_2 - (\text{heat}_1 + \text{heat}_3)|}{\text{heat}_2} \times 100 \text{ percent}$$

4. Would changing the amount of NaOH used in reaction 1 affect the value obtained for the energy given off per mole of NaOH? Explain.

5. State in your own words what is meant by the additive nature of heats of reaction.

Extensions

1. Taking into account your answer to question 4 in the Data Analysis section, explain why you were asked to use exactly 2.00 g of NaOH in reactions 1 and 2, and an equivalent number of moles of NaOH in reaction 3.

2. Design an experiment to determine the specific heats of the solutions used in this experiment. (**Hint:** Review Experiment 15.) Repeat the calculations for this experiment, using the actual specific heats and densities of the solutions, instead of assuming them to be the same as those of pure water.

Experiment

17 Pressure–Volume Relationship for a Gas

Text reference:
Section 11.3

Background

When you squeeze a tennis ball, the ball compresses easily at first. But, as you squeeze harder, the ball becomes harder and harder to compress. You can explain these qualitative observations simply. For example, you know that the gas contained inside the tennis ball is being compressed into a smaller volume. As a result, the harder you squeeze, the smaller the volume and the greater the pressure exerted by the gas pushing outward against the ball. Therefore, the harder you squeeze the ball, the more resistance you encounter. This example suggests a relationship between the volume and pressure of a gas. In this experiment, you will measure the pressure of a gas sample as its volume is changed. You will then analyze your data to determine the relationship that exists between the volume and pressure of a gas.

Goals

- **Collect data** needed to find the relationship between the pressure and the volume of a gas.
- **Make a graph** of pressure versus volume for a gas.
- **Interpret** the relationship between pressure and volume from the graph.

Equipment

safety goggles
plastic tubing, 1-cm × 5-cm length
1 50-cm glass capillary tube, fire-polished
1 500-mL filter flask
1 50-mL graduated cylinder
1 500-mL graduated cylinder
2 ring stands
2 utility clamps
1 centimeter ruler
8 meter sticks/class

1 one-holed rubber stopper, to fit filter flask
1 30-mL plastic syringe
8 glass-marking pencils/class
1 barometer/class
1 pinch clamp
cloth towels

Materials

dibutyl phthalate, $C_6H_4(CO_2C_4H_9)_2$ [T]
glycerin, $C_3H_8O_3$, in dropper bottle
silicone grease

Safety

- Note the Safety Symbols used here and in the Procedure section. Review safety information on pages 7–10.
- Always wear safety goggles when working in the lab.
- Dibutyl phthalate is toxic. Do not come in contact with this chemical.
- Follow directions carefully when inserting the glass tubing into the rubber stopper. Severe cuts may occur if the correct technique is not used.

Procedure

Copy Tables 18.1, 18.2, and 18.3 into your laboratory notebook. As you perform the experiment, record your data in Tables 17.1 and 17.2.

1. Select a one-holed rubber stopper to fit a 500-mL filter flask. The 50-cm capillary tube must fit snugly into the hole of the stopper. Push a 5-cm length of plastic tubing over the sidearm of the flask.

2. Measure 50 mL of dibutyl phthalate (DBP) in a *dry* 50-mL graduated cylinder. Pour this volume into the *dry* filter flask.

3. Use a centimeter ruler to measure and record the outside diameter of the capillary tube. Use a glass-marking pencil to mark the tube at 1-cm intervals. Lubricate one end of the tube with a drop or two of glycerin and *gently* twist the tube into the stopper as shown in Figure 17.1. Insert the rubber stopper, with capillary tube, into the mouth of the 500-mL filter flask. Adjust the capillary tube so that its lower end is about 5 mm below the surface of the DBP. Measure and record the length of the tube that is inside the flask (below the stopper).

4. Obtain a 30-mL syringe and apply a *thin film* of silicone grease so that the plunger operates smoothly. Depress the plunger to the 30-mL

Figure 17.1

Figure 17.2

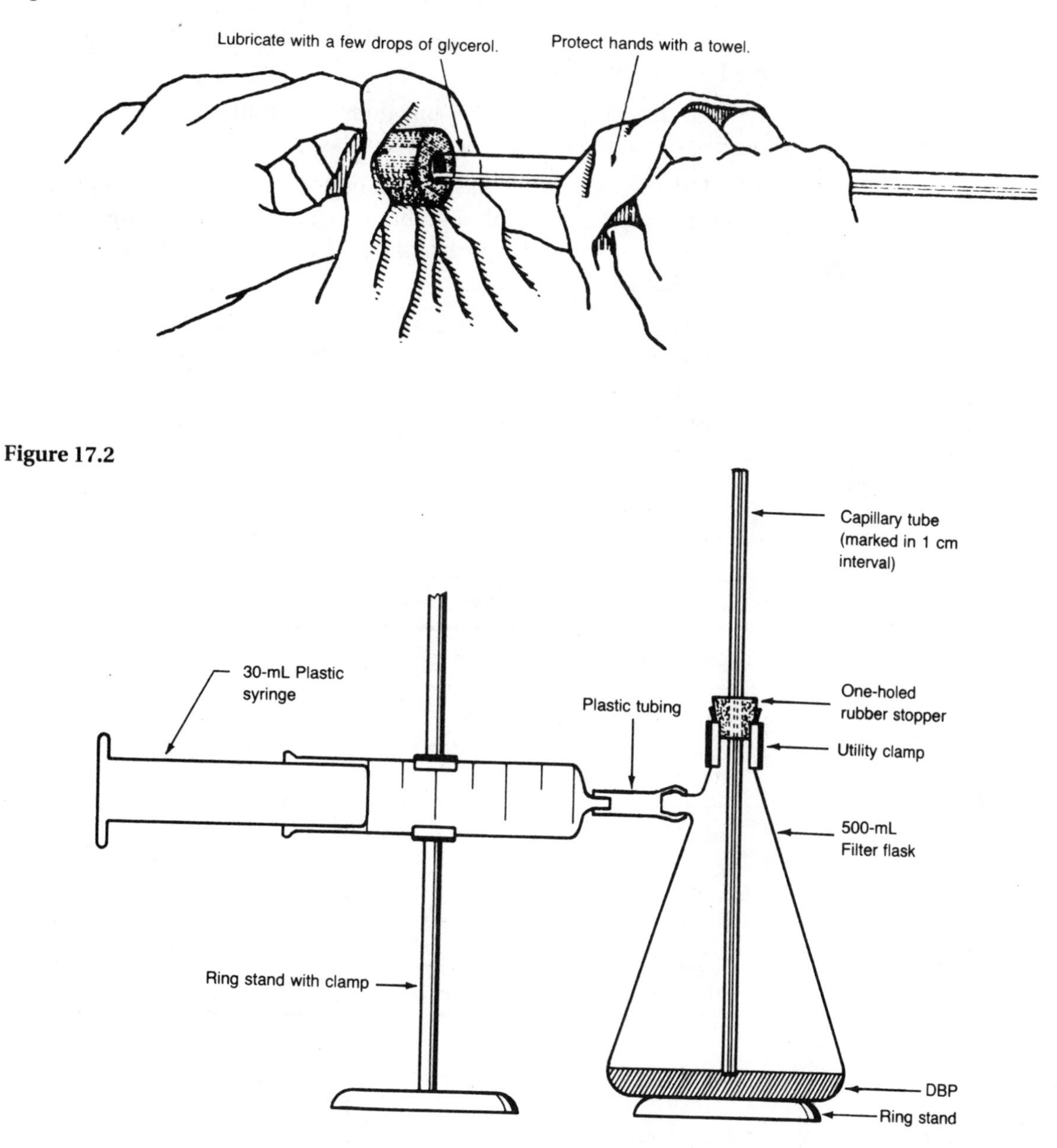

mark. Look at Figure 17.2. Insert the end of the syringe into the plastic tubing attached to the sidearm of the filter flask. Use a utility clamp attached to a ring stand to support the syringe.

5. Adjust the syringe plunger to indicate a volume of 30 mL. Record this reading and the height to which the DBP has risen in the capillary tube in Table 17.2.

6. Depress the plunger to the 25-mL mark. Record this reading. Allow the DBP column to come to rest in the capillary tube. Measure and record the height of the column.

7. Repeat this process at 5-mL intervals, until all the air has been pushed out of the syringe and into the flask.

8. Mark the neck of the flask at the bottom of the rubber stopper. Remove the stopper assembly and the syringe, leaving the plastic tubing in place on the sidearm. Dispose of the DBP and rinse the flask as directed by your teacher.

9. Use a pinch clamp to close the end of the plastic tubing as shown in Figure 17.3. Fill the flask with water to the mark on the neck. Pour this water into a 500-mL graduated cylinder. Record the volume to the nearest milliliter. This is the volume of your flask.

10. Record atmospheric pressure and room temperature in Table 17.1.

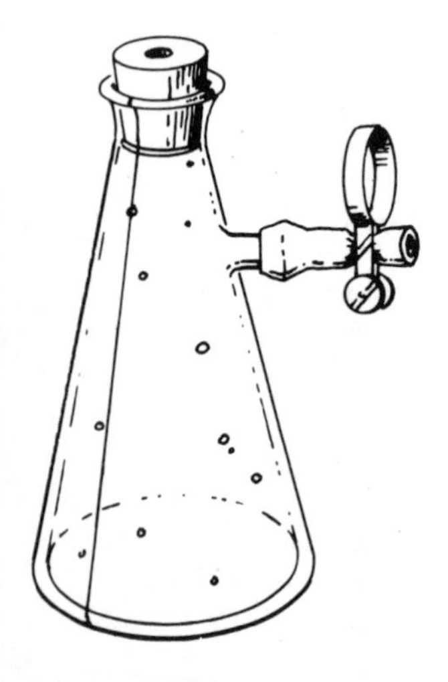

Figure 17.3

Data Record

Table 17.1 Preliminary Measurements
diameter of capillary tube:
length of capillary tube in flask:
barometric pressure:
room temperature:
volume of flask:

Table 17.2 Syringe Volume and DBP Height Readings

Trial 1		Trial 2	
volume (mL)	DBP height (cm)	volume (mL)	DBP height (cm)

Table 17.3 Volume and Pressure Calculations for Air in Flask

Trial 1			Trial 2		
P (mm Hg)	V (mL)	P × V	P (mm Hg)	V (mL)	P × V

Data Analysis

Note, **one page of graph paper** is required for your report.

1. Calculate the volume of air present in your apparatus during the experiment. You must correct the value determined in step 9—that is, for the volume of the flask to account for the following *included volumes*: the volume of the capillary tube in the flask, the volume of the DBP, and the volume of air in the syringe.

First, calculate the volume occupied by the capillary tube, using your measurements for the diameter of the tube and for the length of that part of the tube that was within the flask.

$$\text{volume of capillary tube} = \pi \times \text{radius}^2 \times \text{length}$$
$$= 3.14 \times (\text{diameter}/2)^2 \times \text{length}$$

Next, calculate the volume of air in the flask without the capillary tube or the DBP.

$$\begin{matrix}\text{volume of} \\ \text{air in flask}\end{matrix} = \begin{matrix}\text{volume} \\ \text{of flask}\end{matrix} - \begin{matrix}\text{volume} \\ \text{of DBP}\end{matrix} - \begin{matrix}\text{volume} \\ \text{of tube}\end{matrix}$$

Finally, for each trial, calculate the total volume of the air in the apparatus by adding the volume of the air in the syringe to the volume of air in the flask. Record this volume in Table 17.3.

2. For each trial, calculate the pressure exerted by the air enclosed within the flask. Use millimeters of mercury (mm Hg) as the units of pressure. You have already read the pressure directly in centimeters of DBP (cm DBP), but now you must convert this figure to millimeters of mercury (mm Hg). DBP has a density of 1.05 g/cm^3; while the density of mercury is 13.6 g/cm^3. This means that a pressure that supports a 1-mm column of DBP will support a column of mercury 1.05/13.6 mm (that is, 0.0772 mm) high.

Calculate the pressure of the volume of enclosed air in millimeters of mercury, using this equation:

$$\text{pressure of enclosed air in mm Hg} = \left(\text{height of DBP in mm} \times \frac{0.077\ \text{mm Hg}}{\text{mm DBP}}\right) + \text{room pressure in mm Hg}$$

Record the pressure for each trial in Table 17.3.

3. Calculate the product of the pressure of the enclosed air (see question 2) and the volume of the enclosed air (see question 1) for each trial. Record the results in Table 17.3.

4. Make a graph of pressure versus volume, on a full sheet of graph paper. Draw a best-fit smooth line for your data points.

Conclusions

1. Based on your data, what relationship exists between the pressure and volume of a gas (assuming constant temperature)?

2. Look up a statement of Boyle's law in your textbook. Are your results consistent with Boyle's law? Examine the class data. Is it consistent with the law? Explain.

3. Would your results have been affected if the room temperature had changed during the experiment? Explain.

4. How would your results have been affected if you had used a different gas in the flask? Explain.

Temperature–Volume Relationship for Gases

Text reference:
Section 11.5

Background

Have you noticed that the tires on automobiles appear to be a little flat on a cold winter's day? Conversely, a balloon inflated in a cold room will expand when taken to a warm room. These observations suggest that there is a relationship between the temperature and volume of a gas. If a gas is heated, its volume increases. If a gas is cooled, its volume decreases. In this experiment, you will measure the volume of a sample of air at a variety of temperatures and analyze the data to determine the relationship between the temperature and the volume of a gas. You will also extrapolate from your experimental data to determine absolute zero—the temperature at which a gas theoretically has no volume.

Goals

- **Collect data** relating volume and temperature of a gas.
- **Make a graph** of volume versus temperature for a gas.
- **Interpret** the relationship between volume and temperature from the graph.
- **Interpret** the value of absolute zero by extrapolation based on the graph.

Equipment

safety goggles
2 400-mL beakers
1 glass capillary tube, 2 mm × 20 cm
1 watch glass
1 centimeter ruler
1 thermometer
1 small rubber band
1 test-tube holder
1 forceps
1 ring stand
1 ring support
2 utility clamps
1 wire gauze
1 gas burner
1 dropper pipet
1 heat-resistant ceramic square

Materials

dibutyl phthalate, $C_6H_4(CO_2C_4H_9)_2$ T

ice and water

Safety 

- Note the Safety Symbols used here and in the Procedure section. Review safety information on pages 7–10.
- Always wear safety goggles when working in the lab.
- Dibutyl phthalate is toxic. Do not come in contact with this chemical.
- Hot glass tubing can cause burns. Make certain that any glass you use is cool before you handle it. Remember that hot glass looks the same as cold glass. If you should be burned, hold the burned area under cold running water, until the burning sensation stops. Notify your teacher immediately.

Procedure

Copy Table 18.1 into your laboratory notebook. As you perform the experiment, record your observations in this table.

1. Seal one end of the capillary tube by rotating it in a hot burner flame. Fire polish the open end. **CAUTION:** *Place all hot glassware on a heat-resistant ceramic square to cool.*

2. Using a dropper pipet, place about 2 mL of dibutyl phthalate (DBP) on a clean, dry watch glass.

3. Grasp the capillary tube in a test-tube holder and pass it back and forth through the burner flame for about 5 seconds as shown in Figure 18.1. Remove the tube from the heat and immediately insert the *open end* into the DBP on the watch glass. Allow a 1-cm length of DBP to be drawn up into the tube.

Figure 18.1

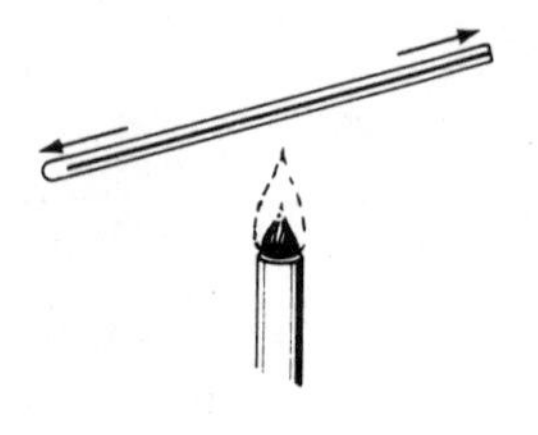

Fanning the capillary tube in flame

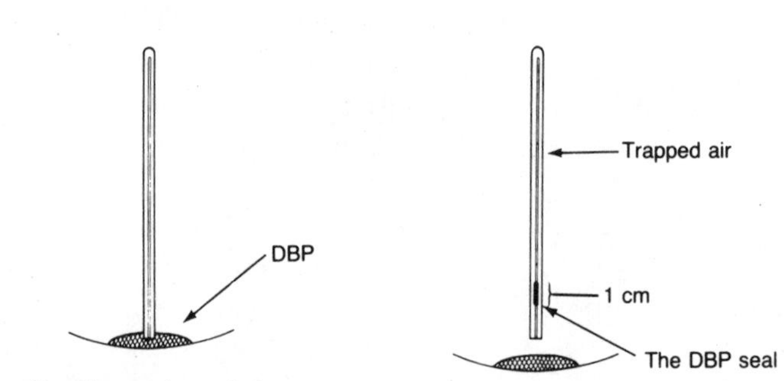

Trapping a volume of air

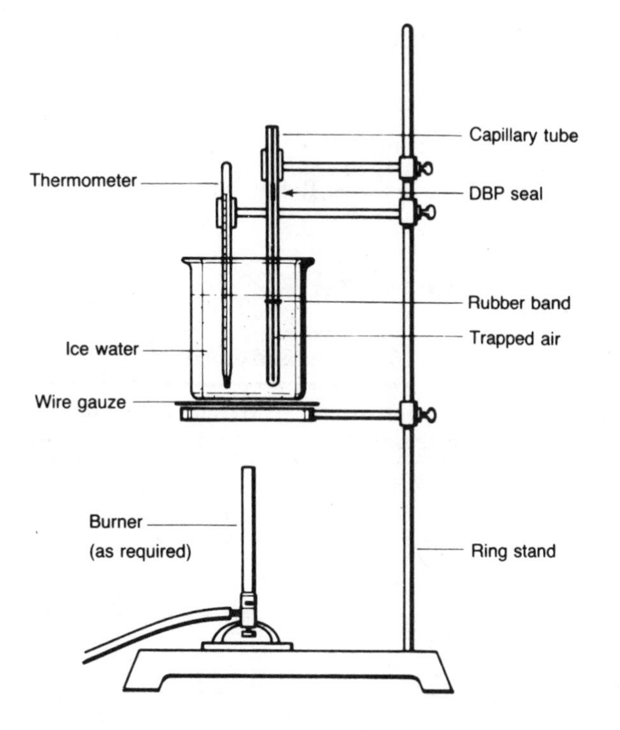

Figure 18.2

4. On a ring stand, clamp the tube vertically, with its *open end up*, and allow the tube to cool to room temperature. The column of trapped air should be between 5 and 10 cm long.

5. Push a small rubber band over the capillary tube until it is about halfway up the tube. This rubber band will serve as a distance marker.

6. Lower the clamped capillary tube, *open end up*, and a thermometer into ice water in a 400-mL beaker so that the entire column of trapped air is submerged as shown in Figure 18.2. Wait several minutes. Without removing the tube from the ice water, use forceps to slide the rubber band to mark the top of the air column. Wait another minute and readjust the band if necessary.

7. Measure and record the height of the column of trapped air inside the capillary tube. Measure and record the temperature of the ice water bath to the nearest 0.1°C.

8. Repeat steps 6 and 7, using a 400-mL beaker filled with water at room temperature.

9. Use a gas burner to heat the water in the beaker to about 40°C. Measure and record the new water temperature and the length of the air column. Repeat this procedure at 20°C intervals, up to 100°C, time permitting.

10. Save the DBP for reuse, or dispose of it as directed by your teacher.

Data Record

Table 18.1 Data and Calculations

Temperature of Water Bath (°C)	Height of Air Column (relative volume) (cm)	Temperature (K)	V/T (cm/K)

Data Analysis

Note, **two pages of graph paper** are required for your report.

1. Convert Celsius temperature to Kelvin and record the results in Table 18.1.

2. The height of the air column is proportional to the volume of air contained in the capillary tube. Therefore, use the height of the air column as the value for the volume of the gas, and calculate the volume/temperature ratio for each trial. Enter your results in Table 18.1.

3. Plot a graph of relative volume (measured in centimeters) versus temperature (in degrees Kelvin). Draw a best-fit straight line through the data points. Should the point (0,0) be on the line?

4. Plot a second graph using the same data, but using degrees Celsius as the unit of temperature. Begin the volume scale at 0 cm, but start the temperature scale at –300°C. Again, draw a best-fit straight line through the data points. Use dashes to extend the straight line from the lowest data point to the horizontal axis. According to your graph, what is the Celsius temperature at which the volume would be equal to 0? How does this value compare with the actual value for absolute zero, in degrees Celsius?

Conclusions

1. Does your data show a volume–temperature relationship for a gas? Explain.

2. The pressure did not vary during the experiment, because all trials were performed at constant room (atmospheric) pressure. If the pressure had varied, how would it have affected your results? Explain.

3. What are some possible sources of error in this experiment?

4. How do the class results for the value of absolute zero compare with the actual value? What factors (besides those mentioned in question 3) could be responsible for any error noted in the class results?

5. Should the V/T ratios for everyone in class be identical? Explain.

Extension

1. Use the data from this experiment to show, through calculations, that the volume of a gas is *not* directly proportional to the Celsius temperature.

Experiment

19 Diffusion of Gases

Text reference: Section 11.1

Background

Have you noticed that, if someone enters a room and sits near you, it can take several minutes before the smell of his or her cologne reaches you? You become aware of the scent because molecules in the cologne diffuse through the surrounding air. Diffusion is the process in which particles in a system move from an area of high concentration to an area of low concentration. Diffusion continues until a uniform concentration of particles is reached throughout the system. The rate at which gas molecules diffuse, at constant temperature, decreases as the molar mass of the gas increases. In fact, the rate of gas diffusion at constant temperature is inversely proportional to the square root of the molar mass of the gas. This proportionality is called Graham's law of diffusion.

$$\text{rate of diffusion} \propto \frac{1}{\sqrt{\text{molecular mass}}}$$

In this experiment, you will determine the relative rates of diffusion of two gases with significantly different molar masses. The gases that you will study are ammonia, $NH_3(g)$, and hydrogen chloride, $HCl(g)$.

Goals

- **Measure** the relative rates of diffusion of ammonia gas and hydrogen chloride gas.
- **Compare** your results to those predicted by Graham's law of diffusion.

Equipment

safety goggles
1 glass tube, 1 cm × 70 cm
2 dropper pipets
2 ring stands
2 utility clamps
2 rubber stoppers
1 meter stick
1 timer, with second hand
1 tweezers

Materials

concentrated hydrochloric acid, 12M $HCl(aq)$ C T

concentrated ammonia, 15M $NH_3(aq)$ C T

cotton

Safety 

- Note the Safety Symbols used here and in the Procedure section. Review safety information on pages 7–10.
- Always wear safety goggles when working in the lab.
- Hydrochloric acid is corrosive and can cause severe burns.
- Concentrated ammonia solution is corrosive. Avoid skin contact. Avoid the inhalation of ammonia fumes.

Procedure

Copy Table 19.1 into your laboratory notebook. As you perform the experiment, record your observations in this table.

1. Use two ring stands and two utility clamps to hold a clean, dry glass tube in a level position as shown in Figure 19.1. Fit a cotton plug snugly into each end of the tube.

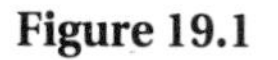

Figure 19.1

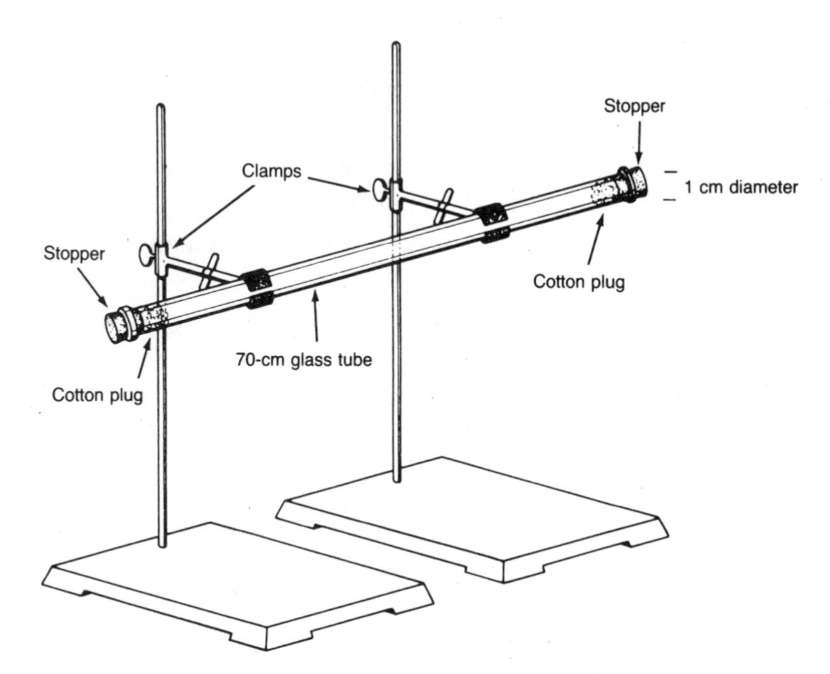

2. Your teacher will come to each lab station with beakers containing HCl and NH_3. **CAUTION:** *HCl(aq) is corrosive. Both HCl(aq) and $NH_3(aq)$ have very pungent and irritating odors. Avoid inhalation of the fumes.* Use droppers to simultaneously add 5 drops of concentrated HCl to the cotton plug at one end of the tube and 5 drops of concentrated NH_3 solution to the cotton plug at the other end. Close the ends with rubber stoppers. Note and record the start time in the data table.

3. Record the time it takes for you to see a white deposit form in the tube. Measure the distances (in centimeters) from the inside end of each cotton plug to the center of the white deposit. Record these measurements in Table 19.1.

4. Your teacher will instruct you how to clean the diffusion tube.

Data Record

Table 19.1 Data and Calculations
start time:
time at deposit formation:
elapsed time:
distance from HCl to product:
distance from NH_3 to product:
rate of diffusion HCl (distance/time):
rate of diffusion NH_3 (distance/time):
experimental ratio of rates (NH_3/HCl):
theoretical ratio of rates (NH_3/HCl):

Data Analysis

1. Calculate the rate of diffusion for each gas by dividing the distance each gas traveled by the time (seconds) required for the appearance of the white deposit. Enter the calculated rates in Table 19.1.

$$\text{rate of diffusion} = \frac{\text{distance traveled by gas}}{\text{time required for product formation}}$$

2. Find the ratio of the rate of diffusion of NH_3 and the rate of diffusion of HCl. (Use the rates calculated in step 1 above.) Record this ratio in Table 19.1.

3. Calculate the theoretical ratio of the rates of diffusion of these gases using the following equation.

$$\frac{\text{diffusion rate of } NH_3}{\text{diffusion rate of HCl}} = \frac{\sqrt{(\text{molar mass HCl})}}{\sqrt{(\text{molar mass } NH_3)}}$$

Enter the value for the theoretical ratio in Table 19.1.

Conclusions

1. Would a change in temperature affect the diffusion rates you calculated? Explain.

2. Would a change in temperature affect the ratio of diffusion rates? Explain.

3. Are the results of this experiment consistent with Graham's law of diffusion? Explain.

4. The white substance in the tube is ammonium chloride, NH_4Cl. It is the only product in the reaction. Write a balanced equation for this reaction. What is the type of the equation?

5. Calculate the percent error in your experimentally determined value for the ratio of diffusion rates of NH_3 and HCl. Use the theoretical ratio calculated in question 3 of the Data Analysis section as the accepted value for the ratio.

$$\text{percent error} = \frac{|\text{theoretical ratio} - \text{experimental ratio}|}{\text{theoretical ratio}} \times 100 \text{ percent}$$

Extension

1. The average speed of a gas particle at room temperature is about 1600 km/h. Convert the rate of diffusion measured in this experiment from centimeters per second to kilometers per hour. Explain why this rate is so much slower than the average speed of a gas particle.

Experiment

20 Flame Tests for Metals

Text reference:
Section 12.6

Background

Have you ever wondered why a candle flame is yellow? The characteristic yellow of a candle flame comes from the glow of burning carbon fragments. The carbon fragments are produced by the incomplete combustion reaction of the wick and candle wax. When elements, such as the carbon fragments, are heated to high temperatures, some of their electrons are excited to higher energy levels. These excited electrons then fall back to lower energy levels, releasing excess energy in packages of light called *photons*, or light quanta. The color of the emitted light depends on its energy. Blue light is more energetic than red light, for example. When heated, each element emits a characteristic pattern of light energies which is useful for identifying the element. The characteristic colors of light produced when substances are heated in the flame of a gas burner are the basis of flame tests for several elements.

In this experiment, you will perform the flame tests used to identify several metallic elements.

Goals

- **Observe** the colors emitted by various metal ions.
- **Identify** metals through flame tests.

Equipment

safety goggles
1 platinum wire or nichrome wire loop
1 50-mL beaker
8 small test tubes
1 test-tube rack
1 scoopula
6 cobalt-blue glasses/class
1 gas burner
paper towels

Materials

6M hydrochloric acid, HCl [C] [T]
potassium nitrate, KNO_3 [T]
calcium nitrate, $Ca(NO_3)_2$ [T]
strontium nitrate, $Sr(NO_3)_2$ [T]
lithium nitrate, $LiNO_3$ [T]
copper(II) nitrate, $Cu(NO_3)_2$ [T]
sodium nitrate, $NaNO_3$ [T]
barium nitrate, $Ba(NO_3)_2$ [T]
unknown salt

Safety

- Note the Safety Symbols used here and in the Procedure section. Review safety information on pages 7–10.
- Always wear safety goggles when working in the lab.
- Hydrochloric acid is corrosive and can cause severe burns.
- Do not at any time touch the end of the wire loop used in the flame tests. This wire gets extremely hot and can cause severe burns. Remember the wire can be hot and yet appear to be cool.

Procedure

Copy Table 20.1 into your laboratory notebook. As you perform the experiment, record your observations in Table 20.1.

1. Place a test-tube rack on a paper towel. Write the chemical name of each of the seven metal salts next to a position in the rack where a test tube will be placed. **CAUTION:** *Do not taste any of the substances or touch them with your hands.* Use a scoopula to place pea-sized samples of each metal salt into a test tube. Place the tubes in a test-tube rack.

2. **CAUTION:** *Hydrochloric acid is corrosive and can cause severe burns.* Pour about 15 mL of 6M HCl into a clean, labeled 50-mL beaker. Dip the wire loop into the 6M HCl and then heat it in the hot flame of a gas burner as shown in Figure 20.1a. Continue this procedure until no color comes from the wire when it is put into the flame.

3. Dip the clean wire loop into a sample of metal salt and heat the sample in the burner flame as shown in Figure 20.1b. Record the color of the flame in Table 20.1. Test the remaining samples, cleaning the wire loop, as described in step 2, before each new sample is tested. Record your observations.

4. View the flame colors produced by $NaNO_3$ and KNO_3 through cobalt-blue glass. Record your observations.

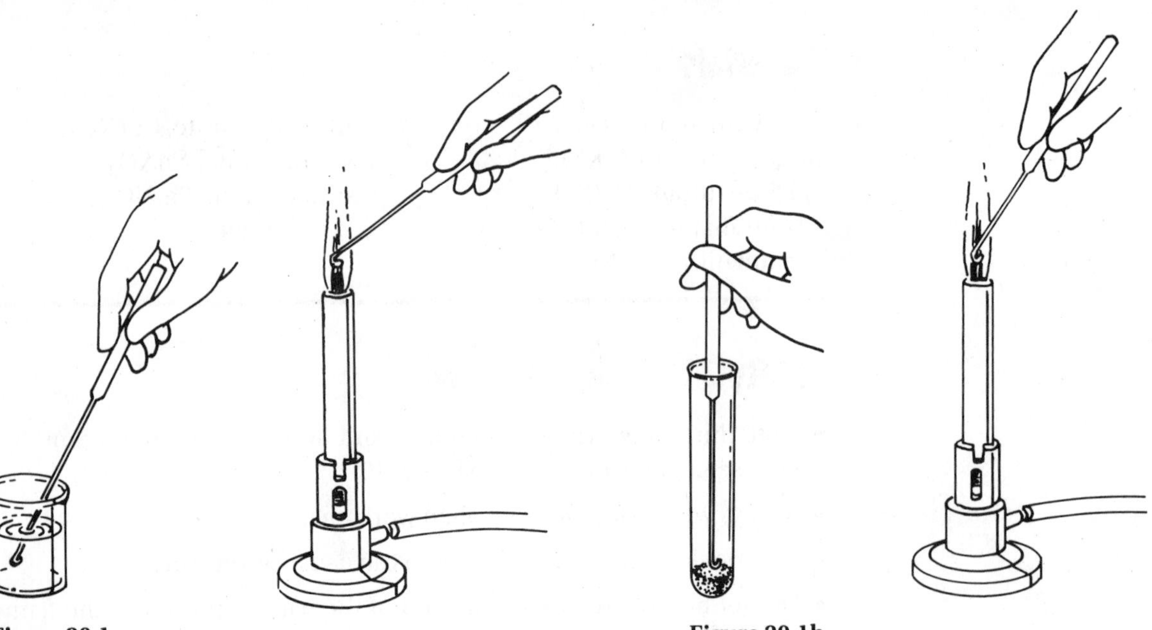

Figure 20.1a

Figure 20.1b

5. Perform a flame test on your unknown salt. Record your observations.

6. Dispose of the unused portions of your samples as directed by your teacher.

Data Record

Table 20.1 Flame Tests

Ion	Flame Color	
Sodium, Na^{+}	orange	pink.
Potassium, K^{+}	pink.	✓ flouresnt.
Calcium, Ca^{2+}	red-violet.	✓
Barium, Ba^{2+}	green	
Strontium, Sr^{2+}	pink.	✓
Lithium, Li^{+}	red.	✓

Table 20.1 (cont.) Flame Tests	
Ion	**Flame Color**
Copper, Cu^{2+}	Green
Sodium, Na^+ (cobalt glass)	orange
Potassium, K^+ (cobalt glass)	yellow pink
Unknown	A: B: Potassium C: D:

Conclusions

1. List the elements that produced the most easily identified colors.

2. Which elements are least easily identified? Explain.

3. Which element produces the most intense color?

4. Would flame tests be useful for detecting metal ions present in a mixture of metal ions? Explain.

5. The energy of colored light increases in the order red, yellow, green, blue, violet. List the metallic elements used in the flame tests in increasing order of the energy of the light emitted.

6. What is the purpose of using the cobalt glass in the identification of sodium and potassium?

Extensions

1. Consider the colors of flames produced by various metal ions. Explain the relationship between the energies of the light emitted and the positions of the elements in the periodic table.

2. Design an experiment to perform flame tests that do not use a nichrome or platinum wire.

Experiment

21 Introduction to the Spectrophotometer

Text reference:
Section 12.6

Background

Many compounds absorb light from regions of the electromagnetic spectrum. A *spectrophotometer* is a device designed to determine the wavelengths of light that a compound absorbs. When an aqueous sample of a compound is placed in the light path of a spectrophotometer, the sample may absorb all the light, some of the light, or no light at all. The absorption of light depends upon the material in the sample and the wavelength of the light. Light absorption occurs at wavelengths whose energy corresponds to the energy necessary to cause electronic excitations of atoms, ions, or molecules in the sample. From the spectrophotometer data, a graph can be made that plots the light intensity transmitted through the sample versus the wavelength of the light; such a graph is called an *absorption spectrum.* The wavelengths absorbed by the sample appear as bands of minimum intensity.

Absorption spectra are useful for two reasons. First, the absorption spectrum of a substance is a unique characteristic of that substance. This makes the spectrum useful for the identification of unknown substances. Second, the intensity of the absorption bands can be related to the concentration of the substance in the sample. Thus, the intensity of the absorption band can be used to determine the amount of a particular substance in a mixture.

In this experiment, you will determine the absorption spectrum of an aqueous solution of chromium(III) ions.

Goal

- **Make a graph** of the wavelenghts of light absorbed by a solution containing chromium(III) ions.

Equipment

safety goggles
4 Spectronic 20 spectrophotometers/class
2 small test tubes or 2 glass cuvettes
1 plastic wash bottle
1 10-mL graduated cylinder

Materials

0.02*M* chromium(III) nitrate, $Cr(NO_3)_3$ T I
distilled water
tissue paper

Safety

- Note the Safety Symbols used here and in the Procedure section. Review safety information on pages 7–10.
- Always wear safety goggles when working in the lab.
- Chromium(III) nitrate is toxic and can irritate your skin.
- Do not pick up dropper bottles by their tops.

Procedure

Copy Table 21.1 into your laboratory notebook. As you perform the experiment, record your percent transmittance data in this table.

1. Turn on the spectrophotometer and allow it to warm up for 20 minutes.

2. Set the wavelength control knob to 375 nanometers (375 nm). Adjust the amplifier control knob to produce 0 percent transmittance (0%T) at this wavelength.

3. Add 3 mL of distilled water to a clean, small test tube. Wipe the outside of the tube with a tissue to make certain that it is clean and dry. Avoid getting fingerprints on the tube. Dislodge any air bubbles present in the water by gently tapping the tube with a finger.

4. Place the tube in the sample holder and close the cover. Adjust the light control knob until the spectrophotometer reads 100%T.

5. Remove the first sample from the spectrophotometer. Add 3 mL of 0.02*M* chromium(III) nitrate, $Cr(NO_3)_3$, to another clean test tube. Use a tissue to clean and dry the tube. Insert the tube of chromium(III) nitrate into the sample holder. Close the cover of the holder. Read the percent transmittance and record in Table 22.1. Remove the sample from the holder.

6. Turn the wavelength dial to 400 nm. Use the amplifier control knob to adjust the percent transmittance to 0%T. Place the water sample in the holder. With the light control knob, adjust the meter to 100%T. Replace the water sample with the chromium(III) nitrate sample. Measure and record the percent transmittance at 400 nm.

7. For the remainder of the wavelengths listed in Table 21.1, continue the procedure of setting 0%T, setting 100%T, and measuring the percent transmittance of the chromium(III) nitrate solution.

8. Unless directed otherwise by your teacher, return the aqueous chromium(III) nitrate to the dropper bottle.

Data Record

Table 21.1 Percent Transmittance of 0.02*M* $Cr(NO_3)_3$ Solution at Various Wavelengths

Wavelength (nm)	% Transmittance (%T)
375	
400	
405	
415	
425	
440	
455	
470	
490	
500	
520	
530	
540	
550	
570	
575	
580	
600	
625	

Data Analysis

Note, **one page of graph paper** is required for your report. Graph percent transmittance versus wavelength. The curve you plot is the absorption spectrum of chromium(III) ions in the visible region of the electromagnetic spectrum.

Conclusions

1. At what wavelengths do chromium(III) ions absorb the maximum amounts of light? What colors of light correspond to these wavelengths?

2. Based on the answer to the previous question, would you expect a red solution to absorb or transmit red light? Explain.

Extensions

1. Starting with a set of solutions of known different concentrations of chromium(III) ions, design an experiment that uses a spectrophotometer to determine the concentration of chromium(III) ions in an unknown solution.

2. The amount of light that is absorbed by a solution is commonly expressed either in terms of percent transmittance (%T), as in this experiment, or in terms of absorbance (A). Absorbance is defined as:

$$\text{Absorbance} = 2 - \log \text{of percent transmittance}$$
$$A = 2 - \log \%T$$

Given the relationship shown in the preceding formula, convert the percent transmittance values in Table 21.1 to absorbance values. Plot a graph of absorbance versus wavelength. Compare and analyze the shapes of the two curves generated. Might it be more useful to use transmittance values sometimes and absorbance values at other times? Explain the advantages and disadvantages of using these different units.

Experiment

22 Energies of Electrons

Text reference:
Sections 12.6, 12.9

Background

You should recall from Experiment 20 that flame tests are useful for identifying metal ions that produce characteristic colors. Separating these characteristic colors into discrete wavelengths of light produces a pattern of individual lines that uniquely identifies the metal ion. This pattern of lines is called an *emission spectrum.* With a reference source of emission spectra, you would find it relatively easy to identify a particular metal ion.

You can separate the lines in the visible region of a flame emission spectrum by using an optical prism or a diffraction grating. A *spectrograph* is an instrument designed to produce electronic excitations, separate the emitted light into its component wavelengths, and then record the wavelengths of emitted light. In this experiment, you will construct a simple spectrograph and measure the wavelength of a strong excitation of sodium ions.

Goals

- **Construct** a simple flame spectrograph.
- **Measure** the wavelength of a strong electronic transition of sodium.

Equipment

safety goggles
2 meter sticks
1 diffraction grating
1 cardboard piece with narrow slit
1 50-mL beaker
1 gas burner
1 platinum or nichrome wire loop
watch glass

Materials

$1M$ sodium chloride, NaCl

$6M$ hydrochloric acid, HCl C T

Safety

- Note the Safety Symbols used here and in the Procedure section. Review safety information on pages 7–10.
- Always wear safety goggles when working in the lab.
- Hydrochloric acid is corrosive and can cause severe burns.
- Do not let your skin or clothing contact the burner flame or the hot wire used in the flame tests.

Procedure

Copy Table 22.1 into your laboratory notebook. As you perform the experiment, record your data and calculation results in this table.

1. Set up the apparatus shown in Figure 22.1.

Figure 22.1

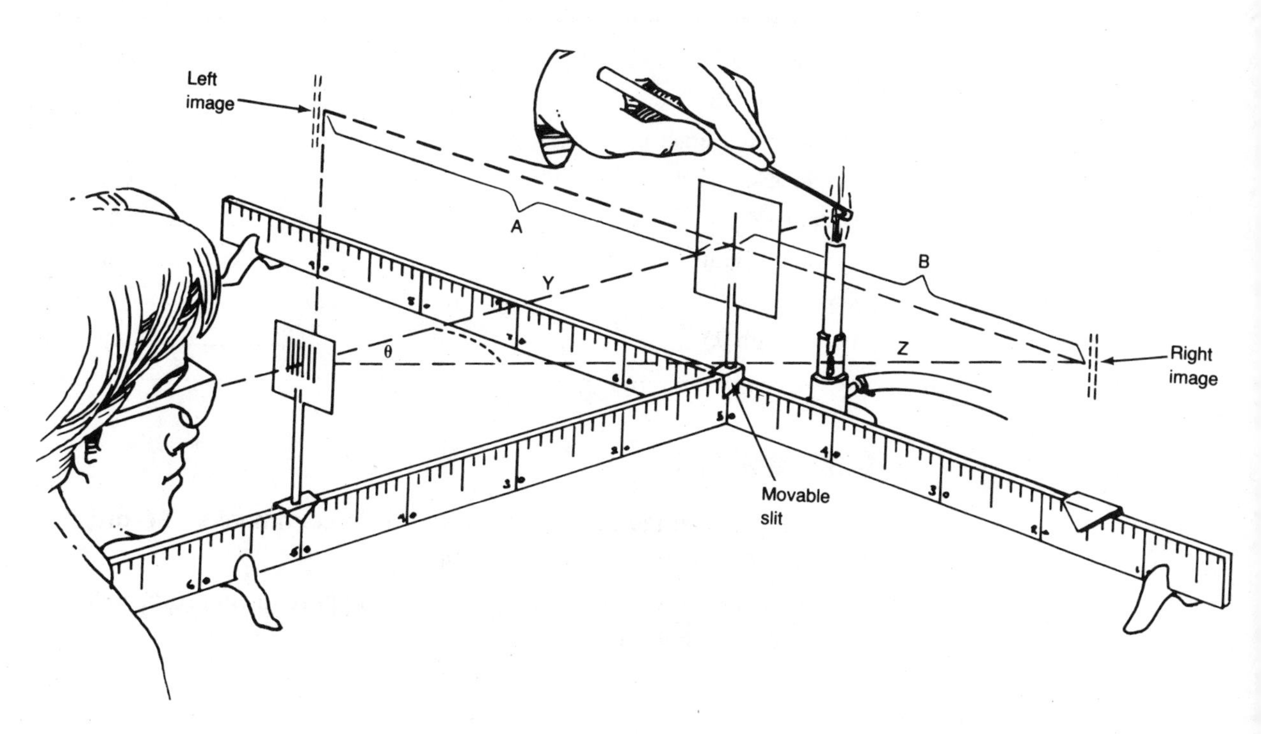

2. **CAUTION:** *Hydrochloric acid is corrosive.* Pour approximately 15 mL of 6*M* hydrochloric acid, HCl, into a 50-mL beaker. Always cover the beaker with a watch glass when it is not being used. Clean the wire loop by first dipping it into the HCl and then heating it in the hot flame of a gas burner. Continue to dip and heat the wire until no color comes from the wire as it is heated.

3. Dip the clean wire loop into the NaCl solution.

4. Place the wire loop in the burner flame. Observe the flame through the slit in the cardboard and the diffraction grating as shown in Figure 22.1. You should see a series of lines to the left and right of the slit. Pick out the brightest line to the left side of the slit and have your partner record this position on the meter stick as position A. Repeat this procedure on the right side of the slit and record this as position B.

5. Measure the distance from the diffraction grating to the slit and record this as distance Y.

6. Dispose of the solutions as directed by your teacher.

Data Record

Table 22.1 Wavelength for the Sodium Emission Line

Left image (A)	________ cm
Right image (B)	________ cm
Distance X (average of left and right images)	________ cm
Distance Y	________ cm
Distance Z	________ cm
Diffracting grating constant (d)	________ cm/line
Sin θ	________
Wavelength (λ)	________ nm

Data Analysis

1. Find the average distance of A and B (in centimeters). Record this answer as distance X in your data table.

2. Calculate the distance Z, using the Pythagorean theorem. Refer to Figure 22.1 for reference.

$$Z = \sqrt{X^2 + Y^2}$$

Record the value of Z in the data table.

3. Calculate $\sin\theta$, using the following relationship:

$$\sin\theta = \frac{X}{Z}$$

Record $\sin\theta$ in the data table.

4. The wavelength (λ) of the sodium flame emission line being investigated in this experiment is given in nanometers by the Bragg equation:

$$\lambda = d \times \sin\theta \times \left(\frac{1 \times 10^{7}\ \text{nm}}{1\ \text{cm}}\right)$$

In the Bragg equation, d represents a diffraction grating constant:

$$d = \frac{1}{n}$$

where n is the number of lines, per centimeter, scribed on the diffraction grating. Calculate the value of d for your grating and enter it in Table 22.1.

5. Compute the wavelength of the bright line you viewed on the meter stick using the Bragg equation. Record this value in the data table.

6. The accepted value of λ for the observed transition is 589.0 nm. Calculate the percent error in your value.

Conclusions

1. Identify the possible sources of error in your determination of λ.

2. How can a spectrographic experiment help identify a particular metal ion?

Extension

1. Measure the predominant visible spectral lines of mercury, helium, and hydrogen using gas discharge tubes as the samples and a high-voltage transformer as the energy source.

Experiment

23 Periodic Properties

Text reference: Section 13.1

Background

When the elements are arranged in order of increasing atomic number, they exhibit a periodic recurrence of properties. This fact led to the grouping of elements as seen in the periodic table. Elements in vertical columns of the periodic table form groups (families) with similar physical and chemical properties. These similarities are due, in large part, to the fact that all the elements within a group have the same outer-shell electron configuration. You can also find periodic trends in certain properties, such as the densities and solubilities of compounds that contain elements in the same group.

In this experiment, you will investigate the periodic variation of density and solubility of compounds within groups. More specifically, you will determine the densities of certain Group 4A elements and the solubilities of certain salts of Group 2A elements. Using your results, you will predict the densities of other Group 4A elements and the solubility of an unknown Group 2A salt.

Goals

- **Measure** the densities of certain elements in Group 4A.
- **Measure** the solubilities of certain salts of Group 2A elements.
- **Describe** the periodic variation of the density and solubility of compounds.
- **Predict** the densities of untested Group 4A elements.
- **Predict** the solubility of an unknown Group 2A salt.

Materials

lead shot, Pb [T]
silicon, Si
tin, Sn
0.1 *M* barium nitrate, $Ba(NO_3)_2$ [T] [I]
1 *M* sulfuric acid, H_2SO_4 [T] [C]

$0.1M$ magnesium nitrate, $Mg(NO_3)_2$
$0.1M$ calcium nitrate, $Ca(NO_3)_2$
$0.1M$ strontium nitrate, $Sr(NO_3)_2$ [T]
$1M$ sodium carbonate, Na_2CO_3
$1M$ potassium chromate, K_2CrO_4 [T] [C]
unknown salt solution [T] [I]
distilled water

Equipment

safety goggles
8 centigram balances/class
4 small test tubes or 1 spot plate
1 test-tube rack
1 plastic wash bottle
1 50-mL graduated cylinder
1 dropper pipet

Safety

- Note the Safety Symbols used here and in the Procedure section. Review safety information on pages 7–10.
- Always wear safety goggles when working in the lab.
- A number of the chemicals used in this experiment are toxic and/or irritating to the skin. Avoid skin contact with these chemicals.
- Sulfuric acid is corrosive and can cause severe burns.
- Wash your hands thoroughly after completing this experiment.

Procedure

Copy Tables 23.1 and 23.2 into your laboratory notebook. As you perform the experiment, record your data in these tables.

Part A. Densities of Group 4A Elements

1. Determine the densities of the tin (Sn), lead (Pb), and silicon (Si) samples by the water displacement method described in Experiment 4. Record the data in Table 23.1. Note the appearance of these elements.

Part B. Solubilities of Salts of Group 2A Elements

2. CAUTION: *Soluble salts of barium and strontium are extremely toxic.* Add 1 mL (20 drops) of $Mg(NO_3)_2$ solution to a small test tube. Add 1 mL of $Ca(NO_3)_2$ solution to a second tube, 1 mL of $Sr(NO_3)_2$ solution to a third, and 1 mL of $Ba(NO_3)_2$ solution to a fourth.

3. **CAUTION:** *At a concentration of 1M, sulfuric acid, H_2SO_4, is a severe skin irritant.* Add 1 mL (20 drops) of 1*M* H_2SO_4 to each tube to provide sulfate ions for reaction with the Group 2A metal ions. If the salt ($MgSO_4$, $CaSO_4$, $SrSO_4$, or $BaSO_4$) is insoluble in water, a precipitate will be formed. Record the solubility of each metal sulfate salt in Table 23.2 using the following letter codes: S = soluble, I = insoluble.

4. Dispose of the materials in the test tubes as directed by your teacher. Rinse the test tubes with distilled water and dispose of the rinse water as directed by your teacher.

5. Repeat step 2, then repeat step 3 using 1*M* Na_2CO_3 in place of 1*M* H_2SO_4.

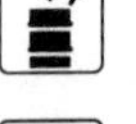

6. Repeat step 4.

7. **CAUTION:** *Chromates are both toxic and irritating.* Repeat step 2, then repeat step 3 using 1*M* K_2CrO_4 in place of 1*M* H_2SO_4.

8. Repeat step 4.

9. Obtain an unknown salt solution from your teacher. The solution will contain ions of a Group 2A metal. Perform the solubility tests to identify the unknown ion. Treat the unknown as if it were toxic and irritating.

10. Dispose of the materials as directed by your teacher.

Data Record

Table 23.1 Densities of Group 4A Elements

	Sn	Pb	Si
mass of metal (mL)			
volume of water alone (mL)			
volume of water + metal (mL)			
volume of metal (mL)			
density of metal (mass/volume)			
appearance			

Table 23.2 Solubilities of Salts of Group 2A Elements

	SO_4^{2-}	CO_3^{2-}	$C_2O_4^{2-}$	CrO_4^{2-}
Mg^{2+}				
Ca^{2+}				
Sr^{2+}				
Ba^{2+}				
Unknown				

Unknown # ______________

Identity of cation of unknown ______________

Data Analysis

Note, **one page of graph paper** is required for your report.

1. Calculate and record the densities of the tin, silicon, and lead samples in Table 23.1.

2. Prepare a graph of density versus period number for tin, silicon, and lead.

Conclusions

1. Based on your graph, estimate the density of germanium, Ge. Compare your estimate with the accepted density of germanium (5.46 g/cm^3). Give possible sources of any errors.

2. Calculate the percent error between your estimated value and the accepted value for the density of germanium.

$$\text{percent error} = \frac{|\text{accepted value} - \text{estimated value}|}{\text{accepted value}} \times 100 \text{ percent}$$

3. Describe any relationship that you see in Table 23.2, between the solubility of salts containing alkaline earth metal ions and the position of the metals in the periodic table.

4. Based on the data in Table 23.2, you may not have been able to identify your unknown specifically. Explain.

Extensions

1. Construct data tables for (a) the elements in Group 1A and (b) the elements in Period 3. In the tables, include information on the following physical properties: melting point, boiling point, density, hardness, electrical conductivity, physical state, and appearance. Do you see any evidence of periodic trends? If so, describe them.

2. Choose three properties, other than those in the preceding question, that demonstrate periodic trends within groups 1A and 2A. Include elements with atomic numbers up to 56. Plot on the same graph the values of properties for both Group 1A and Group 2A. Comment on the results.

Experiment

24 Crystal Structures

Text reference:
Section 14.5

Background

The regular geometric shapes of crystals reflect the orderly arrangement of the atoms, ions, or molecules making up the crystal lattice. In this experiment, you will gain insight into the ways crystals are formed. To do this, you will model crystal structures using Styrofoam spheres. Using the models, you will determine the number of nearest neighbors (the coordination number) of the particles in each of these structures. The effect of the size of the anions and cations in the crystal structure on determining the coordination number will also be investigated. Your investigation will include three types of packing: hexagonal closest packing, face-centered cubic packing, and body-centered cubic packing.

Goals

- **Make models** of some crystal structures.
- **Identify** the coordination number of atoms in a crystal structure.

Equipment

safety goggles
62 plastic-foam balls, 2-inch diameter
13 plastic-foam balls, 1-inch diameter
13 plastic-foam balls, 3/4-inch diameter
1 box of toothpicks, or 3 packs of plastic coffee stirrers, or 1 box of pipe cleaners
1 scissors/class
1 centimeter ruler

Safety

- Always wear safety goggles when you are working in the lab.

Procedure

As you perform the experiment, answer the questions in the Conclusions section in your laboratory notebook.

Part A. Hexagonal Closest Packing

1. Use toothpicks (or plastic coffee stirrers) to connect three sets of 2-inch-diameter spheres as shown in Figure 24.1.

Figure 24.1

2. Place one of the sets of three spheres on a table. This is the first layer.

3. Place the set of seven spheres on the three spheres so that its center sphere fits snugly into the depression in the first layer.

4. Place the second set of three spheres over the center sphere of the second layer. The spheres in this third layer should be directly above the spheres in the first layer. The arrangement you have constructed, hexagonal closest packed, is found in crystals of zinc, magnesium, and many other metals. Record the number of nearest neighbors (the coordination number) of the central sphere in the structure you formed. Retain your model for Part C.

Part B. Face-Centered Cubic Packing

5. Construct the layers shown in Figure 24.2. Use 2-inch-diameter foam spheres and toothpicks as before.

Figure 24.2

6. Place the first layer (five spheres) on the table. Place the second layer (four spheres) over the first in such a way that the spheres of the second layer rest in the spaces between the corner spheres of the first layer.

7. Place the third layer on the second layer so that the spheres of the third layer are directly over the spheres in the first layer. Study this model carefully to determine why crystals with this structure are described as face-centered cubic. This is the type of packing that is found in copper, silver, aluminum, and many other metals.

Part C. Comparison of Hexagonal Closest Packing and Face-Centered Cubic Packing

8. Rearrange the model from Part A so the top layer (three spheres) is no longer directly over the first layer, but is rotated 60° with respect to it.

9. Rotate this rearranged model and look for four spheres forming a square facing you. Once you have found the four-sphere square, obtain the model made in Part B. Remove the top layer of the Part B model and place it over the four-sphere square of rearranged model A. Note that this new model contains a face-centered cube, just as model B did.

Part D. Body-Centered Cubic Packing

10. Use 2-inch foam spheres to construct the layers depicted in Figure 24.3. Leave a space of approximately 0.5 cm between the spheres.

Figure 24.3

11. Place the single sphere in the center of the first layer and then position the third layer in such a way that its spheres are directly over the spheres of the first layer. Examine the symmetry of this model and comment on the term body-centered cubic. This type of packing is typical of the alkali metals, which include sodium and potassium.

Part E. The Sodium Chloride Lattice

12. Ionic crystals are formed by packing positive and negative ions alternately into a lattice. A single sodium ion has a diameter of 0.19 nm; a chloride ion has a diameter of 0.36 nm. Because the diameters are in a ratio of roughly 1:2, the relative sizes of Na^+ and Cl^- can be approximated by using 1-inch and 2-inch spheres.

13. Use model B, with its 2-inch spheres, to represent the face-centered cubic arrangement of the chloride ions in a sodium chloride crystal. Insert thirteen 1-inch spheres, representing sodium ions, into the holes between the chloride ions in each layer. Note that the sodium chloride lattice is an interpenetrating set of face-centered cubes, one set of cubes made up of Na^+ ions and the other made up of Cl^- ions.

Part F. The Zinc Sulfide (Wurtzite) Lattice

14. Because each individual zinc ion has a diameter of 0.15 nm and the diameter of the sulfide ion is 0.37 nm, we shall use 3/4-inch spheres for the Zn^{2+} ion and 2-inch spheres for the S^{2-} ion to approximate the relative sizes of these ions.

15. Use model A, with its hexagonal closest-packing orientation, to represent the lattice of the larger sulfide ions. Secure one 3/4-inch sphere directly above each of the larger spheres in each of the three layers of model A. The 3/4-inch spheres represent Zn^{2+} ions.

16. Place the largest layer of spheres on the table, with the small spheres pointed down. Place one of the smaller layers on top of this layer in such a way that the smaller spheres fit into alternate depressions. Invert the two layers and place the other small layer, with small spheres upward, above the larger layer so that the spheres on the top layer are directly above the spheres on the bottom layer.

Conclusions

Part A. Hexagonal Closest Packing

1. What is the coordination number of the central atom in the model of hexagonal closest packing?

Part B. Face-Centered Cubic Packing

2. Explain the appropriateness of this name for describing the model you constructed.

Part C. Comparison of Hexagonal Closest Packing and Cubic Closest Packing

3. Compare the coordination numbers for the two types of closest packing.

4. If both a hexagonal closest-packed model and a cubic closest-packed model were constructed from spheres of the same size and mass, would the densities of the models differ?

Part D. Body-Centered Cubic Packing

5. Below 906°C, metallic iron crystallizes in a body-centered cubic form called alpha-ferrite. Above this temperature, the stable form is gamma-ferrite, which is a face-centered cubic. At 140°C, the crystal form changes back to a body-centered cubic form called delta-ferrite. What is the coordination number of iron in each of these forms?

Part E. The Sodium Chloride Lattice

6. What ions most closely surround each Na^+ ion? What ions most closely surround each Cl^- ion?

7. What is the coordination number of the Na^+ ions? What is the co- ordination number of the Cl^- ions?

Part F. The Zinc Sulfide (Wurtzite) Lattice

8. What is the coordination number of the Zn^{2+} ions?

Extension

1. Use Styrofoam balls and toothpicks to explore some other types of crystal structures. Possibilities include cesium chloride (both ions have a coordination number of 8) and titanium dioxide (coordination numbers of 6 and 3, respectively).

Experiment

25 Molecular Models

Text reference:
Chapter 15

Background

You can represent a molecule on paper with either a molecular formula or a structural formula. However, molecular formulas, such as NH_3, provide no information concerning the actual arrangement of atoms in the molecule. Structural formulas, such as the following, give some information about the arrangement of atoms in the molecule.

```
                                       H
                                       |
H—O—H      H—N—H      H—C—H
              |                        |
              H                        H
```

However, these structural formulas provide only limited information since they are two-dimensional. Actual molecular shapes are three-dimensional. A molecular model is far superior to a structural formula when it comes to visualizing atomic arrangement. Compared to molecular formulas and structural formulas, molecular models show much more information about the true shapes of the molecules.

In this experiment, you will use ball-and-stick models to help you visualize the shapes of molecules. The balls are color-coded and sized to represent different atoms. The balls are also drilled with holes to accept the sticks and springs; the number of holes in the ball represents the maximum number of bonds a given atom can have. Single bonds are represented by short wooden sticks, double and triple bonds are represented by springs.

Goals

- **Make models** of molecules using ball-and-stick model kits.
- **Convert** three-dimensional molecular models to two-dimensional molecular drawings.

Equipment

1 ball-and-stick model set/6-student group

Safety

- Always wear safety goggles when working in the lab.

Procedure

Table 25.1 shows color codes for balls representing different atoms. As you build the models, draw the structural formulas of the molecules in your laboratory notebook. You will make the following molecular models: H_2O, NH_3, CH_4, H_2S, CCl_4, CCl_2F_2, C_2H_6, N_2, CO_2, O_2, C, $CO(NH_2)_2$, CHBrClF, and C_4H_{10}.

Table 25.1

Atom	Symbol	Color of Ball	Number of Holes	Maximum Number of Bonds
Hydrogen	H	yellow	1	1
Carbon	C	black	4	4
Oxygen	O	red	2	2
Nitrogen	N	blue	3 or 5*	3
Chlorine	Cl	green	1	1
Bromine	Br	orange	1	1
Iodine	I	purple	1	1

1. Using the ball-and-stick model set, construct models of water, H_2O; ammonia, NH_3; and methane, CH_4. Draw a sketch of each molecule in your laboratory notebook. The shape shown by the water molecule is described as *bent,* the shape of the ammonia molecule is called *trigonal pyramidal,* and the shape of the methane molecule is termed *tetrahedral.* Write these names below the matching structures you have drawn.

2. Construct models of hydrogen sulfide, H_2S; carbon tetrachloride, CCl_4; dichlorodifluoromethane, CCl_2F_2; and ethane, C_2H_6. Give the molecular formula for each of these compounds and draw a sketch of each molecule in your laboratory notebook. Name the shape of each molecule.

3. The air above a burning candle contains nitrogen gas, carbon dioxide gas, oxygen gas, and soot. Construct models of these substances and draw a sketch of each molecule.

4. The compound urea has the molecular formula $CO(NH_2)_2$. The structural formula of urea is:

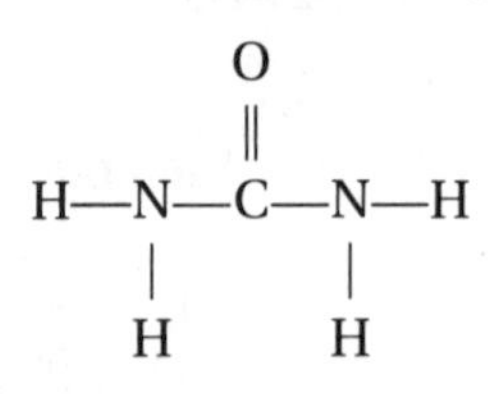

Construct a model of urea and sketch its shape in your laboratory notebook.

5. Construct a model of butane, C_4H_{10}. (**Hint:** The carbons are bonded to one another in a continuous, unbranched chain.) Draw a sketch of this molecule. Can you construct a model of a different molecule that has the same molecular formula as butane? Make a model of such a molecule and sketch its structure. The two different compounds having the molecular formula C_4H_{10} are called *structural isomers.* They have identical molecular formulas but different structural formulas. They also have different physical and chemical properties. Structural isomers play a very important role in organic chemistry.

6. Construct a model of bromochlorofluoromethane, CHBrClF. Sketch the compound. Can you construct an isomer of this compound? (**Hint:** Is your left hand identical to your right?) Draw the new compound if you can.

The compound and the isomer have the same molecular formula, CHBrClF, but they are different from each other in the way that a left hand is different from a right hand. The compounds are mirror images of each other and are called *stereoisomers.* The phenomenon of "handedness" exhibited by pairs of stereoisomers is very important in organic chemistry and biochemistry.

Extension

1. Construct models of all the structural isomers of heptane, C_7H_{16}. Draw a structural formula for each isomer. Watch for duplicates.

Experiment

26 The Solvent Properties of Water

Text reference:
Section 16.7

Background

"Oil and water don't mix!" You've probably heard this phrase before. Though this phrase is true, there are plenty of substances that do dissolve in water. The polar nature of the water molecule is largely responsible for its remarkable solvent action. Because of its polarity, water is able to dissolve ionic compounds, such as sodium chloride and copper sulfate, and polar covalent compounds, such as sugar and ammonia. Many chemical reactions and most biochemical reactions take place in water.

Similarly, many substances dissolve in oily, nonpolar solvents, such as gasoline and kerosene. In general, only nonpolar molecules will dissolve in nonpolar solvents.

In this experiment, you will examine the relationship between a compound's polarity and its solubility in water.

Goal

- **Compare** the solubilities in water of compounds having different polarities.

Equipment

safety goggles
1 spatula
1 dropper pipet
10 small test tubes
1 test-tube rack
1 plastic wash bottle

Materials

sodium chloride, $NaCl$
sucrose, $C_{12}H_{22}O_{11}$
sodium thiosulfate, $Na_2S_2O_3$
calcium carbonate, $CaCO_3$
hexane, C_6H_{14} [F] [T]
kerosene, C_{12}–C_{15} [F] [T]
1,1,2-trichloro-1,2,2-trifluoroethane (TTE), $C_2Cl_3F_3$ [T] [I]

potassium sulfate, K_2SO_4 T
ethanol, C_2H_5OH F T
glycerin, $C_3H_8O_3$
distilled water

Safety 

- Note the Safety Symbols used here and in the Procedure section. Review safety information on pages 7–10.
- Always wear safety goggles when working in the lab.
- Ethanol, hexane, and kerosene are flammable. Do not use these substances near open flames.

Procedure

Copy Table 26.1 into your laboratory notebook. As you perform the experiment, record your results and observations in this table.

1. Record in Table 26.1 the chemical formula, physical state, and color of each of the substances in the Materials section, with the exception of distilled water.

2. Test each of the substances for water solubility. Add 3–4 mL of distilled water to each small test tube. Add a very small quantity of the substance to be tested to an individual test tube. For solids, use a sample about the size of a match head. For liquids, use one drop. Be careful not to contaminate the chemicals with one another.

Flick the test tube gently and note what happens. If all of the substance dissolves, add another small quantity and flick gently. Repeat the process several more times if the material continues to dissolve. Describe each substance as insoluble, slightly soluble, or very soluble, based on its behavior. Record these descriptions in Table 26.1.

3. Dispose of the hexane, kerosene, and TTE samples as directed by your teacher. Dispose of all other samples by flushing them, with water, down the drain. Rinse the test tubes.

Data Record

Table 26.1 Results and Observations			
Substance	**Formula**	**Physical State**	**Solubility in Water**
sodium chloride			
glycerin			
sucrose			
sodium thiosulfate			
calcium carbonate			
hexane			
potassium sulfate			
ethanol			
TTE			
kerosene*			

*mixture of hydrocarbons

Conclusions

1. Polar and ionic substances generally dissolve in water; nonpolar substances do not. Explain.

2. Based on the fact that calcium carbonate is an ionic compound, you may be puzzled by your experimental results for this compound. Propose an explanation for the solubility of calcium carbonate.

3. What basis can you use to decide whether the liquids tested are polar or nonpolar?

4. Which of the liquid substances tested are polar? Which are nonpolar?

Extension

1. Give the structural formulas of the four liquids other than kerosene that were tested in this experiment. Do these structural formulas support the solubility data obtained? Explain.

Experiment

27 Distillation

Text reference:
Sections 16.7, 1.6

Background

Pure water is a valuable commodity, as anyone who has experienced flooding and a contaminated water supply knows. Because water is an excellent solvent, it never exists in its pure state in nature. Even water purified for drinking contains a number of dissolved substances, such as minerals. However, pure water can be obtained from aqueous solutions through a process called distillation. In distillation a solution is boiled, vaporizing the water and leaving behind any dissolved solid material. The vapor is directed through a condenser consisting of a straight glass tube encased by an outer glass jacket. Cold water circulates through the outer jacket, causing the water vapor in the inner tube to condense on the cold walls. The purified condensed liquid, called the *distillate*, can then be collected.

In this experiment, you will distill a solution of water that contains one volatile and one nonvolatile impurity.

Goal

- **Apply** the distillation process to an aqueous solution containing one volatile and one nonvolatile impurity.

Equipment

safety goggles
1 250-mL beaker
2 100-mL beakers
1 100-mL graduated cylinder
3 medium test tubes
1 250-mL distillation flask
1 condenser
2 rubber hoses for condenser
1 thermometer
2 one-holed rubber stoppers
1 dropper pipet
1 ring stand
1 ring support
1 wire gauze
1 gas burner
2 utility clamps
1 spatula
1 long-stemmed funnel
1 towel

Materials

glycerin
$6M$ ammonia, NH_3 T I
sodium chloride, NaCl
$0.1M$ silver nitrate, $AgNO_3$ T I
$3M$ nitric acid, HNO_3 C T
1% phenolphthalein solution I
boiling chips
universal indicator paper

Safety

- Note the Safety Symbols used here and in the Procedure section. Review safety information on pages 7–10.
- Always wear safety goggles when working in the lab.
- Nitric acid is corrosive and can cause severe burns.
- Ammonia is an irritant. Avoid inhaling the fumes of this chemical.
- Silver nitrate can stain skin and clothing.
- Mercury is extremely toxic, and a mercury spill is very difficult to clean up. If you break a mercury thermometer, report it to your teacher immediately.
- Be very careful when putting glass tubing or a thermometer into a rubber stopper. Wrap the glassware in a towel to prevent cutting yourself in case of breakage. Grasp the thermometer close to the rubber stopper and twist gently when inserting.

Procedure

Copy Table 27.1 into your laboratory notebook. As you perform the experiment, record your observations in this table.

1. Study the distillation apparatus shown in Figure 27.1. First, support the condenser with a utility clamp and ring stand. Connect a length of rubber hose from the cold-water tap to the "Cooling water in" connection on the condenser. Connect another length of rubber hose to the "Cooling water out" connection on the condenser, and run the hose into the sink. Turn on the cold water and check for leaks. The water should flow steadily through the outer tube of the condenser and into the sink. Turn off the water.

CAUTION: *Use glycerin or water to lubricate the thermometer.* Insert the thermometer into a one-holed rubber stopper that securely fits the neck of the round-bottomed 250-mL distillation flask. Insert the thermometer into the stopper by twisting the thermometer and stopper in opposite directions. Adjust the position of the thermometer so the

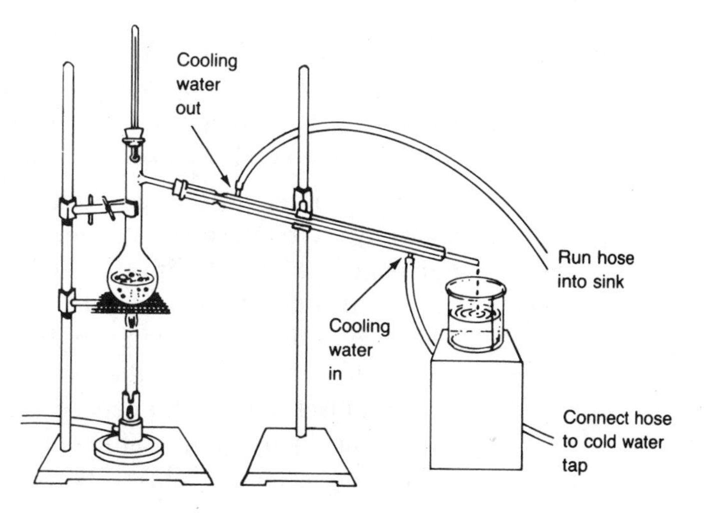

Figure 27.1

thermometer bulb reaches just to the sidearm of the distillation flask when the stopper is in position. *Wait until the entire distillation apparatus is assembled before inserting the stopper and thermometer into the flask.*

CAUTION: *Use glycerin or water to lubricate the sidearm.* Insert the sidearm of the distillation flask into a one-holed rubber stopper that fits the neck of the condenser. The stopper should be positioned far enough in so that the sidearm extends into the straight portion of the inner condenser tube.

Finish assembling the distillation apparatus shown in Figure 27.1. Tighten the utility clamps on the condenser and the flask only enough to gently support the apparatus. **CAUTION:** *Do not tighten the clamp too tightly; otherwise the glass will break.* The apparatus should be *secure,* but *not rigid.* Insert the rubber stopper and thermometer into the distillation flask.

2. Dissolve about 1 g of NaCl in 100 mL of water in a 250-mL beaker. Add 2 drops of phenolphthalein solution and 2 drops of 6*M* NH_3 to the solution. Note the color of the solution. **CAUTION:** *Aqueous ammonia is an irritant. Do not inhale its vapors.*

3. Remove the thermometer and stopper from the distillation flask and pour the colored solution through a long-stemmed funnel into the flask. Add three or four boiling chips to the solution.

4. Turn on the cooling water. Add 2 drops of phenolphthalein solution to a clean 100-mL beaker and position it at the end of the condenser to catch the distillate. Use the gas burner to gently heat the contents of the distillation flask. Record the temperature at which liquid begins to drip from the condenser. Adjust the burner flame to keep the solution boiling steadily. Note any color changes that occur during the distillation.

5. Continue distillation until about 25 mL of distillate has been collected. Remove the collection beaker from under the condenser and replace it with another clean 100-mL beaker. Add 2 drops of phenolphthalein solution to this beaker and collect another 25 mL of distillate.

6. While waiting for the second distillate to accumulate, perform the following tests on the first distillate. Compare the color of the distillate to the color of the mixture in the flask.

CAUTION: *HNO_3 is corrosive and can cause burns.* Add 3 mL of this distillate to a medium test tube and test for the presence of chloride ions by adding 10 drops of $3M$ HNO_3 and 5 drops of $0.1M$ $AgNO_3$. Test the pH of the distillate in the beaker with a piece of universal indicator paper. Test for the presence of ammonia in the distillate by using the wafting technique to detect ammonia fumes. Record your results and observations in Table 27.1.

7. When the second 25-mL of distillate has been collected, turn off the gas burner. Repeat the procedure in step 6 for the second distillate, and record your results and observations in Table 27.1.

8. Allow the apparatus to cool completely before carefully taking it apart. If time permits, perform the tests in step 6 on the solution that remains in the distillation flask.

9. Discard the solutions as directed by your teacher. Save the boiling chips for future use.

Data Record

Table 27.1 Distillation Data for Aqueous Solution of NaCl, NH_3, and Phenolphthalein

Temperature at which distillation began: ______ °C

Test	Solution before Distillation	Solution after First Distillation	Solution after Second Distillation	First Distillate	Second Distillate
Color					
Cl^-					
pH					
NH_3 fumes					

Conclusions

1. For each of the solutes used in this experiment, state whether it is volatile or nonvolatile. Give evidence for your answer.

2. Should you have tested for sodium ion in the distillate? Explain.

Extension

1. Start with a higher concentration of ammonia and modify this experiment to quantitatively follow the collection of ammonia in the distillate.

Experiment

28 Water of Hydration

Text reference: Section 16.10

Background

Have you ever had your arm put in a plaster cast? If you have, then you already know something about hydrates. Plaster of paris is the hemihydrate of calcium sulfate, $CaSO_4 \cdot \frac{1}{2}H_2O$. When you add water to plaster of paris and allow it to set, it is gradually transformed into a hard crystalline compound, calcium sulfate dihydrate, $CaSO_4 \cdot 2H_2O$. Water is an integral part of many ionic solids, and such ionic solids are called *hydrates.* The water in these solids is called *water of hydration.*

The water of hydration is more loosely bound in the hydrated crystal than the ions are. Thus, you can usually drive off the water by heating the crystals. The material that remains after the water is gone is called the *anhydrous salt.*

In this experiment, you will heat several hydrates and observe the appearance of the reactants and products involved. You will also heat a nonhydrated compound as a basis for comparison.

Goal

- **Observe** the effect of heat on several hydrates.

Equipment

safety goggles
4 medium test tubes
1 gas burner
1 test-tube holder
1 spatula
2 glass-marking pencils/class

Materials

copper(II) sulfate pentahydrate, $CuSO_4 \cdot 5H_2O$ T I
magnesium sulfate heptahydrate, $MgSO_4 \cdot 7H_2O$
sodium carbonate decahydrate, $Na_2CO_3 \cdot 10H_2O$ I
sodium chloride, NaCl

Safety 

- Note the Safety Symbols used here and in the Procedure section. Review safety information on pages 7–10.
- Always wear safety goggles when working in the lab.
- Copper compounds are toxic. Avoid contact with copper(II) sulfate pentahydrate.

Procedure

Copy Table 28.1 into your laboratory notebook. As you perform the experiment, record your observations in this table.

1. Label four clean dry test tubes with the numbers 1–4. To separate test tubes add about 1 g of each of the following substances.

tube 1	$CuSO_4 \cdot 5H_2O$
tube 2	$NaCl$
tube 3	$MgSO_4 \cdot 7H_2O$
tube 4	$Na_2CO_3 \cdot 10H_2O$

2. Grasp tube 1 in a test-tube holder. Hold the tube almost horizontally and heat it *gently* in a burner flame, as shown in Figure 28.1. **CAUTION:** *Never point the mouth of the tube at yourself or at anyone else.* Record what you observe near the mouth of the test tube, and note any change in the appearance of the crystals.

3. Repeat step 2 for tubes 2, 3, and 4. Record your observations.

4. Follow your teacher's instructions for proper disposal of the materials.

Figure 28.1

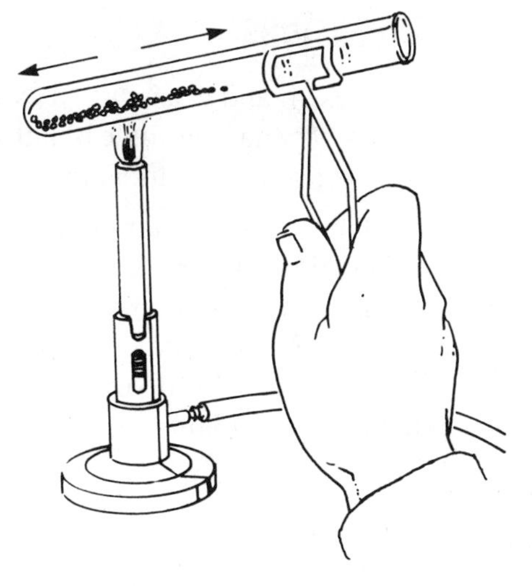

Data Record

Table 28.1 Observations		
Tube	**Substance**	**Observations**
1		
2		
3		
4		

Data Analysis

1. In which tubes did you observe a change near the test tube's mouth?

2. In which tubes did the appearance of the crystals change?

Conclusions

1. Write a general statement to describe what you would expect to observe when a hydrate is heated.

2. For any substance that was a hydrate, write a balanced equation for the change that took place when the substance was heated. In each case assume that the anhydrous salt was formed.

Extensions

1. Design and carry out an experiment for determining the number of moles of water per mole of anhydrous salt in an unknown hydrate. You will be given the formula mass of the anhydrous salt, but not its formula.

2. Find out the water pollution standards for copper in your area. Calculate the total amount of copper used in your school for this experiment. What additional information would you need to determine whether this amount of copper would exceed the amount allowed in the water outflow from your school? Obtain the needed information and report your findings.

Experiment

29 Electrolytes and Nonelectrolytes

Text reference: Section 16.8

Background

If an electrical device accidentally falls into water in which you're standing, you could receive a severe or even fatal shock. This is possible because small amounts of dissolved ions in the water allow it to conduct electricity. Thus, in the case of an electrical device accidentally dropped into water, the electricity normally conducted to the device is instead conducted into you. Substances that dissolve in water to produce electrically conductive solutions are called *electrolytes.* If, when dissolved, the substance is a good conductor of electricity, it is called a *strong electrolyte.* In general, strong electrolytes are almost completely ionized when dissolved in solution. If, when dissolved, the substance is a poor conductor of electricity, it is called a *weak electrolyte.* In general, weak electrolytes are only slightly ionized when dissolved in solution. Substances that dissolve in water without ionizing will not conduct electricity and are called *nonelectrolytes.*

In this experiment, you will observe as your teacher tests several solutions for conductivity. You will classify the solute in each solution as a strong electrolyte, a weak electrolyte, or a nonelectrolyte.

Goals

- **Classify** solutes as strong electrolytes, weak electrolytes, or nonelectrolytes.
- **Explain** conductivity data in terms of chemical bonding.

Equipment

safety goggles
1 conductivity apparatus, including light bulbs
1 100-mL beaker
paper towels
1 plastic wash bottle

Materials

5% sodium chloride solution, NaCl(*aq*)
sodium chloride, NaCl
5% sucrose solution, $C_{12}H_{22}O_{11}$ (*aq*)
ethanol, C_2H_5OH [F] [T]
kerosene [F] [T] [I]
1*M* hydrochloric acid, HCl [T] [I]
1*M* sodium hydroxide, NaOH [C] [T]

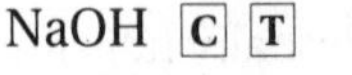

glacial ethanoic acid, $HC_2H_3O_2$ [C]
6*M* ethanoic acid, $HC_2H_3O_2$ [C]
6*M* ammonia, NH_3(*aq*) [T] [I]
1*M* ammonia, NH_3(*aq*) [T]
distilled water
tap water

Safety

- Note the Safety Symbols used here and in the Procedure section. Review safety information on pages 7–10.
- Always wear safety goggles when working in the lab.
- Hydrochloric and ethanoic acid are irritating and corrosive and can cause severe injury, depending on concentration.
- Ammonia is an irritant and has a choking smell. Avoid inhalation and skin contact with this chemical.
- Sodium hydroxide is corrosive and can cause severe burns.
- Note that the teacher will always be sure that the switch is turned off and the plug is removed from the outlet before handling the conductivity apparatus. This is done to prevent electric shock.

Procedure

Copy Table 29.1 into your laboratory notebook. As this demonstration is conducted by your teacher, record your observations in this table.

1. The apparatus commonly used in determining electrical conductivity is shown in Figure 29.1. **CAUTION:** *The plug of the conductivity apparatus should be removed from the outlet and the switch should be turned off except when making a test.*

2. Your teacher will put about 20 mL of the 5% sodium chloride solution into a 100-mL beaker. The beaker will be positioned so that the electrodes are immersed to a depth of 0.5–1 cm in the solution. The apparatus will then be plugged in and the switch turned on. Record your

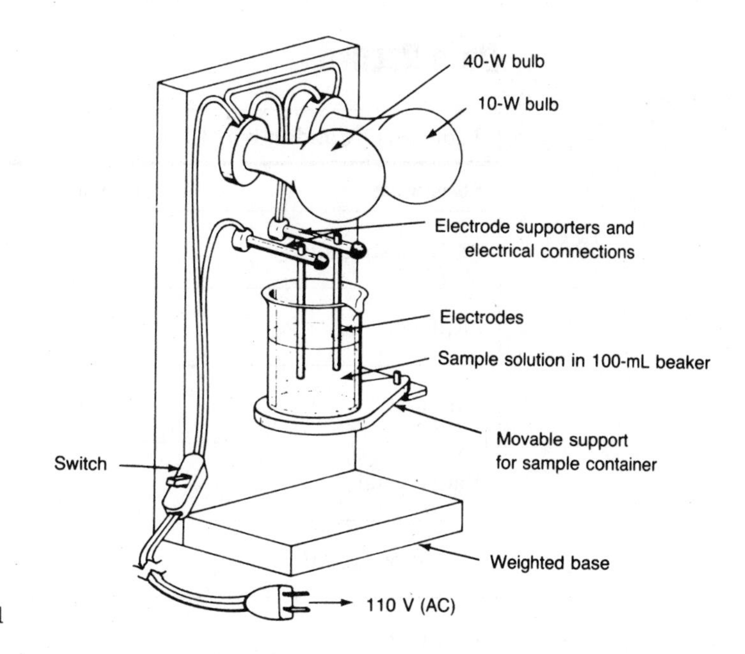

Figure 29.1

observations in Table 29.1. The apparatus will then be turned off and unplugged.

3. Your teacher will clean and dry the electrodes and repeat step 2, testing each of the substances listed in the Materials section. For liquids a 20-mL sample will be used; for solids, a depth of 1 cm, in a *dry* beaker, will be used.

4. Your teacher will properly dispose of the materials.

Data Record

Table 29.1 Conductivity Data		
Substance	**Observation**	**Comments**
5% NaCl solution		
distilled water		
tap water		
NaCl crystals		
5% sucrose solution		
kerosene		
1*M* HCl		
1*M* NaOH		
glacial CH_3COOH		
6*M* CH_3COOH		
6*M* NH_3		
1*M* NH_3		

Data Analysis

1. In Table 29.1, identify each substance tested as a strong electrolyte, a weak electrolyte, or a nonelectrolyte.

2. For each electrolyte, either strong or weak, write the formulas of the ions that are present in a solution of the substance.

Conclusions

1. Based on the type of bonding present in hydrochloric acid, the results of the conductivity test may have been unexpected. Explain.

2. Compare the conductivity of solid sodium chloride and a 5% solution of a sodium chloride. Explain any difference.

3. Glacial ethanoic acid is ethanoic acid that is at least 99.8% pure, that is, it contains no more than 0.2% water. Compare the conductivity of glacial ethanoic acid with that of 6*M* ethanoic acid and explain the difference.

4. Compare the conductivity of 6*M* ammonia and 1*M* ammonia. Explain any difference.

5. What types of bonding do compounds have that are electrolytes?

Extension

1. Many people are concerned about their salt (sodium chloride) intake. Would it be possible to test for the amount of salt in foods, using a device based on conductivity measurements? Point out some potential pitfalls in a device of this type.

Experiment

30 Factors Affecting Solution Formation

Text reference:
Section 17.1

Background

When you put a spoonful of sugar into a glass of iced tea, you probably begin to stir it up immediately. Why? If your reply is that the sugar will sink to the bottom and not easily dissolve if it is not stirred, you already understand an important fact about solution formation. Stirring is one of several factors that determines how fast a substance will dissolve and form a solution.

A solution consists of a *solute*, the material that is dissolved, and a *solvent*, the material that the solute is dissolved in. In this experiment, you will investigate the effects of stirring, temperature, and particle size on the rate of dissolution.

Goal

- **Observe** the effect of particle size, degree of mixing, and temperature on the rate of dissolution.

Equipment

safety goggles
7 large test tubes
1 test-tube rack
2 100-mL beakers
1 50-mL graduated cylinder
1 ring stand
1 ring support
1 wire gauze
1 gas burner
1 mortar and pestle
1 spatula
1 thermometer
1 glass-marking pencil

Materials

sodium chloride, NaCl
copper(II) sulfate pentahydrate,
  $CuSO_4 \cdot 5H_2O$ T I
crushed ice
paper towels
weighing paper
distilled water

Safety

- Note the Safety Symbols used here and in the Procedure section. Review safety information on pages 7–10.
- Always wear safety goggles when working in the lab.
- Copper compounds are toxic. Avoid contact with copper(II) sulfate pentahydrate.

Procedure

Copy Tables 30.1 and 30.2 into your laboratory notebook. As you perform the experiment, record your observations in these tables.

Part A. Effects of Particle Size and Mixing

1. Label four large test tubes with the numbers 1–4. **CAUTION:** *$CuSO_4 \cdot 5H_2O$ is toxic and irritating. Avoid contact with this material.* Use a spatula to put four pea-sized crystals of copper(II) sulfate pentahydrate, $CuSO_4 \cdot 5H_2O$, on a piece of weighing paper.

2. Put one crystal of $CuSO_4 \cdot 5H_2O$ into tube 1 and another crystal into tube 2. Crush a third crystal with the mortar and pestle and pour the powder into tube 3. Crush the fourth crystal and pour the powder into tube 4.

3. Fill each of the four test tubes about one-third full of water. Place tubes 1 and 3 in the test-tube rack *without* shaking them. Flick tubes 2 and 4. Note how long it takes for the contents of each of the four tubes to dissolve. Record your observations in Table 30.1.

4. Follow your teacher's instructions for proper disposal of the materials.

Part B. Effect of Temperature

5. Add 50 mL of distilled water to a 100-mL beaker. Using a gas burner, heat the water until it is almost boiling. While the water is heating, proceed to step 6.

6. Half-fill a 100-mL beaker with crushed ice and then add approximately 30 mL of distilled water to the beaker. While the water is chilling, proceed to step 7.

7. Label three large test tubes with the numbers 1–3. Add 5 g of sodium chloride to each test tube. Place the tubes in a test tube rack.

8. Fill tube 1 one-third full of ice-cold water (see step 6). Fill tube 2 one-third full with distilled water at room temperature. Fill tube 3 one-third full with hot water (see step 5). **CAUTION:** *Pour the hot water from the beaker, using a paper towel handle as illustrated in Figure 30.1.* Gently flick the contents of the test tubes. Note how long it takes for the contents of each tube to dissolve. Record your observations in Table 30.2.

9. Dispose of the contents of the three test tubes by pouring them down the drain.

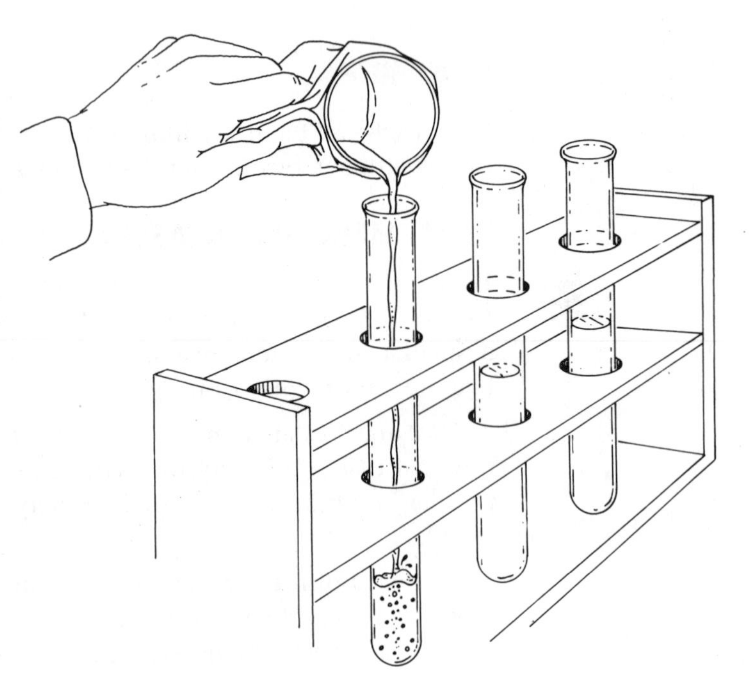

Figure 30.1

Data Record

Table 30.1 Effects of Particle Size and Mixing on Solution Formation				
Tube	**Particle Size**	**Mixed?**	**Time to Dissolve**	**Observations**
1				
2				
3				
4				

Table 30.2 Effects of Temperature on Solution Formation			
Tube	**Temperature**	**Time to Dissolve**	**Observations**
1			
2			
3			

Conclusions

1. What effects does particle size appear to have on the rate at which a solute dissolves? Why should particle size make a difference in the rate of dissolving?

2. Does shaking the test tube affect the rate at which a solute dissolves? Explain your results.

3. Using kinetic theory, explain the effect of temperature on the dissolution rate of a solute.

Extensions

1. Devise an experiment to discover if there is a linear relationship between increasing temperature and the rate of dissolving. Use a temperature range from 0°C to 100°C. Test at least three different solutes.

2. Temperature affects not only the rate of dissolving, but also the amount of solute that will dissolve in a given volume of solvent. Design an experiment to quantitatively determine the solubilities of sodium chloride, sucrose, and potassium sulfate in water at 0°C, 25°C, and 100°C.

Experiment

31 Supersaturation

Text reference:
Section 17.3

Background

Perhaps you've made rock candy by placing a string in a sugar solution and letting the sugar crystallize on the string. But did you know this candy-making method will work only with a particular kind of sugar solution? Under certain conditions, a solution may contain more solute than is normally contained in a saturated solution at the same temperature. This type of solution is unstable and is called *supersaturated.* The addition of a single crystal of solute often causes the excess solute to crystallize. You must use a supersaturated solution when making rock candy. The addition of a string disturbs the unstable solution and begins the crystallization.

The solubility of most substances decreases as temperature decreases. This fact sometimes leads to the formation of supersaturated solutions. As the solution cools, the excess solute may or may not crystallize out. If the excess solute remains in the solution, the solution becomes supersaturated.

In this experiment you will make a supersaturated solution and observe the effect of adding a seed crystal to it.

Goals

- **Prepare** a supersaturated solution of sodium sulfate.
- **Observe** the effect of seeding the supersaturated solution.

Equipment

safety goggles
1 medium test tube
1 test-tube rack
1 test-tube holder
1 100-mL beaker
1 10-mL graduated cylinder
1 gas burner
8 centigram balances/class

Materials

sodium sulfate decahydrate, $Na_2SO_4 \cdot 10H_2O$

ice

distilled water

Safety

- Note the Safety Symbols used here and in the Procedure section. Review the safety information on pages 7–10.
- Always wear safety goggles when working in the lab.

Procedure

Copy Table 31.1 into your laboratory notebook. As you perform the experiment, record your observations in this table.

1. Place 5 g of $Na_2SO_4 \cdot 10H_2O$ in a clean medium-sized test tube. Add 10 mL of distilled water.

2. Hold the test tube in a test tube holder and heat it in a burner flame, agitating the mixture *gently* until all of the solid has dissolved. **CAUTION:** *When heating a test tube, never point the mouth of the tube at yourself or anyone else. Make sure to warm the bottom and sides of the tube evenly. Never heat only the bottom of the tube.* Place the test tube in a test-tube rack. Add one more crystal of $Na_2SO_4 \cdot 10H_2O$ to the warmed solution and gently agitate it. Record your observations in Table 31.1.

3. Place the test tube and contents in a beaker of ice water to cool. Be careful not to disturb the test tube during the cooling process. If crystals begin to form as it is cooling, reheat the tube to redissolve the crystals, and cool the tube again.

4. When the solution is cold, gently remove the tube from the ice water bath and put it in the test-tube rack. Add one small crystal of $Na_2SO_4 \cdot 10H_2O$. Describe what you see. Touch the bottom of the test tube to the palm of your hand. Record your observations in Table 31.1.

5. Follow your teacher's instructions for the proper disposal of the materials.

Data Record

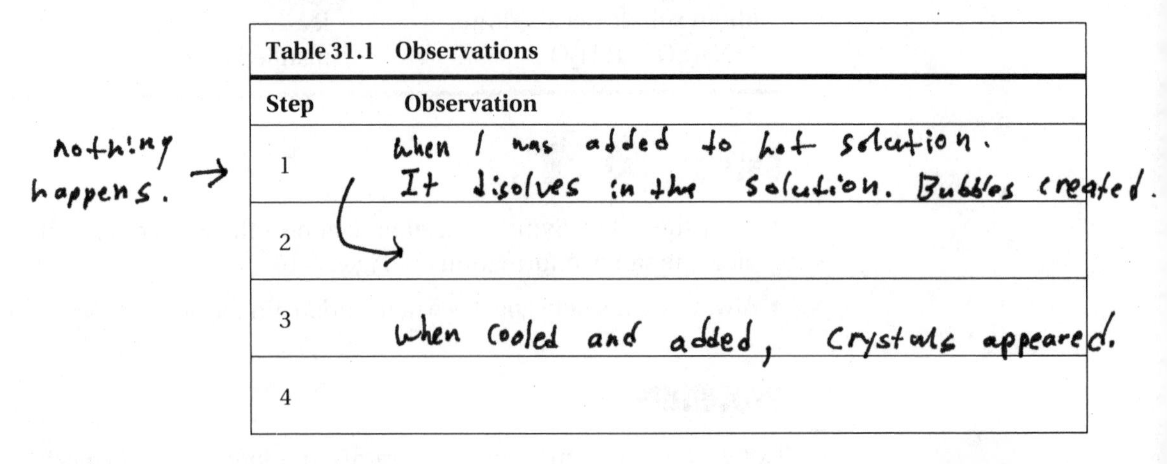

Table 31.1 Observations	
Step	**Observation**
1	when I was added to hot solution. It disolves in the solution. Bubbles created.
2	nothing happens.
3	when cooled and added, crystals appeared.
4	

Conclusions

1. Why is it necessary to heat the mixture in step 2 of the procedure?

2. Is the solution unsaturated, saturated, or supersaturated at the end of step 2? Explain.

3. Is the solution unsaturated, saturated, or supersaturated at the end of step 3? Give evidence for your answer.

4. At the end of step 4, when crystallization is complete, is the solution unsaturated, saturated, or supersaturated? Explain.

5. Describe a simple test to determine whether a solution is unsaturated, saturated, or supersaturated. Explain how to interpret the test.

Extensions

1. Devise an experiment to discover whether the rate of cooling of a supersaturated solution affects its stability.

2. The concepts explored in this experiment are used in growing crystals. Find instructions for several crystal-growing labs. Ask your teacher which of these you can do in your school laboratory and which you can do at home. After you have successfully grown some crystals, design a crystal-growing lab for others in your class.

Experiment

32 Introduction to Chromatography

Text reference: Chapter 16

Background

You've probably seen different colors mixed together to form a new color. The mixing of paint is a common example: Red and yellow paints are mixed to make orange paint. Have you ever thought of how you might separate the orange paint to get original colors back? Separations similar to this are often performed in chemistry. Chemical separations might be performed to answer questions dealing with determining the ingredients in a pill or measuring the amount of cholesterol in a sample of fat. *Chromatography* is a commonly used method for separating substances in a mixture. The name of the method is derived from the fact that chromatography was first applied to separating colored substances. In Greek, *chromos* means color. Although the effectiveness of the separation is most easily detected if the components of the mixture are colored, the method is commonly applied to separating many kinds of mixtures.

In this experiment, you will separate the dyes of various food coloring by paper chromatography.

Goal

- **Observe** the separation of a mixture of substances by paper chromatography.

Equipment

safety goggles
3 large test tubes
3 cork stoppers
1 test-tube rack
1 10-cm ruler
3 capillary tubes
1 plastic wash bottle
1 pencil
3 wire paper clips

Materials

filter paper strips, 1 cm × 15 cm

yellow, blue, and green food coloring

Safety

- Note the Safety Symbol used here. Review safety information on pages 7–10.
- Always wear safety goggles when working in the lab.

Procedure

Copy Table 32.1 into your laboratory notebook. As you perform the experiment, record your data in this table.

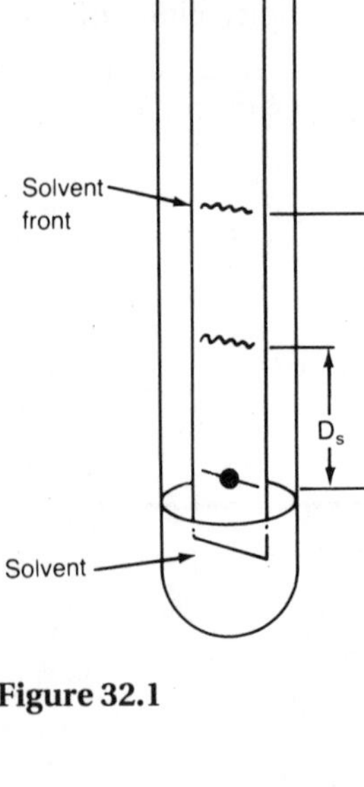

Figure 32.1

1. Your teacher will show you how to use a capillary tube to apply dye (food coloring) to the filter paper strips. Use a pencil to mark a small circle, the size of the printed letter *o*, about 2 cm from one end of each of three filter paper strips. The penciled circle is the point of origin. Use a capillary tube to put one drop of dye at the point of origin on one of the filter strips. Repeat this procedure for the other dyes.

2. Fill each of three large test tubes with water, to a depth of approximately 2 cm. Use a cork stopper to suspend each filter paper strip in a test tube, as shown in Figure 32.1. The end of the paper strip should be below the water level; the dye spot should be above the water level. Put each tube, as it is prepared, in the test-tube rack.

3. Permit the solvent in each tube to rise up the filter paper until it is about 2 cm from the top of the paper.

4. Remove the strips from the tubes. Using a pencil, mark on each strip the distance the water has traveled from the point of origin. Record these distances as D_f in the data table.

5. Measure on each paper strip the distance each dye spot has traveled. Record these distances as D_s. If the original dye spot has separated into several spots, measure and record the D_s for each spot.

6. Dispose of the water in the sink and the solids in the trash.

Data Record

Table 32.1 Paper Chromatography of Food Dyes			
Dye	D_f value (cm)	D_s value (cm)	R_f value (cm)
yellow			
blue			
green			

Data Analysis

1. Calculate the R_f value for each substance that produces a spot in your paper chromatograms. The formula for R_f follows:

$$R_f = D_s / D_f$$

D_s is the distance traveled by the solute and D_f is the distance traveled by the solvent. Record the R_f values in the data table.

Conclusions

1. Do the yellow and blue dyes appear to be composed of a single colored compound? Explain your reasoning.

2. Does the green dye appear to be composed of a single colored compound? Explain.

3. Would it be a problem to use an ink pen or a marking pen instead of a pencil as directed in step 1 of the procedure? Explain.

4. Consider the molecular interactions that might occur between the dye, the solvent, and the paper and suggest an explanation for the different R_f values for different dyes.

5. Blue ink from two different pens appears to be the exact same color. Explain how to determine whether the inks are identical.

Extensions

1. Chromatography on paper can be done using solvents besides water. Consult college laboratory texts in organic chemistry to find and try a method for the separation of chlorophyll and other leaf pigments.

2. Try simple spot paper chromatography by placing a large spot of a mixture of several dyes in the center of a circle of ordinary filter paper and observing the result.

Experiment

33 Freezing Point

Text reference: Section 17.9

Background

If you live in an area that has cold winters, you know that salt is often applied to the roads when it snows. Since the salt causes corrosion problems for the vehicles that use the salted roads, what is the reason for its use? From Experiment 14 you know that a pure liquid freezes to a solid at a constant temperature unique to that substance. But what happens to the freezing point if a solute is dissolved in the pure liquid? Will the solution freeze at a higher or lower temperature than the pure liquid? Will the temperature remain constant throughout the freezing process?

In this experiment you will investigate the effect of a solute on the freezing behavior of a solution. When you are done, you should understand why salt is used on roads in the winter.

Goals

- **Measure** the freezing point of pure benzoic acid and of a benzoic acid solution containing a solute.
- **Observe** the effect of a solute on the freezing point of benzoic acid.
- **Describe** the effect of solute concentration on the freezing point of benzoic acid.

Equipment

safety goggles
1 large test tube
1 thermometer
1 3-pronged jaw clamp
1 copper wire stirrer (from Experiment 14)
1 gas burner
1 ring stand and utility clamp
1 spatula
1 timer with second hand
4 centigram balances/class

Materials

benzoic acid, C_6H_5COOH T I F

one of the following solutes:

camphor, $C_{10}H_{16}O$ F T I
urea, $CO(NH_2)_2$ I
potassium ethanoate, CH_3COOK I

Safety

- Note the Safety Symbols used here and in the Procedure section. Review safety information on pages 7–10.
- Always wear safety goggles when working in the lab.
- Benzoic acid is an irritant and is mildly toxic.
- Mercury is extremely toxic and a mercury spill is very difficult to clean up. If you break a mercury thermometer, report it immediately to your teacher.

Procedure

Copy Tables 33.1 and 33.2 into your laboratory notebook. As you perform the experiment, record your observations in Table 33.1.

Part A. The Freezing Point of Pure Benzoic Acid

1. Measure out 10.0 grams of benzoic acid, to the nearest 0.1 g. Place the benzoic acid in a large clean, dry test tube.

2. Secure the test tube in a utility clamp attached to a ring stand. Place the stirrer around the thermometer. With a three-pronged clamp, clamp the thermometer above the test tube so it rests on the solid benzoic acid.

3. **CAUTION:** *Do not heat the benzoic acid above 140°C. Above 140°C benzoic acid gives off toxic fumes.* Gently heat the benzoic acid to melting, using the gas burner.

4. Lower the thermometer into the molten benzoic acid so that the bulb is immersed and the stirrer surrounds the thermometer, as shown in Figure 33.1. Secure the thermometer clamp.

5. Stir the molten benzoic acid. When the temperature of the benzoic acid reaches 140°C, discontinue heating and turn off the gas burner.

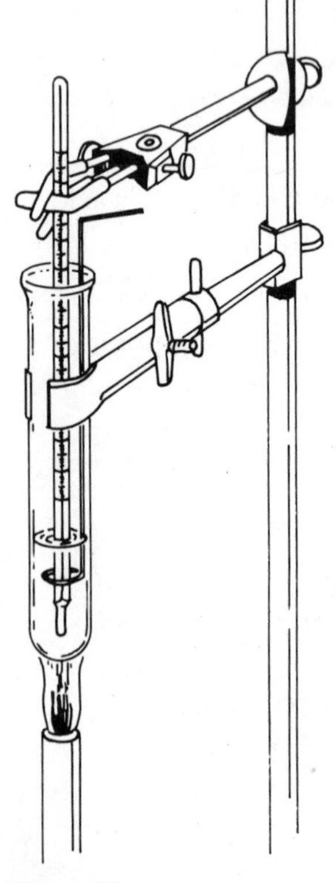

Figure 33.1

6. As the benzoic acid cools, take temperature readings every 30 seconds for the first 3 minutes and then every minute. Record all temperatures to the nearest 0.5°C. Stir for as long as possible, but do not force the stirrer. Collect data until the temperature drops to about 100°C.

Part B. The Freezing Point with 0.0050 Mole of Solute

7. Calculate the mass of 0.0050 mole of the solute assigned to you by your teacher. Measure out this calculated mass to the nearest 0.01 g and record the measurement.

8. Transfer the weighed solute to the test tube of benzoic acid used in Part A. Carefully reheat the mixture, stirring constantly as it melts and the solute dissolves. Heat the mixture to about 140°C.

9. Repeat step 6 for this mixture.

Part C. The Freezing Point with 0.010 Mole of Solute

10. Using the mixture from Part B, repeat step 7 (add another 0.0050 mole of the same solute). The solution now contains 0.010 moles of solute.

11. Remelt the mixture and heat it to 140°C. When all of the solute has dissolved, turn off the burner and repeat step 6.

12. Follow your teacher's instructions for the proper disposal of the materials.

Data Record

Table 33.1 Cooling of Benzoic Acid and Benzoic Acid Plus Solute

Time (min)	Temperature (°C) of Benzoic Acid	Temperature (°C) of Benzoic Acid Plus 0.0050 mol Solute	Temperature (°C) of Benzoic Acid Plus 0.010 mol Solute
0			
0.5			
1			
1.5			
2			
2.5			
3			
4			
5			
6			
7			
8			
9			
10			
11			

Table 33.2 Class Averages for Freezing-Point Depressions		
Solute	**Average ΔT_1 (°C)**	**Average ΔT_2 (°C)**
camphor		
urea		
potassium ethanoate		

Data Analysis

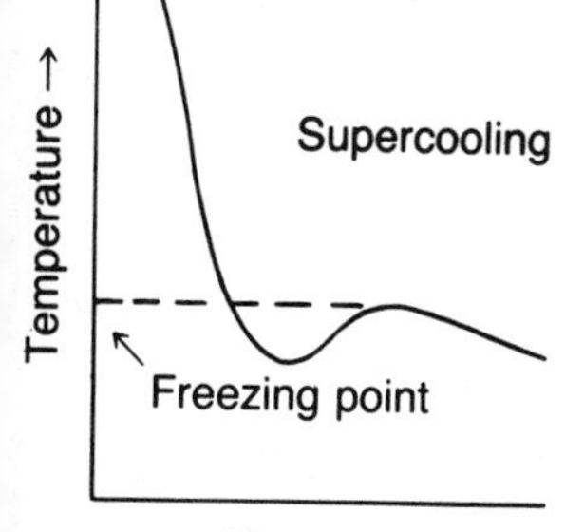

Figure 33.2

Note, **one page of graph paper** is required for your report.

1. Plot a graph of temperature (°C) versus time (minutes) for all three freezing-point determinations. Plot and label all three curves on the same graph, connecting the points for each determination in a smooth curve. If your graph shows a dip similar to the one in Figure 33.2, it is likely that your solution supercooled. The true freezing point of the solution can be found by disregarding the dip and extrapolating from the highest point of the horizontal portion of the graph to the vertical axis.

2. From your graph, determine the freezing point of the pure benzoic acid and of the two solutions.

3. What was the magnitude of the freezing-point depression, ΔT_1, caused by the addition of the first 0.0050 moles of solute?

4. What was the magnitude of the freezing-point depression, ΔT_2, of pure benzoic acid, caused by the addition of 0.010 moles of solute?

5. Average all the ΔT_1 values obtained in the class for camphor. Do the same for ΔT_2. Repeat these calculations for each solute used. Record the results in Table 33.2.

Conclusions

1. Compare ΔT_1 to ΔT_2 for each solute in this experiment. What general statement can you make concerning the relationship between doubling the number of moles of solute and the magnitude of the freezing-point depression?

2. Compare the freezing-point depression caused by urea to that caused by camphor. Does your data support the idea that the freezing point depression depends only on the number of moles of particles in the solution? Explain.

3. The freezing-point depression of potassium ethanoate is greater than that of the other two solutes when an equal number of moles of each is used. Explain.

4. The freezing point of benzoic acid remains relatively constant throughout the freezing process. Is the same true for the freezing point of a solution? Explain any difference.

Extensions

1. If you have made homemade ice cream, you depended on the freezing point depression of the salt-ice-water mixture to freeze your ice cream. Design a quantitative experiment to determine the optimal amount of salt to add to the ice-water mixture.

2. Design an experiment to determine how the boiling point of a solution compares to the boiling point of the pure solvent.

Factors Affecting Reaction Rates

Text reference:
Sections 18.1, 18.2

Background

You may have noticed that chemical reactions occur at different speeds. The explosion of fireworks is instantaneous; the rusting of an iron gate is relatively slow. In most situations, you would like to make the rusting of iron proceed as slowly as possible. On the other hand, a chemical company might want to speed up the reactions that produce the chemicals they sell. In order to understand how the rates of chemical reactions can be controlled, it is necessary to understand the factors that influence the rates of chemical reaction.

In this experiment, you will study the effect that temperature, reactant concentration, particle size, catalysts, and surface area have on chemical reaction rates.

Goals

- **Observe** the effects of temperature, concentration, particle size, surface area, and catalysts on the rates of chemical reactions.
- **Explain** these effects in terms of kinetic-molecular theory.

Equipment

safety goggles
1 10-mL graduated cylinder
1 100-mL graduated cylinder
16 medium test tubes
1 test-tube rack
2 250-mL beakers
4 centigram balances/class
1 crucible tongs
1 thermometer
1 250-mL plastic bottle
1 ring stand
1 ring support
1 wire gauze
1 gas burner
1 dropper pipet
1 metal cutter/class
watch or timer
tape, for label

Materials

0.1*M* iron(III) chloride, $FeCl_3$ [T] [I]
0.1*M* iron(III) nitrate, $Fe(NO_3)_3$ [T]
0.1*M* sodium chloride, NaCl
0.1*M* calcium chloride, $CaCl_2$ [T]
0.1*M* potassium nitrate, KNO_3
0.1*M* manganese chloride, $MnCl_2$ [T]
3% hydrogen peroxide, H_2O_2
6*M* hydrochloric acid, HCl [C] [T]
3*M* hydrochloric acid, HCl [C] [T]
1*M* hydrochloric acid, HCl [T] [I]
0.1*M* hydrochloric acid, HCl [T] [I]
zinc strips, Zn, 0.25 mm × 0.50 mm × 2.00 cm
powdered zinc [F] [T]
wood splints
steel wool
ice cubes
aluminum foil
paper towels
distilled water

Safety

- Note the Safety Symbols used here and in the Procedure section. Review the safety information on pages 7–10.
- Always wear safety goggles when working in the lab.
- Hydrochloric acid is corrosive and can cause severe burns.
- Iron(III) chloride is an irritant.
- Mercury is extremely toxic and a mercury spill is very difficult to clean up. If you break a mercury thermometer, report it immediately to your teacher.

Procedure

Copy Tables 34.1, 34.2, 34.3, and 34.4 into your notebook. As you perform the experiment, record your data and observations in these tables.

Part A. Effect of Temperature on Reaction Rate

The reaction of zinc metal with hydrochloric acid will be examined.

1. **CAUTION:** *Hydrochloric acid is corrosive.* Pour 5.0 mL of 6*M* hydrochloric acid into each of three clean test tubes. Place one of the tubes in an ice water bath (ice-water mixture in 250-mL beaker). Place another in a hot water bath, maintained at 50°C (heat the water in a 250-mL beaker over a gas burner). Place the third tube in a test-tube rack, at room temperature. Allow about 10 minutes for the tubes to reach the temperature of their surroundings.

2. Clean a zinc strip with steel wool. Cut three small pieces of zinc to the same size. Each piece should be approximately 0.5 cm × 2.0 cm. Save the remainder of the strip for step 8.

3. Note the time in Table 34.1, and drop one piece of zinc into each of the three test tubes containing hydrochloric acid. Cover each tube loosely with a piece of aluminum foil and wait for 2 minutes. Test for the identity of the gas produced by using tongs to hold a burning splint near the mouth of each of the tubes. Note the time at which each reaction ceases.

Part B. Effect of a Catalyst on Reaction Rate

The decomposition of hydrogen peroxide will be studied.

4. Measure 90 mL of distilled water into a clean 250-mL plastic bottle and add 10 mL of 3% hydrogen peroxide solution. Label it as 0.3% hydrogen peroxide. This will be your test solution.

5. Rinse seven clean test tubes and a 10-mL graduated cylinder with the 0.3% hydrogen peroxide. Discard the rinses. Measure 5 mL of 0.3% hydrogen peroxide into each of the seven test tubes. Place the test tubes in a rack.

6. Add 5 drops of each of the following solutions to separate test tubes of the hydrogen peroxide: 6*M* hydrochloric acid, 0.1*M* iron(III) chloride, 0.1*M* sodium chloride, 0.1*M* iron(III) nitrate, 0.1*M* calcium chloride, 0.1*M* potassium nitrate, 0.1*M* manganese chloride. Flick each tube to mix its contents. Observe each solution and report the rate of gas evolution from each. Use the terms *fast, slow, very slow,* or *none* to describe the rate of gas evolution. Describe the catalytic activity as *high, low,* or *none.* Record your observations in Table 34.2.

Part C. Effect of Concentration on Reaction Rate, at Constant Temperature

The reactions of zinc metal with hydrochloric acid solutions of varying concentrations will be examined.

7. **CAUTION:** *Hydrochloric acid is corrosive.* Pour 5 mL of each of the following hydrochloric acid solutions into separate clean test tubes: 0.1*M*, 1*M*, 3*M*, and 6*M*.

8. Cut four small pieces (1 cm × 1 cm) from the zinc strip you cleaned in Part A. (Save the remainder of the zinc strip for use in Part D.) Drop one piece of zinc into each of the acid solutions. Record the start time and the end time of each reaction. Record your observations in Table 34.3.

Part D. Effect of Particle Size or Surface Area on Reaction Rate

The reaction of zinc metal with hydrochloric acid will be used to study the effect of particle size and surface area on the rate of reaction.

9. Cut a piece of zinc (0.5 cm × 2.0 cm) from a clean strip of the metal. Determine the mass of the piece of zinc to the nearest 0.01 g and record. Place the piece of zinc in a clean dry test tube.

10. CAUTION: *Powdered zinc is flammable; keep it away from open flames.* Measure an equal quantity of powdered zinc into a second clean dry test tube.

11. Place both test tubes in a rack, and add 5 mL of 1*M* hydrochloric acid to each. Observe the reactions for several minutes and record your observations in Table 34.4.

12. Follow your teacher's instructions for proper disposal of the materials.

Data Record

Table 34.1 Effect of Temperature on Reaction Rate

Reaction Condition	Time Reaction Started	Time Reaction Ended	Reaction Duration	Burning Splint Test Result
ice water 0°C				
room temp. _____ °C				
hot water 50°C				

Table 34.2 Effect of a Catalyst on Reaction Rate

Test	HCl 6*M*	$FeCl_3$ 0.1*M*	NaCl 0.1*M*	$Fe(NO_3)_3$ 0.1*M*	$CaCl_2$ 0.1*M*	KNO_3 0.1*M*	$MnCl_2$ 0.1*M*
oxygen evolution							
catalytic activity							

Table 34.3 Effect of Concentration on Reaction Rate

Reaction Condition	Time Started	Time Ended	Reaction Duration	Observations
0.1 M HCl				
1 M HCl				
3 M HCl				
6 M HCl				

Table 34.4 Effect of Surface Area on Reaction Rate

Substance Tested	Observations
sheet zinc	
powdered zinc	

Data Analysis

1. Write a balanced chemical equation for the reaction between hydrochloric acid and zinc metal.

2. Write a balanced chemical equation for the decomposition of hydrogen peroxide.

3. Which ionic compounds used in Part B were effective catalysts?

4. Examine the data in Table 34.2 and identify the ion responsible for the catalytic activity.

5. Many reaction rates approximately double for every 10°C increase in temperature. Are the results you obtained in Part A consistent with this general statement?

6. How does the surface area of a substance change as it is broken into smaller pieces?

Conclusions

1. Describe in your own words the effect of temperature on the rate of a reaction. Explain this effect in terms of the collision theory of reactions.

2. Describe in your own words the effect of concentration on the rate of a reaction. Explain this effect in terms of the collision theory of reactions.

3. Describe in your own words the effect of particle size or surface area on the rate of a reaction. Explain this effect in terms of the collision theory of reactions.

4. Describe in your own words the effect of a catalyst on the rate of a reaction. Explain this effect in terms of the collision theory of reactions.

Extensions

1. Devise an experiment to study the effect of changing temperature on the rate of evolution of gas from an Alka-Seltzer tablet dropped in water.

2. For each part of this experiment, identify the independent (manipulated) variable, the dependent (responding) variable, and the variables that must be controlled.

Experiment

35 The Clock Reaction

Text reference:
Section 18.2

Background

Suppose you work in a chemical plant that produces a valuable compound. The compound is produced at specific conditions, but now your company has asked you to increase the manufacturing speed of the compound. Can you change the conditions to make the reaction faster? In order to speed up the reaction, you must know something about the factors that influence reaction rates. To test the influence of these factors on the rate of your reaction, you must be able to find out how long it takes to produce a certain amount of the product, or how long it takes to use up a certain amount of one of the reactants.

The time it takes for a reaction to go to completion is easy to measure if a color change signals when one of the reactants is used up. This kind of reaction is called a *clock reaction*. To tell how long a clock reaction takes, all you need to do is time the reaction from the moment the reactants are mixed to the moment that the color appears.

In this experiment, you will conduct a quantitative study of the effect of concentration on the rate of a clock reaction.

Goals

- **Measure** the time required to produce a specific amount of product in a chemical reaction.
- **Explain** how concentration of reactants affects the rate of the reaction.
- **Make a graph** of the results of these rate studies.

Equipment

safety goggles
3 25-mL graduated cylinders
1 100-mL beaker
1 stirring rod
1 thermometer
1 dropper pipet
1 stopwatch
1 plastic wash bottle
1 box safety labels/class

Materials

Solution A: 0.20*M* potassium iodide, KI [T]

Solution B: 0.0050*M* sodium thiosulfate, $Na_2S_2O_3$

Solution C: 0.10*M* ammonium peroxydisulfate, $(NH_4)_2S_2O_8$ [I]

soluble starch

distilled water

Safety

- Note the Safety Symbols used here and in the Procedure section. Review safety information on pages 7–10.
- Always wear safety goggles when working in the lab.
- Mercury is extremely toxic and a mercury spill is very difficult to clean up. If you break a thermometer, report it immediately to your teacher.

Procedure

Copy Tables 35.1, 35.2, and 35.3 into your notebook. As you perform the experiment, record your data and observations in Table 35.2.

Procedure note: Seven mixtures of solutions A, B, and C will be used in this experiment. The compositions of the mixtures are given in Table 35.1. Mixture 1 has the maximum concentration of each reactant. In mixtures 2, 3, and 4, solution A is diluted to vary the concentration of the iodide ion. In mixtures 5, 6, and 7, solution C is diluted to vary the concentration of the peroxydisulfate ion. All the solutions should be at room temperature.

Table 35.1 Proportions for Mixtures

Mixture	Solution A (I^-)	Solution B ($S_2O_3^{2-}$)	Solution C ($S_2O_8^{2-}$)
1	20.0 mL	10.0 mL	20.0 mL
2	15.0 mL + 5.0 mL water	10.0 mL	20.0 mL
3	10.0 mL + 10.0 mL water	10.0 mL	20.0 mL
4	5.0 mL + 15.0 mL water	10.0 mL	20.0 mL
5	20.0 mL	10.0 mL	15.0 mL + 5.0 mL water
6	20.0 mL	10.0 mL	10.0 mL + 10.0 mL water
7	20.0 mL	10.0 mL	5.0 mL + 15.0 mL water

1. Label three clean, dry graduated cylinders with the letters *A, B, C*. Pour the solutions given for mixture 1 into these cylinders. Measure all volumes to the nearest 0.5 mL.

2. Pour the 10.0 mL of solution B into a clean 100-mL beaker. Add 5 drops of starch solution with a dropper pipet. One person should be ready to signal the other person when to pour solutions A and C into the beaker. At the signal, the other person should pour the solutions into the beaker and stir the mixture occasionally until a blue color appears. Note the exact time that the solutions were poured together and the exact time that the blue appears. Record the temperature of the solution and the time required, in seconds, for blue to appear in Table 35.2.

3. Discard the solution as directed by your teacher. Wash the beaker and rinse it well with distilled water. Shake it as dry as possible. Repeat the reaction with mixture 1 until you can obtain two approximately equal reaction times (trial 1, trial 2).

4. Repeat the experiment, using any mixture assigned by your teacher. Try to predict the outcome of each trial before you do it.

Data Record

Table 35.2 Data

Mixture	Temperature (°C)	Time Solutions Mixed	Time Color Appears	Total Time of Reaction (sec)
1				42 sec
2				58 sec.
3				2 minutes (120 sec)
4				4 min 54 sec (294 sec.)
5				1 min 10 se (70 sec.)
6				1 min 40 sec (110 sec.)
7				5 min 31 sec (331 sec.)

Data Analysis

Class Data on the Effect of Concentration

1. Use class data to complete Table 35.2. If more than one trial was done for a mixture, compute the average of the reaction times.

2. Calculate the number of moles of iodide ion and peroxydisulfate ion in each of the seven mixtures studied. Enter these results in Table 35.3.

3. For each of the mixtures used, the total volume was 50.0 mL. Using this volume and the number of moles calculated in the previous problem, determine the initial concentration of iodide and peroxydisulfate ions in each reaction mixture. Enter these initial concentrations in Table 35.3.

4. Plot a graph of iodide ion concentration versus reaction time. Use the data and calculated concentrations for mixtures 1, 2, 3, and 4. Choose a scale that will fill a page of graph paper and allow you to plot the curve the next question will ask you to draw. Connect the plotted points with a smooth curve.

5. On the same graph that you made for question 4, plot a curve representing the concentration of peroxydisulfate versus time. Use the data and calculated concentrations for Mixtures 1, 5, 6, and 7.

Table 35.3 Calculations

Mixture	Mol I^-	Initial Concentration I^- (mol/L)	Mol $S_2O_8^{2-}$	Initial Concentration $S_2O_8^{2-}$ (mol/L)
1				
2				
3				
4				
5				
6				
7				

Conclusions

1. Describe the relationship between reactant concentration and reaction rate.

Extensions

1. Design and carry out an experiment to determine how an increase in the concentration of thiosulfate ions will affect the rate of this reaction.

2. Design and carry out an experiment to measure the effect of temperature, over a range of 5°C to 45°C, on the rate of this reaction.

Experiment

36 Disturbing Equilibrium

Text reference:
Section 18.4

Background

Imagine you are starting a terrarium. You add dirt, plants, and water, then seal the container. Some of the water in the terrarium will vaporize. Soon the air in the terrarium will hold as much water as possible. At this point some of the vapor will begin to condense. Eventually, as much water is condensing as is vaporizing; the liquid water and its vapor are in *equilibrium.* What happens to the equilibrium if the conditions change? A change of conditions in the system is called a stress. For example, if the terrarium gets colder (undergoes a stress) some of the water vapor will condense. In response to the stress a new equilibrium will be established. The new equilibrium will have less water vapor and more liquid water than the old equilibrium.

Are there any rules to help predict what happens when a stress is applied to physical and chemical systems in equilibrium? Yes, Le Chatelier's principle applies to systems in equilibrium. It states that, if a stress is placed on a system at equilibrium, the system will change in a way that relieves the stress.

In this experiment you will impose stresses on physical and chemical systems at equilibrium to see how the systems change in response to the stresses.

Goals

- **Observe** the effect of a change in conditions on a system at equilibrium.
- **Explain** the effects observed by applying Le Chatelier's principle.

Equipment

safety goggles
5 medium test tubes
1 test-tube rack
1 dropper pipet
1 spatula
1 50-mL graduated cylinder

1 100-mL beaker
1 250-mL beaker
1 white card, 3 in. × 5 in.

Materials

saturated potassium nitrate solution, KNO_3 [T]
0.1*M* iron(III) chloride, $FeCl_3$ [I]
0.1*M* potassium thiocyanate, KSCN [T]
potassium chloride crystals, KCl
potassium nitrate crystals, KNO_3 [T]
ice
distilled water

Safety 

- Note the Safety Symbols used here and in the Procedure section. Review the safety information on pages 7–10.
- Always wear safety goggles when working in the lab.
- Aqueous iron(III) chloride is an irritant. Avoid skin contact with this chemical.

Procedure

Copy Table 36.1 into your laboratory notebook. As you perform the experiment, record your observations in this table.

Part A. Effect of Temperature on a Physical Equilibrium

1. Add 2–3 mL of saturated potassium nitrate solution to a clean test tube. Using a spatula, add one crystal of potassium nitrate to the solution to act as a seed crystal.

2. Cool the test tube in a 250-mL beaker of ice water for 10 minutes. Record the results.

3. Remove the tube from the ice water and place it in the test-tube rack. Record what happens as the solution warms to room temperature.

Part B. Common Ion Effect on a Chemical Equilibrium

4. Use a graduated cylinder to add 50 mL of distilled water to a 100-mL beaker. Add 1 mL of 0.1*M* iron(III) chloride, $FeCl_3$, and 1 mL of 0.1*M* potassium thiocyanate to the water; stir. The color that appears is due to the presence of ferrothiocyanate ions, $FeSCN^{2+}$. Your teacher will write on the board the reaction that is observed. Record your observations.

5. Label four identical clean, dry test tubes with the numerals 1–4. Pour 5 mL of the mixture from step 4 into each. Hold the tubes over a white background and look down into them, as shown in Figure 36.1. The solutions should appear equally dark.

6. Tube 1 is the control in this experiment. To tube 2, add 20 drops of 0.1*M* iron(III) chloride. To tube 3, add 20 drops of 0.1*M* potassium thiocyanate. Flick each tube to mix the solutions. To tube 4, add 1 g of potassium chloride crystals. Flick the tube to dissolve the crystals. Compare the colors of the solutions in tubes 2, 3, and 4 with the color of the solution in the control tube (tube 1). Record your observations.

7. Discard the solutions as directed by your teacher.

Data Record

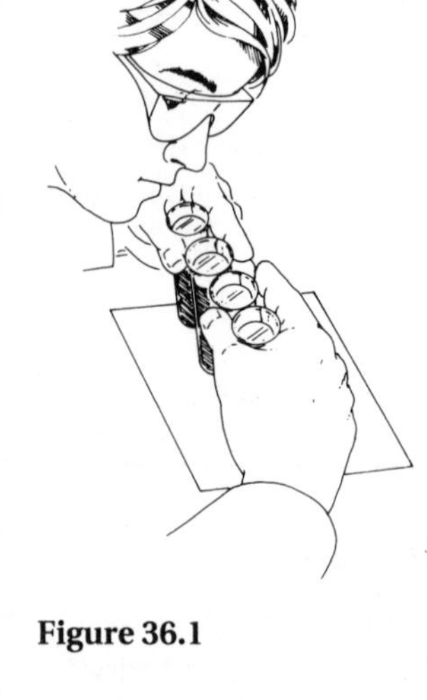

Figure 36.1

Table 36.1 Observations

System	Observations
KNO_3 (sat.) cooled	
KNO_3 (sat.) warmed	
Fe^{3+}/SCN^- reaction	
Fe^{3+}/SCN^- mixture + additional Fe^{3+}	
Fe^{3+}/SCN^- mixture + additional SCN^-	
Fe^{3+}/SCN^- mixture + KCl(*s*)	

Conclusions

1. Write a balanced equation for the equilibrium that existed before the saturated potassium nitrate was cooled.

2. Did lowering the temperature (step 2) affect the equilibrium? Explain your answer.

3. Did increasing the temperature (step 3) disturb the equilibrium? What evidence do you have for your answer?

4. Explain what happened in the potassium nitrate system in terms of Le Chatelier's principle.

5. Write a balanced equation for the equilibrium that existed after the ferric and thiocyanate ions were combined in the beaker.

6. What evidence was there that the equilibrium shifted when iron(III) chloride was added? In which direction did it shift?

7. What evidence was there that the equilibrium shifted when potassium thiocyanate was added? In which direction did it shift?

8. Explain the effect of adding potassium chloride to the system.

9. Explain the changes observed in the ferrothiocyanate ion system in terms of Le Chatelier's principle.

Experiment

37 Estimation of pH

Text reference:
Section 19.4

Background

If you are interested in gardening, you may know that plants such as azaleas and rhododendrons prefer acidic soils. A part of soil testing consists of the measurement of the pH of the soil. The pH is important in many other applications in the home and in industry. For example, maintenance of the proper pH of water is important in caring for swimming pools. There are several ways to test pH. One of the most important ways is by means of acid–base indicators such as phenolphthalein. In neutral and acidic solutions, phenolphthalein is colorless. In alkaline solutions, it is pink. By adding a few drops of a weak solution of the indicator to a solution to be tested, you can tell immediately whether the test solution is alkaline. Other acid–base indicators change colors at different pH values. By systematically testing a solution with a series of indicators, you can often arrive at a good estimate of the pH of a solution.

In this experiment, you will estimate the pH of several solutions by using acid–base indicators. You will then use the same indicators to test the pH of several common household chemicals.

Goals

- **Observe** the characteristic color changes of several acid–base indicators.
- **Estimate** the pH of solutions, using acid–base indicators.

Equipment

safety goggles
5 small test tubes
1 test-tube rack
1 stirring rod
1 plastic wash bottle
1 pH meter/class (optional)

Materials

0.1M hydrochloric acid, HCl [I]
0.1M ethanoic acid, CH_3COOH
0.1M ammonia, NH_3 [T]
0.1M sodium hydroxide, NaOH [I]
methyl red solution
litmus solution (or litmus paper)
bromthymol blue solution
phenolphthalein solution
distilled water

household chemicals, an assortment such as:

lemon juice
vinegar
bleach
baking soda
carbonated beverage
shampoo
cold tea
aspirin
milk
liquid antacid

Safety

- Note the Safety Symbols used here and in the Procedure section. Review the safety information on pages 7–10.
- Always wear safety goggles when working in the lab.
- Hydrochloric acid and sodium hydroxide are irritants at the concentrations used in this experiment.
- Ammonia is an irritant. Do not inhale ammonia fumes.

Procedure

Copy Tables 37.2 and 37.3 into your laboratory notebook. As you perform the experiment, record your observations in these tables.

1. Add 1–2 mL of the following to five separate, clean test tubes: 0.1M hydrochloric acid, 0.1M ethanoic acid, 0.1M ammonia, 0.1M sodium hydroxide, and distilled water. **CAUTION:** *Even the dilute acids and bases used in this experiment can irritate your skin and damage your clothes.*

2. Add 2 drops of methyl red indicator solution to each tube. Flick to mix the contents. Record the final color in Table 37.2 and estimate the pH of the solution by referring to Table 37.1.

3. Using fresh samples of the solutions, repeat the procedure for each of the other indicators named in Table 37.1. If you are using paper indicator strips, use a glass rod to transfer a drop of the solution to the indicator strip. Record the results of all the tests in Table 37.2.

4. Test the commonhousehold chemicals that are available to you. Test liquids directly. Solidsshould be dissolved or suspended in water before testing. Record your results in Table 37.3.

5. If a pH meter is avalable, use it to determine the pH of the household chemicals.

6. Follow your teacher's instructions for proper disposal of the materials.

Data Record

Table 37.1 Common Acid–Base Indicators

Indicator	Color in Acid (H*In* form)	Color in Base (*In*⁻ form)	pH Range
Methyl red	Red	Yellow	4.8–6.0
Litmus	Red	Blue	5.2–7.5
Bromthymol blue	Yellow	Blue	6.0–7.6
Phenolphthalein	Colorless	Pink	8.2–10.0

Table 37.2 Indicator Reactions with Standard Solutions

Solution	Methyl Red	Litmus	Bromthymol Blue	Phenolphthalein	Estimated pH
0.1*M* HCl	red	red.	Yellow	colorless	
0.1*M* acetic acid	red	red	Yellow	colorless	
distilled water	Yellow	neutral.	Yellow	colorless	
0.1*M* ammonia	Yellow	blue	Blue	Pink	
0.1*M* NaOH	Yellow.	blue.	Blue.	Pink	

Table 37.3 Indicator Reactions with Household Chemicals						
Substance	**Methyl Red**	**Litmus**	**Bromthymol Blue**	**Phenolphthalein**	**Estimated pH**	**Measured pH**
milk.	Yellow	blue.	Yellow,	Colorless		
shampoo	red	red.	Yellow	Colorless.		
lemon juice	red.	red	yellow	clear.		
Asprin	red.	red.	Yellow	clear		
Baking soda.	Yellow	blue	blue.	pink		

Conclusions

1. Compare the pH of 0.1M ethanoic acid with that of 0.1M hydrochloric acid. Compare the pH of 0.1M ammonia with that of 0.1M sodium hydroxide. Explain any differences.

2. Which of the indicators used in this experiment could most accurately identify a neutral solution? Explain.

3. Are the household chemicals you tested acidic, basic, or neutral?

Extension

1. Obtain a sample of a universal indicator. Explore its properties and uses. Explain the meaning of "universal."

Reactions of Acids

Text reference:
Section 19.1

Background

Because of its usefulness in many industrial processes, sulfuric acid is the most important bulk chemical produced today. The uses of acids are not limited to industry, however. Artists pull beautiful prints from metal lithographic plates that have been etched with hydrochloric acid. Hydrofluoric acid is used to etch designs on glass. You encounter natural acids when you pour vinegar (which contains ethanoic acid) on a salad or eat a tart apple (contains malic acid). Acids can also cause problems. Acid rain can corrode metal, dissolve marble and limestone statues, and even damage buildings.

In this experiment, you will investigate some common reactions of acids. These characteristic reactions are often used to test for certain ions or metals.

Goals

- **Observe** several common reactions involving acids.
- **Identify** the gas produced by the reaction of several metals with acid.
- **Identify** the gas produced by the reaction of a carbonate and a bicarbonate with acid.

Equipment

safety goggles
6 small test tubes
1 test-tube rack
1 test-tube holder
1 gas burner
1 forceps
1 dropper pipet
1 spatula
8 glass-marking pencils/class

Materials

iron wire or small nails, Fe
copper wire, Cu
zinc strips, Zn,
    0.25 mm × 0.5 cm × 2 cm
magnesium ribbon, Mg [F]
6*M* hydrochloric acid,
    HCl [C] [T]

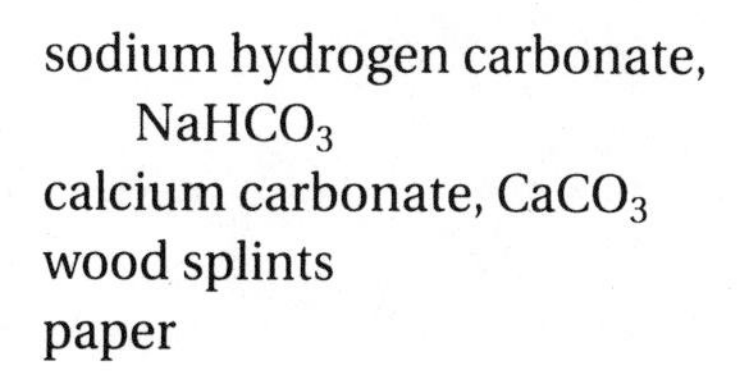

sodium hydrogen carbonate,
    $NaHCO_3$
calcium carbonate, $CaCO_3$
wood splints
paper

Safety

- Note the Safety Symbols used here and in the Procedure section. Review safety information on pages 7–10.
- Always wear safety goggles when working in the lab.
- Hydrochloric acid is corrosive and can cause severe burns.
- Magnesium is flammable. Keep it away from open flames.

Procedure

Copy Table 38.1 into your laboratory notebook. As you perform the experiment, record your observations in this table.

1. CAUTION: *Hydrochloric acid is corrosive.* Label six small test tubes with the numbers 1–6 and place them in a test tube rack. Add 2 mL of 6*M* hydrochloric acid to each tube.

2. Obtain the items indicated below and place them on labeled pieces of paper. **CAUTION:** *Magnesium is flammable.* Using forceps, carefully transfer the materials to the numbered test tubes, as the following list indicates.

tube 1	2-cm length of clean iron wire or a small nail
tube 2	2-cm length of copper wire
tube 3	2-cm length of magnesium ribbon
tube 4	small strip of zinc

Using a spatula, transfer the materials to the numbered test tubes, as the following list indicates.

tube 5	pea-sized quantity of sodium hydrogen carbonate
tube 6	pea-sized piece of calcium carbonate

3. Observe the tubes for several minutes to determine if a gas is evolving. Attempt to identify any gas evolved by holding a burning wood splint at the mouth of the test tube. If it appears no gas is evolving, hold the test tube in a holder and warm it gently, *without boiling*, in a burner flame. **CAUTION:** *Do not point the mouth of the tube toward yourself or anyone else.* Remove the tube from the flame and test for the presence of evolving gas. Record your observations.

4. Follow your teacher's instructions for proper disposal of the materials.

Data Record

Table 38.1 Reactions with Hydrochloric Acid	
Substance	**Observations and Results**
iron	
copper	
magnesium	
zinc	
sodium carbonate	
calcium carbonate	

Conclusions

1. List the four metals tested in order of increasing reactivity with hydrochloric acid. List any nonreactive metals first, then the least reactive, and so on, up to the most reactive.

2. Was the same gas produced when all the metals reacted with hydrochloric acid? What was the gas? How did you identify this gas?

3. Write a balanced equation for the reactions of the two metals that reacted most vigorously with hydrochloric acid.

4. Was the same gas produced when sodium hydrogen carbonate and calcium carbonate reacted with hydrochloric acid? What was the gas? How did you identify this gas?

5. Write balanced equations for the reactions of sodium hydrogen carbonate and calcium carbonate with hydrochloric acid.

Extension

1. Repeat the experiment, using dilute sulfuric and dilute ethanoic acid. Compare the results of using all three acids and comment on any differences.

Experiment

39 Neutralization Reactions

Text reference:
Section 20.1

Background

Early chemists discovered that sour acids and bitter bases combine to form relatively bland-tasting (neutral) salts. (**CAUTION:** *Never taste any chemical in the laboratory.*) For example, equivalent amounts of hydrochloric acid and sodium hydroxide combine to form neutral water and neutral sodium chloride, common table salt.

$$HCl(aq) + NaOH(aq) \rightarrow NaCl(aq) + H_2O(l)$$

In this reaction, the H^+ and OH^- ions, which are responsible for the properties of the acid and base, respectively—combine to produce water. The products of the reaction do not have the properties of an acid or a base. The reaction is, therefore, called a *neutralization reaction.*

In this experiment, you will use a neutralization reaction between a strong acid and a strong base to make a salt.

Goal

- **Produce** a salt by neutralizing a base with an acid.

Equipment

safety goggles
1 10-mL graduated cylinder
1 50-mL beaker
1 250-mL beaker
1 evaporating dish
1 glass stirring rod
1 ring stand
1 ring clamp
1 crucible tongs
1 wire gauze
1 gas burner
1 dropper pipet

Materials

$1M$ hydrochloric acid, HCl [T] [I]
$1M$ sodium hydroxide, NaOH [C] [T]
phenolphthalein solution

Safety

- Note the Safety Symbols used here and in the Procedure section. Review safety information on pages 7–10.
- Always wear safety goggles when working in the lab.
- Hydrochloric acid is an irritant at the concentration used in this experiment.
- Sodium hydroxide is corrosive and can cause severe burns.

Procedure

Copy Table 39.1 into your laboratory manual. As you perform the experiment, record your observations in Table 39.1.

1. Fill a 250-mL beaker three-fourths full with water and set up a boiling water bath. While the water is heating, proceed to the next step.

2. **CAUTION:** *Sodium hydroxide is corrosive.* Pour 5.0 mL of $1M$ sodium hydroxide solution into a 50-mL beaker. Add 1 or 2 drops of phenolphthalein indicator solution to the sodium hydroxide.

3. Add, drop by drop, $1M$ hydrochloric acid to the beaker, using a dropper pipet. Stir constantly while adding the acid. Continue adding acid until the color of the solution just disappears.

4. Transfer about 5 mL of the neutralized solution to a clean evaporating dish. Place the evaporating dish over the boiling water bath as shown in Figure 39.1. Evaporate the solution to dryness. **CAUTION:** *Be careful not to be burned by the steam coming from the water bath.*

5. Turn off the gas burner and remove the evaporating dish from the beaker, using tongs. Examine the residue in the evaporating dish. **CAUTION:** *Do not touch or taste the residue.*

6. Follow your teacher's instructions for proper disposal of the materials.

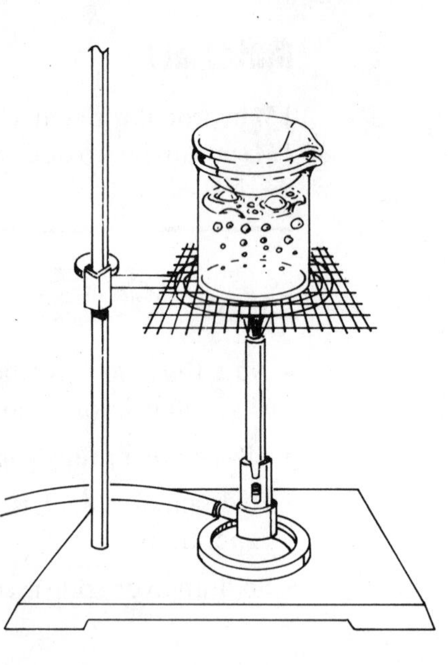

Figure 39.1

Data Record

Table 39.1 Observations	
Step	**Observation**
2	The sodium turns pink.
3	The sodium turns clear
5	white residue is on side of evaporation dish.

Conclusions

1. Write a balanced equation for the neutralization reaction that took place in this experiment.

2. How does the product that was prepared in this experiment compare with the same product as it is prepared commercially?

3. Why should you not taste the residue from this reaction, even though you know that the salt produced is commonly used in food?

4. How could you determine whether the phenolphthalein remains in the residue of the reaction?

Extensions

1. Design an experiment in which you produce and examine the products of several other neutralization reactions. Include in your procedure a step in which you determine whether the product is truly free of all traces of acid or base.

2. Design and carry out an experiment to test the effectiveness of various antacid products in neutralizing acid.

Acid–Base Titrations

Text reference:
Section 20.2

Background

Every day scientists in many fields conduct experiments designed to answer one question: How much acid or base does this solution contain? The chemical reactions used to answer this question are, for the main part, neutralization reactions, and *titration* is the method generally used.

You can neutralize an acid with a base very precisely by using the technique of titration. To conduct a titration, a solution of known acidity (a standard solution) is gradually added to a solution of unknown basicity. At the point of neutralization, the number of equivalents of acid must be equal to the number of equivalents of base. Thus, titration tells you the equivalents of base in your unknown solution. The neutralization, or equivalence point, of the reaction is estimated by the color change of an acid–base indicator or by a neutral reading (pH 7.0) on a pH meter. You can also reverse the titration procedure so a standard base solution is used to titrate an unknown acidic solution.

In this experiment, you will prepare a standard solution of an acidic compound, potassium hydrogen sulfate ($KHSO_4$). You will then use this solution to make a standard solution of sodium hydroxide by titration. Finally, you will use your standardized sodium hydroxide solution to titrate vinegar, a dilute solution of ethanoic acid, CH_3COOH.

Goals

- **Prepare** a standard base solution by titration with a standard acid solution.
- **Measure** the normality of vinegar with the standard base solution.

Equipment

safety goggles
1 10-mL graduated cylinder
1 100-mL graduated cylinder
1 ring stand
1 double buret clamp
1 spatula

2 50-mL burets
1 10-mL pipet
1 25-mL pipet
1 pipet suction bulb
1 100-mL beaker
1 100-mL volumetric flask
1 250-mL volumetric flask
2 250-mL Erlenmeyer flasks
3 250-mL plastic bottles
8 centigram balances/class
1 filter funnel
2 rubber stoppers, for volumetric flasks
1 weighing bottle
1 plastic wash bottle
1 box of labels/class
1 sheet white paper, 25 cm × 25 cm

Materials

potassium hydrogen sulfate, $KHSO_4$ [T]
6*M* sodium hydroxide, NaOH [C] [T]
phenolphthalein solution
vinegar, dilute ethanoic acid, CH_3COOH
distilled water

Safety

- Note the Safety Symbols used here and in the Procedure section. Review safety information on pages 7–10.
- Always wear safety goggles when working in the lab.
- Potassium hydrogen sulfate is a toxic substance.
- Sodium hydroxide is corrosive and can cause severe burns.

Procedure

Copy Tables 40.1, 40.2, and 40.3 into your laboratory notebook. As you perform the experiment, record your data and observations in these tables.

Part A. Preparation of a Standard Solution of Potassium Hydrogen Sulfate

1. Determine the mass of a sample of potassium hydrogen sulfate (the *acid*) in a weighing bottle, using the most accurate balance available to you. Using a funnel and a spatula, transfer 3–4 g of the acid to a clean 250-mL volumetric flask. Remeasure the mass of the weighing bottle and remaining sample. The difference between the two mass values is the mass of the acid in the flask.

3.5 g, Acid

2. Add about 100 mL of distilled water to the flask, washing into the flask any acid crystals clinging to the funnel. Remove the funnel and gently swirl the flask to dissolve the acid. When the acid is completely dissolved, fill the flask to the 250-mL mark with distilled water.

3. Stopper and mix the contents thoroughly by inverting the flask and swirling the mixture. Transfer the solution to a clean, dry 250-mL plastic bottle labeled "approximately 0.1N $KHSO_4$" and mark the label with your initials.

Part B. Standardization of a Solution of Sodium Hydroxide

4. **CAUTION:** *Sodium hydroxide is corrosive.* Using a 10-mL graduated cylinder, measure out 5 mL of 6M sodium hydroxide. Transfer this solution to a clean dry 250-mL plastic bottle labeled "approximately 0.1N NaOH" and mark the label with your initials. Add 250 mL of distilled water to the bottle, cap it, and shake it to mix the contents.

5. Clean and mount two 50-mL burets, as shown in Figure 40.1. Place a white sheet of paper or a white plastic base each buret. Label the left buret "acid" and the right buret "base."

6. Rinse the "acid" buret with three 5-mL portions of the standard solution of potassium hydrogen sulfate. Let each portion drain out of the buret before adding the next rinse. Discard these rinses. Fill the buret with the potassium hydrogen sulfate solution. Before beginning the titration remove any bubbles trapped in the tip of the buret and the stopcock.

7. Using the sodium hydroxide solution, rinse and fill the "base" buret. Use a wash bottle of distilled water to rinse off the tip of each buret; catch the runoff in a 100-mL beaker. Record the initial volume in each buret to the nearest 0.01 mL.

8. Add 10–12 mL of the acid solution to a clean 250-mL Erlenmeyer flask. Use the wash bottle to rinse the last drop of acid from the tip of the buret into the flask. Add 50 mL of distilled water and 1–2 drops of phenolphthalein to the flask.

9. Now, slowly add sodium hydroxide solution from the "base" buret to the flask. As you add the base, gently swirl the solution in the flask. A pink color will appear and quickly disappear as the solutions are mixed. As more and more base is added, the pink color will persist for a longer time before disappearing. This is a sign that you are nearing the equivalence point, also called the end point. Wash down the sides of the flask and the tip of the buret with distilled water from the wash bottle. Continue to add sodium hydroxide more slowly, until a single drop of base turns the solution a pale pink color that persists for 15–30 seconds.

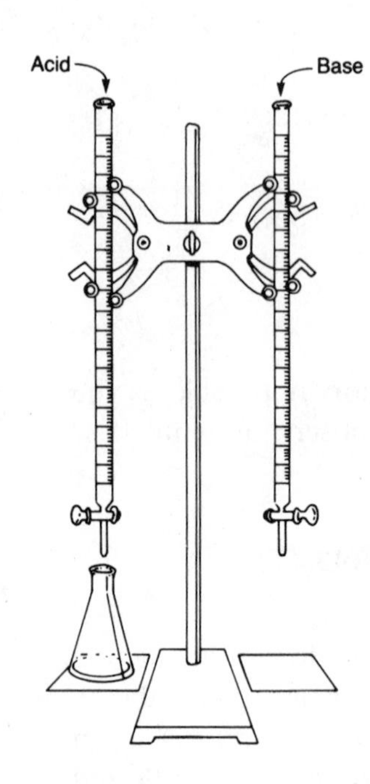

Figure 40.1

10. If you overshoot the end point—that is, if you add too much base so that the solution turns bright pink—simply add a few drops of acid from the acid buret to turn the solution colorless again. Approach the end point again, adding base drop by drop, until one drop causes the color change to pale pink.

11. When you are sure that you have achieved the end point, record the final volume reading of each buret. Note: Do not allow the level of the solution in either buret to go below the 50-mL mark. If you do, you will have to discard your sample and begin again.

12. Discard the solution in the Erlenmeyer flask as directed by your teacher, and rinse the flask well with distilled water. Refill both burets, if necessary. Read the initial volume in each buret and do another titration, as described in steps 9–11.

13. Before proceeding, calculate the normality of the sodium hydroxide solution for each titration, as described in Data Analysis, questions 1–6. If the normalities obtained from the two titrations do not agree within 1%, perform a third titration.

Part C. Determination of the Normality of Ethanoic Acid in Vinegar

14. Using a clean, dry pipet and suction bulb, transfer 10 mL of commercial vinegar into a clean 100-mL volumetric flask. Fill the flask to the 100-mL mark with distilled water. Stopper the flask and mix the solution by inverting the flask 20–30 times. Transfer this solution to a clean, dry 250-mL plastic bottle. Label the bottle "10% vinegar" and mark the label with your initials.

15. Using a clean, dry 25-mL pipet, transfer a 25-mL sample of the diluted vinegar to a clean 25-mL Erlenmeyer flask. Add 50 mL of distilled water and 1–2 drops of phenolphthalein to the flask. Titrate the vinegar with the sodium hydroxide solution that you standardized in Part B. Note: If you overshoot the end point in these titrations, you will have to discard the sample and begin again. Do at least two titrations that agree.

16. Follow your teacher's instructions for proper disposal of the materials.

Data Record

Table 40.1 Normality of Potassium Hydrogen Sulfate	
initial mass of weighing bottle and $KHSO_4$:	
final mass of weighing bottle and $KHSO_4$:	
mass of $KHSO_4$ used:	
gram equivalent mass of $KHSO_4$:	
equivalents of $KHSO_4$ used in 250 mL:	
normality of $KHSO_4$:	

Table 40.2 Normality of Sodium Hydroxide

	Trial 1		Trial 2		Trial 3	
	Acid	Base	Acid	Base	Acid	Base
final volume:	[illegible]					25
initial volume:	0					13.
volume used:	10 [illegible] ml	13.5 ml	10	12.5	10	12.
normality of NaOH:						
average normality of NaOH:						

Table 40.3 Normality of Vinegar

	Trial 1		Trial 2		Trial 3	
	Vinegar	Base	Vinegar	Base	Vinegar	Base
final volume:	—		—		—	
initial volume:	—		—		—	
volume used:						
normality of vinegar:						
average normality of 10% vinegar:						

Data Analysis

As you do the following calculations, enter the results in Table 40.1, Table 40.2, or Table 40.3.

1. Determine the mass of potassium hydrogen sulfate used.

2. Find the gram equivalent mass of potassium hydrogen sulfate.

$$\text{gram equivalent mass} = \frac{\text{gram formula mass}}{\text{number of equivalents per mole}}$$

3. Calculate the number of equivalents of potassium hydrogen sulfate used.

$$\text{number of equivalents} = \frac{\text{mass}}{\text{gram equivalent mass}}$$

4. Determine the normality of your standard solution of potassium hydrogen sulfate. Be sure to use units properly in your calculation.

$$\text{normality} = \frac{\text{number of equivalents}}{\text{volume}}$$

5. Determine the volumes of acid and base used in each titration performed in Part B.

6. The normality of the sodium hydroxide solution is calculated with this equation:

$$\text{normality}_{\text{base}} = \text{normality}_{\text{acid}} \times \frac{\text{volume}_{\text{acid}}}{\text{volume}_{\text{base}}}$$

Calculate the normality of your sodium hydroxide solution for each titration. Record the value obtained for each trial, as well as the average value for all trials.

7. Determine the volume of 10% vinegar and sodium hydroxide solutions used in each titration.

8. Using the average normality of sodium hydroxide that was calculated in question 6 of this section, determine the normality of your 10% vinegar solution (ethanoic acid).

$$\text{normality}_{\text{acid}} = \text{normality}_{\text{base}} \times \frac{\text{volume}_{\text{base}}}{\text{volume}_{\text{acid}}}$$

Record the value for each trial, and the average value.

Conclusions

1. Examine the class results for the normality of vinegar. Account for any difference among these values.

2. Explain why the plastic bottles into which you transferred your potassium hydrogen sulfate and vinegar solutions had to be dry, but you could add distilled water to the titration flask at any time and not affect your results.

3. Why are the burets rinsed with the acid and base solutions before filling?

Extensions

1. Use your data from this experiment to calculate the mass/volume percent of ethanoic acid present in commercial, undiluted vinegar.

2. Explain why you cannot prepare a standard sodium hydroxide solution by weighing the solid and dissolving it in a measured amount of water, as you did with the potassium hydrogen sulfate.

Experiment

41 Salt Hydrolysis

Text reference:
Section 20.5

Background

Neutralization of strong acids by strong bases produces neutral salts. However, salts formed in the neutralization reactions of other types of acids and bases can yield solutions that are not neutral. The salt of a strong acid and a weak base, for instance, yields an acidic solution in water. Other reactions can produce basic solutions. The acidic or basic character of these nonneutral solutions is the result of a phenomenon called *salt hydrolysis.* In salt hydrolysis, one of the ions of the dissolved salt reacts with water to produce hydronium or hydroxide ions.

In this experiment you will measure the pH of solutions of various salts. You will analyze your results to determine if one of the ions produced in solution can react with water to produce hydronium ions or hydroxide ions.

Goals

- **Measure** the pH of aqueous solutions of several salts.
- **Explain** the formation of nonneutral salt solutions by writing chemical equations for salt hydrolysis.

Equipment

safety goggles
7 small or medium test tubes
1 test-tube rack
1 spatula
1 dropper pipet
1 10-mL graduated cylinder

Materials

freshly boiled distilled water
sodium chloride, $NaCl$
sodium ethanoate, CH_3COONa I
sodium hydrogen carbonate, $NaHCO_3$
sodium phosphate, Na_3PO_4 I

ammonium chloride,
NH_4Cl T I
sodium carbonate, Na_2CO_3
wide-range indicator solution or
wide-range pH test paper
(pH 1–14)

Safety

- Note the Safety Symbols used here and in the Procedure section. Review safety information on pages 7–10.
- Always wear safety goggles when working in the lab.

Procedure

Copy Table 41.1 into your laboratory notebook. As you perform the experiment, record your pH measurements in this table.

1. Place small quantities (less than pea-size) of sodium chloride, sodium ethanoate, ammonium chloride, sodium carbonate, sodium hydrogen carbonate, and sodium phosphate into separate labeled test tubes. Place the tubes in a test-tube rack.

2. Add about 5 mL of cool, previously boiled distilled water to each tube. Flick each tube gently to dissolve the sample.

3. Add 2 drops of wide-range indicator solution to each tube, or dip a small piece of wide-range pH test paper into each tube.

4. Determine the pH of the solution in each tube by comparing the color of the solutions or test papers to a standard chart of indicator reactions.

5. Measure the pH of the boiled, distilled water.

6. Dispose of the liquid wastes down the drain.

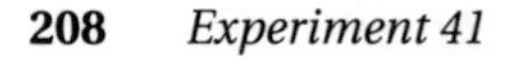

Data Record

Table 41.1 Measurement of pH of Salt Solutions		
Aqueous Solution	**Chemical Formula**	**Approximate pH**
sodium chloride		
sodium ethanoate		
ammonium chloride		
sodium carbonate		
sodium hydrogen carbonate		
sodium phosphate		
boiled distilled water (control)		

Data Analysis

1. Which salts produce neutral aqueous solutions?
2. Which salts produce acidic aqueous solutions?
3. Which salts produce basic aqueous solutions?

Conclusions

1. Why is it important to know the pH of the boiled distilled water?

2. For each salt, write a balanced equation to show how it ionizes in solution.

3. For each salt whose solution is acidic, write an additional equation to show which ion in solution reacts with water to produce the hydronium ion.

4. For each salt whose solution is basic, write an additional equation to show which ion in solution reacts with water to produce the hydroxide ion.

5. What do all the acids of the anions identified in the previous question have in common?

6. Would you expect a sodium salt to produce an acidid solution? Explain.

Extensions

1. Predict whether solutions of the following salts would be acidic, basic, or neutral. Write balanced equations to justify your answers for those solutions you believe will be acidic or basic.

a. sodium nitrated
b. sodium sulfate
c. ammonium sulfate
d. potassium sulfate
e. potassium hydrogen carbonate

2. Use a pH meter to test your predictions for solutions of the salts in question 1.

Experiment

42 Buffers

Text reference: Section 20.6

Background

Your blood must be maintained at pH 7.35–7.45 for you to stay healthy. However, chemical reactions taking place in your body are continuously pumping a stream of hydrogen ions into your blood. Your body maintains the proper blood pH, in spite of the hydrogen ions, due to blood buffers. *Buffered solutions* maintain a relatively constant pH when limited amounts of acid or base are added to them.

What are buffers? They usually consist of solutions of a weak acid and its salt or of a weak base and its salt. For example, a solution containing ethanoic acid, (CH_3COOH), and its salt, sodium ethanoate (CH_3COONa), is a buffer. A solution containing ammonia (NH_3) and its salt, ammonium chloride (NH_4Cl), is also a buffer. Sodium ethanoate is formed by the neutralization of ethanoic acid by sodium hydroxide. Ammonium chloride is formed by the neutralization of ammonia by hydrochloric acid. In other words, a buffer can be created by the partial neutralization of a weak acid by a strong base or by partial neutralization of a weak base by a strong acid.

In this experiment, you will examine the effectiveness of different buffering systems in resisting changes in pH.

Goals

- **Measure** the pH changes that occur when acids and bases are added to buffered and unbuffered solutions.
- **Hypothesize**, using chemical equations, the reasons that buffers keep the pH of solutions relatively constant.

Equipment

safety goggles
7 medium test tubes
1 test-tube rack
2 50-mL beakers
2 dropper pipets
1 10-mL graduated cylinder

Materials

1 M hydrochloric acid, HCl I
1 M sodium hydroxide, $NaOH$ I
0.1 M sodium carbonate, Na_2CO_3
0.1 M sodium hydrogen carbonate, $NaHCO_3$
0.1 M sodium monohydrogen phosphate, Na_2HPO_4 I
0.1 M sodium dihydrogen phosphate, NaH_2PO_4 I
boiled distilled water
wide-range indicator solution (pH 1–14) or wide-range pH paper (pH 1–14)
paper towels

Safety

- Note the Safety Symbols used here and in the Procedure section. Review safety information on pages 7–10.
- Always wear safety goggles when working in the lab.
- Hydrochloric acid and aqueous sodium hydroxide are irritants at the concentrations used in this experiment.
- Never pick up a dropper bottle by its cap. Always hold a dropper with the tip lower than the rubber bulb so that the liquid does not run into the bulb.

Procedure

Copy Table 42.1 into your laboratory notebook. As you perform the experiment, record your results in this table.

1. Label seven medium test tubes with the numbers 1–7.

2. Mix 5 mL of 0.1 M Na_2CO_3 and 5 mL of 0.1 M $NaHCO_3$ in a 50-mL beaker. This is a carbonate/hydrogen carbonate (CO_3^{2-}/HCO_3^-) buffer. Divide this buffer solution equally between test tubes 1 and 2.

3. Mix, in another 50-mL beaker, 5 mL of 0.1 M Na_2HPO_4 and 5 mL of 0.1 M NaH_2PO_4. This is a monohydrogen phosphate/dihydrogen phosphate ($HPO_4^{2-}/H_2PO_4^-$) buffer. Divide this buffer solution equally between test tubes 3 and 4.

4. Put 5 mL of 0.1 M $NaHCO_3$ in test tube 5, 5 mL of 0.1 M NaH_2PO_4 in test tube 6, and 5 mL of cool, previously boiled distilled water in test tube 7.

5. Use a dropper to add 3 drops of wide-range indicator to each test tube. Estimate the pH of each solution by comparing your result with those in the color chart supplied with the indicator. Record the results in Table 42.1.

6. **CAUTION:** *1M HCl is an irritant.* Use a dropper to add 1 drop of 1*M* HCl to tubes 1, 3, 5, 6, and 7. Flick the test tubes to mix, note the color changes, and record the results.

7. **CAUTION:** *1M sodium hydroxide is corrosive and an irritant.* Use a dropper to add 2 drops of 1*M* NaOH to tubes 1, 3, 5, 6, and 7 that received the HCl solution. Flick the test tubes to mix and note the color changes. Estimate and record the pH.

8. (Optional) Add hydrochloric acid, drop by drop, to tubes 2 and 4. Flick the test tubes, to mix, until the pH drops to about 2. Record the number of drops required for this to occur.

9. Follow your teacher's instructions for proper disposal of the materials.

Data Record

Table 42.1 Effects of Acid and Base on Buffered and Unbuffered Solutions

Tube	Contents of Tube	Initial pH	pH After Adding 1 Drop HCl	pH After Adding 2 Drops NaOH	Number of Drops HCl Added (Optional)
1	CO_3^{2-}/HCO_3^-				
2	CO_3^{2-}/HCO_3^-				
3	$HPO_4^{2-}/H_2PO_4^-$				
4	$HPO_4^{2-}/H_2PO_4^-$				
5	0.1*M* $NaHCO_3$				
6	0.1*M* NaH_2PO_4				
7	Boiled distilled water				

Conclusions

1. Based upon your experimental evidence, how effective are the CO_3^{2-}/HCO_3^- and $HPO_4^{2-}/H_2PO_4^-$ buffer systems? Explain your answer.

2. Do $0.1M$ $NaHCO_3$ and $0.1M$ NaH_2PO_4 solutions buffer as effectively as the CO_3^{2-}/HCO_3^- and $HPO_4^{2-}/H_2PO_4^-$ systems? Explain your answer.

3. Write equations for the reaction of the $HPO_4^{2-}/H_2PO_4^-$ buffer system with an acid and a base.

4. Write equations for the reaction of the CO_3^{2-}/HCO_3^- buffer system with an acid and a base.

Extensions

1. Consider the CO_3^{2-}/HCO_3^- buffer system. Suppose that you wish this system to buffer against addition of small amounts of both strong acids and strong bases. What would be the best molar ratio of Na_2CO_3 and $NaHCO_3$ to use in making the most efficient buffer solution?

2. Do all buffers maintain the pH in the same range? In a chemistry handbook look up the pH range of buffers in the list that follows. Prepare and measure the pH of each buffer solution. How do your experimental results compare to the published values? Which of these buffer systems would be effective at pH 5.0?

monohydrogen phosphate/dihydrogen phosphate
ethanoate/ethanoic acid
carbonate/hydrogen carbonate
phosphate/monohydrogen phosphate

Experiment

43 A Solubility Product Constant

Text reference: Section 20.7

Background

From everyday experiences you are familiar with several substances that are very soluble in water. Table sugar (sucrose) and salt (NaCl) are examples of soluble compounds. Many other substances, such as limestone ($CaCO_3$) and gasoline, are quite insoluble. *Solubility* and *insolubility* are relative terms, however. Almost all substances have at least a slight solubility in water. If you put a slightly soluble substance in water, a dynamic equilibrium is established between the dissolved substance and its solid form. In this equilibrium, the rate of dissolution of ions from the solid equals the rate of precipitation of the ions from the solution. How can you express in numerical terms the fraction of dissolved substance in the solution? One way is to use the K_{sp}, the solubility product constant.

In this experiment, you will find the K_{sp} of a slightly soluble salt, lead(II) chloride ($PbCl_2$). You will precipitate Pb^{2+} ions as lead(II) chromate, $PbCrO_4$, from a saturated solution of lead(II) chloride. The amount of lead chromate precipitated will tell you the concentration of Pb^{2+} ions in the saturated solution. When you know the concentration of lead ions, you can calculate the concentration of chloride ions and compute the K_{sp} for lead(II) chloride.

Goals

- **Measure** the concentration of Pb^{2+} ions in a saturated solution of lead (II) chloride.
- **Compute** the K_{sp} of lead(II) chloride.

Equipment

safety goggles
2 250-mL beakers
1 100-mL graduated cylinder
1 glass stirring rod
1 filter funnel
1 plastic wash bottle

1 ring stand
1 ring support
1 wire gauze
1 gas burner
8 centigram balances/class
2 drying ovens/class or 2 heat lamps/class

Materials

saturated lead(II) chloride solution, $PbCl_2(aq)$ T
0.5*M* potassium chromate, K_2CrO_4 T
filter paper
distilled water

Safety

- Note the Safety Symbols used here and in the Procedure section. Review safety information on pages 7–10.
- Always wear safety goggles when working in the lab.
- Lead compounds and chromate compounds are toxic.

Procedure

Copy Table 43.1 into your laboratory notebook. As you perform the experiment, record your data in this table.

1. Place a filter paper in a clean, dry 250-mL beaker. Determine the combined mass to the nearest 0.01 g and record the measurement in Table 43.1. Remove the filter paper from the beaker.

2. Slowly, to avoid disturbing the crystals, decant 100 mL of clear supernatant from the saturated $PbCl_2$ solution into the beaker. Add 20 mL of 0.5*M* K_2CrO_4 to the solution in the beaker.

3. Using a gas burner, heat the mixture in the beaker to the boiling point while occasionally stirring. Allow the mixture to cool, undisturbed, for 5 minutes.

4. Using the filter paper from step 1, assemble a filtration setup. (Refer to Figure 2.2).

5. Decant the liquid from the beaker into the filter funnel. Avoid transferring the precipitate to the filter paper. Wash the precipitate in the beaker by adding 30 mL of distilled water and swirling the mixture gently. Again decant the liquid into the filter funnel. Repeat the washing procedure once more.

6. Place the filter paper and any solid material retained on it in the beaker that contains the washed precipitate.

7. The contents of the beaker will now be dried according to your teacher's instructions.

8. Determine the combined mass of the beaker and its dry contents to the nearest 0.01 g and record the measurement.

9. Dispose of the filtrate and precipitate as instructed by your teacher.

Data Record

Table 43.1 Determination of the Mass of Lead Chromate
Mass of beaker + filter paper
Mass of beaker + filter paper + precipitate
Mass of precipitate ($PbCrO_4$)
Volume of saturated $PbCl_2$ solution used
Gram formula mass $PbCrO_4$
Gram formula mass $PbCl_2$

Data Analysis

1. Write a balanced equation for the reaction of Pb^{2+} and CrO_4^{2-} ions.

2. Calculate the moles of $PbCrO_4$ obtained in the experiment.

3. Determine the concentration (mol/L) of Pb^{2+} ions in the saturated $PbCl_2$ solution.

4. Find the Cl^- concentration (mol/L) in the saturated solution.

5. Calculate the K_{sp} for $PbCl_2$.

Conclusions

1. Calculate the percent error in your results. Use a chemistry handbook to look up the accepted K_{sp} values for $PbCl_2$ and $PbCrO_4$.

2. Suggest likely sources of error in this experiment.

Extensions

1. Devise and carry out an experiment to determine the solubility product of calcium hydroxide. Use a saturated solution of calcium hydroxide and titrate it with a standardized hydrochloric acid solution. Compare your result with the value reported in a chemistry handbook.

2. Barium ions are extremely toxic. Yet patients in hospitals are required to drink a suspension of barium sulfate in order to have their stomachs and intestinal tracts X-rayed. Find the K_{sp} value for barium sulfate and explain why patients are not at risk with this treatment.

Experiment

44 Oxidation–Reduction Reactions

Text reference:
Sections 21.1, 21.2

Background

The rusting of iron and the combustion of gasoline are common examples of oxidation–reduction reactions. Oxidation reactions are also thought to be partly responsible for the aging of the human body. Every oxidation reaction involves a transfer of electrons from the substance oxidized to the substance reduced. A substance undergoing oxidation gives up, or loses, electrons; a substance undergoing reduction gains electrons. The ease with which a substance oxidizes depends on the substance. For instance, iron oxidizes more easily than either silver or gold.

In this experiment you will study some oxidation–reduction reactions that occur between metals and metal ions. On the basis of your experiments, you will organize these substances into a series according to their relative ease of oxidation.

Goals

- **Observe** several oxidation–reduction reactions.
- **Classify** the substances tested in terms of ease of oxidation.

Equipment

safety goggles
9 small test tubes
1 test-tube rack
1 plastic wash bottle
1 10-mL graduated cylinder

Materials

3 strips of copper (Cu), each
0.25 mm × 0.50 cm × 2.00 cm
3 strips of lead (Pb), each
0.25 mm × 0.50 cm × 2.00 cm
0.1 *M* lead(II) nitrate, $Pb(NO_3)_2$ T
0.1 *M* zinc nitrate, $Zn(NO_3)_2$ I
steel wool

3 strips of zinc (Zn), each
0.25 mm × 0.50 cm × 2.00 cm

0.1M copper(II) nitrate, $Cu(NO_3)_2$ T

8 glass-marking pencils/class

distilled water

Safety

- Note the Safety Symbols used here and in the Procedure section. Review safety information on pages 7–10.
- Always wear safety goggles when working in the lab.
- Copper and lead compounds are toxic.

Procedure

Copy Table 44.1 into your laboratory notebook. As you perform the experiment, record your observations in this table.

1. Polish the small metal strips of copper, lead, and zinc with steel wool.

2. **CAUTION:** *Copper(II) nitrate is toxic.* Label three test tubes 0.1M $Cu(NO_3)_2$. Add 3 mL of 0.1M copper(II) nitrate to each test tube. In one tube place a strip of copper. In another place a strip of lead. In the third place a strip of zinc. Put the tubes in a test-tube rack.

3. **CAUTION:** *Lead nitrate is toxic.* Repeat step 2, labeling the tubes 0.1M $Pb(NO_3)_2$ and using 0.1M lead(II) nitrate in place of copper(II) nitrate.

4. Repeat step 2, labeling the tubes 0.1M $Zn(NO_3)_2$ and using 0.1M zinc nitrate in place of copper(II) nitrate.

5. Allow the test tubes to stand undisturbed for 5–10 minutes. Record your observations in Table 44.1, briefly describing evidence of any reaction.

6. Return the metal strips for reuse and dispose of the solutions as instructed by your teacher.

Data Record

Table 44.1 Part A. Reactions of Metals and Metal Ions			
	Cu^{2+}	Pb^{2+}	Zn^{2+}
Cu(*s*)			
Pb(*s*)			
Zn(*s*)			

Conclusions

1. Write balanced equations for any reactions that you observed between solid metals and metal ions.

2. Which metal was oxidized by both of the other two metals?

3. Which metal was oxidized by only one of the other two metals?

4. Which metal was oxidized by neither of the other metals?

5. Write balanced *half-reactions* for the *reduction* of each of the three metal ions used in this experiment. Write the equations so that the metal ions are shown as reactants and the solid metals are shown as products. List these half-reactions so that the most easily oxidized metal is given last.

Extension

1. The relative ease of oxidation of the halogens is in this order: chlorine, bromine, iodine, with iodine the most easily oxidized. Design an experiment that would allow you to determine if the halogens are less or more easily oxidized than the metals used in this experiment.

Experiment

45 Corrosion

Text reference:
Section 22.8

Background

Each year, the corrosion of metals does untold damage to cars, homes, and factories. *Corrosion* is a complex reduction–oxidation (redox) reaction in which metals are changed to their oxides or other compounds. In a corrosion reaction, electrons flow from the anode to the cathode. The anode and the cathode may be two different parts of the metal being corroded, or the cathode may be a different object that is in electrical contact with the metal being corroded.

In this experiment you will study a variety of factors involved in the corrosion of iron.

Goals

- **Observe** how different chemical environments affect corrosion.
- **Infer** whether structural stress influences corrosion.
- **Predict** whether copper or zinc can be used to protect iron from corrosion.

Equipment

safety goggles
6 small test tubes
1 test-tube rack
1 250-mL beaker
2 petri dishes, with lids
1 ring stand
1 ring support
1 wire gauze
1 gas burner
1 glass stirring rod
2 pliers/class
1 dropper pipet

Materials

9 uncoated iron nails, Fe
thin zinc strip, Zn
copper wire, Cu
steel wool
agar, powdered
distilled water
litmus paper or Hydrion paper
phenolphthalein solution
0.1*M* iron(II) sulfate, $FeSO_4$ [T]
0.1*M* potassium ferricyanide, $K_3Fe(CN)_6$ [T]

Solution Set 1

0.1*M* sodium hydroxide, NaOH [I]
0.1*M* sodium dichromate, $Na_2Cr_2O_7$ [T] [I]
0.1*M* sodium chloride, NaCl
0.1*M* hydrochloric acid, HCl [I]

Solution Set 2

0.1*M* potassium hydroxide, KOH [C]
0.1*M* sodium carbonate, Na_2CO_3
0.1*M* potassium nitrate, KNO_3 [I]
0.1*M* nitric acid, HNO_3 [C]

Solution Set 3

0.1*M* sodium phosphate, Na_3PO_4 [I]
0.1*M* sodium oxalate, $Na_2C_2O_4$ [T]
0.1*M* sodium thiocyanate, NaSCN [T]
0.1*M* sulfuric acid, H_2SO_4 [C]

Safety

- Note the Safety Symbols used here and in the Procedure section. Review safety information on pages 7–10.
- Always wear safety goggles when working in the lab.
- Sodium oxalate and sodium dichromate are toxic. Avoid contact with these chemicals.
- Nitric, hydrochloric, and sulfuric acids are irritating and corrosive.
- Sodium hydroxide is an irritant at the concentration used in this experiment.
- Never pick up a dropper bottle by its cap.
- Potassium ferricyanide can react with acids and chromates to produce toxic fumes. Read all labels carefully and mix chemicals only according to directions.

Procedure

Copy Table 45.1 into your laboratory notebook. As you perform the experiment, record your observations in this table.

Day 1 Experiments

Part A. Reaction of Iron with Aqueous Solutions

1. Clean five iron nails with steel wool. Place each nail in a separate small test tube.

2. Your teacher will assign you one of the three sets of chemicals listed in the Materials section. Fill each of four test tubes with a different solution from the set, until each nail is just covered. Fill the fifth tube with distilled water. Put the tubes in a test-tube rack.

3. Use litmus or Hydrion paper to determine whether each solution is acidic, basic, or neutral. Record the results in Table 45.1.

4. Allow the test tubes to stand overnight. You will study them tomorrow, when you begin with step 10.

Part B. Effects of Stress; Protection by Other Metals

5. Heat 100 mL of distilled water to boiling in a 250-mL beaker. Remove the gas burner. **CAUTION:** *Hot agar causes severe burns to the skin.* Add, while stirring, 1 g of powdered agar. Replace the burner; heat and stir the mixture until the agar forms a suspension. Be careful not to burn the agar. Stop heating and turn off the gas burner.

6. Add 5 drops of 0.1*M* potassium ferricyanide and 3 drops of phenolphthalein to the agar suspension. Stir to mix thoroughly. Allow the agar to cool, but not set, while you proceed to the next step.

7. Clean four iron nails with steel wool. Place one nail in a petri dish. Use pliers to bend a second nail into a right angle. Place the bent nail beside, but not touching, the straight nail as shown in Figure 45.1. Tightly wrap a 10-cm piece of copper wire around a third nail. Wrap the fourth nail tightly with a thin strip of zinc metal. Place these two metal-wrapped nails in a second petri dish. Be sure that the nails do not touch.

8. Pour the warm agar suspension into the petri dishes. The nails and attached pieces of metal should be covered by agar to a depth of at least 2 mm.

9. View the dishes against a white background and make observations at the end of the class period. Cover the dishes and keep them undisturbed overnight. You will observe them again tomorrow.

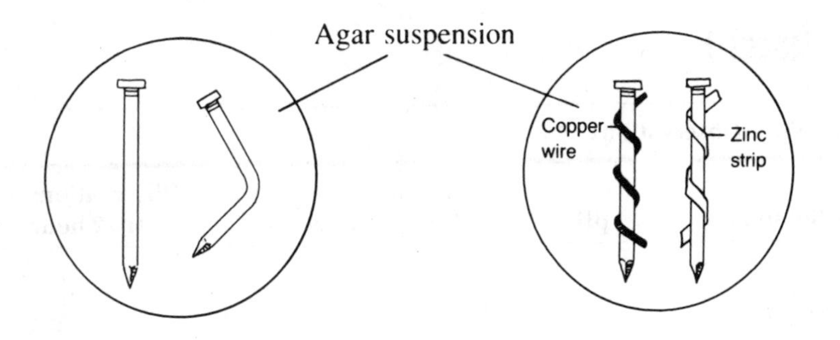

Figure 45.1

Day 2 Observations

Part A

10. Observe the test tubes that have stood overnight against a white background. Record any evidence of reaction in Table 45.1.

11. Test for the presence of ferrous ions, Fe^{2+}. In a separate small test tube, add one drop of 0.1*M* potassium ferricyanide to 1 mL of 0.1*M* iron(II) sulfate. Record your observations.

12. Now, test each of the five test tubes containing the nails for the presence of ferrous ions by adding 1 or 2 drops of 0.1*M* potassium ferricyanide. Record your observations. The presence of ferrous ions in the test tubes is evidence that corrosion has occurred.

Part B

13. Observe the dishes against a white background. Record your observations by sketching the dishes. Show the location and color of any reaction products.

14. Follow your teacher's instructions for proper disposal of the materials.

Data Record

Table 45.1 Observations

Test Solution	pH	Initial Observations	Observations After 12 hours	*Test with $Fe(CN)_6^{3-}$
Set I NaOH				
$Na_2Cr_2O_7$				
NaCl				
HCl				
Set II KOH				
Na_2CO_3				
KNO_3				
HNO_3				
Set III Na_3PO_4				
$Na_2C_2O_4$				
NaSCN				
H_2SO_4				
Controls H_2O				
$FeSO_4$	reference test for presence of Fe^{2+} ions			

*Positive: production of blue color indicates presence of Fe^{2+} ions in solution. Negative: no blue color.

Data Analysis

1. Obtain class data for the two sets of chemicals that you did not use in Part A. Enter this data in Table 45.1.

2. List the chemicals used in Part A for which there was no evidence of corrosion.

3. List the chemicals used in Part A for which there was evidence of corrosion.

4. Did either copper or zinc appear to protect the iron nail against corrosion? Explain.

5. Explain how the colors that developed in the petri dishes identify the anode and cathode for each reaction.

6. What were the usual sites where corrosion took place for the nails embedded in the agar?

Conclusions

1. Examine the data for Part A. Are there any ions that seem to inhibit corrosion or to promote it? Try to explain these effects.

2. Explain the results obtained in distilled water.

3. Consider your answer to question 6 in Data Analysis. What effect does bending seem to have on the tendency of iron to corrode?

4. Explain the effects caused by wrapping the nails with zinc or copper. Discuss the relative ease of oxidation of iron, zinc, and copper in your answer.

5. Is it correct to say that corrosion did not take place in the nail wrapped with zinc? Explain.

Extensions

1. Design an experiment to test other ways of preventing the corrosion of iron. Methods might include the use of various types of coatings, by adjusting pH, or by using so-called sacrificial metals.

2. Do some library research on corrosion effects that are due to air pollution. Design an experiment to test some of the effects that you learn about.

Experiment

46 Electrochemistry

Text reference:
Section 22.9

Background

It is common for manufactured products to be coated with a very thin layer of metal. For example, maybe you've eaten with silver-plated tableware. Your watch band, belt buckle, or jewelry may be gold-plated. All these plated items were produced using the electroplating process. *Electroplating* consists of depositing a thin layer of metal on another metal, either to protect the surface from corrosion or for a decorative effect. An electrolytic cell set up to electroplate a fork with a silver coating is shown in Figure 46.1. When the fork is being silver-plated, the anode metal is silver, the electrolytic solution is aqueous silver nitrate, and the cathode is the fork. The fork becomes silver-plated as a result of the reduction of Ag^+ ions, from the solution, at the cathode.

$$Ag^+(aq) + e^- \rightarrow Ag(s) \quad \text{reduction}$$

At the same time, the silver ions are replenished by oxidation of silver atoms at the anode.

$$Ag(s) \rightarrow Ag^+(aq) + e^- \quad \text{oxidation}$$

In this experiment, you will electroplate a metal object, using a typical electrolytic cell. You will then remove the plating by reversing the direction of flow of electrons in the electrolytic cell.

Figure 46.1

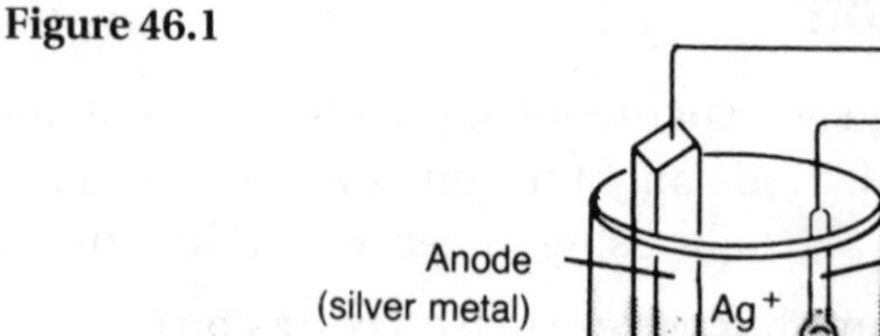

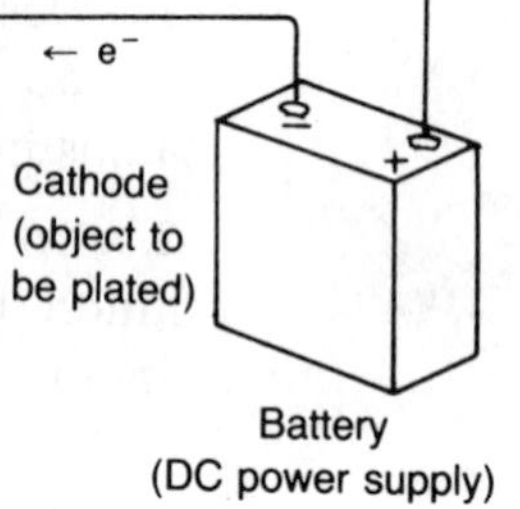

Goals

- **Construct** a typical electrolytic cell
- **Apply** the electroplating process to an object.
- **Apply** the electroplating process to reverse the plating process.

Equipment

safety goggles
1 250-mL beaker
1 100-mL graduated cylinder
2 copper wire lengths, 25 cm
4 alligator clips
1 6-volt battery

Materials

1*M* copper(II) sulfate, $CuSO_4$ T
copper strip, Cu, 1 × 5 cm
silver coin
steel wool
paper towels

Safety

- Note the Safety Symbol used here. Review safety information on pages 7–10.
- Always wear safety goggles when working in the lab.
- Use a piece of paper to hold the steel wool to avoid getting metal slivers in your hands.

Procedure

Copy Table 46.1 into your laboratory notebook. As you perform the experiment, record your observations in this table.

1. Thoroughly clean a small silver object, such as a coin, with steel wool. Securely attach, with an alligator clip, a 25-cm length of copper wire to the object.

2. Polish a 1-cm × 5-cm strip of copper with steel wool. Use an alligator clip to attach a 25-cm length of copper wire to the strip.

3. Add 100 mL of 1*M* $CuSO_4$ to a 250-mL beaker and set up a system similar to that shown in Figure 46.2.

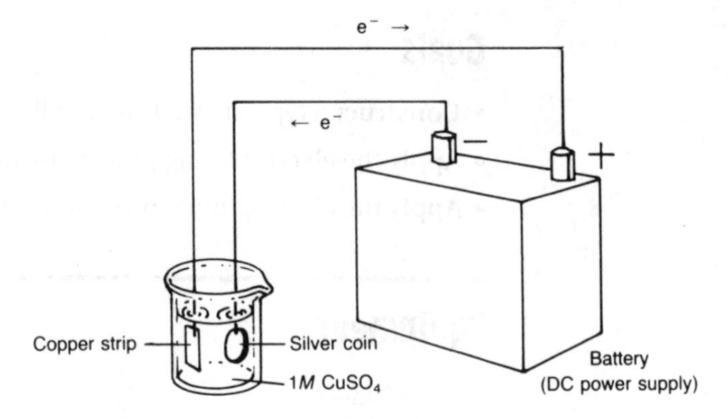

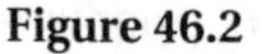
Figure 46.2

4. Use an alligator clip to connect the wire attached to the object to the negative terminal of a 6-volt battery. Use another alligator clip to connect the wire attached to the copper strip to the positive terminal. The object and the copper strip should not touch. Record your observations after 5 minutes have elapsed.

5. Reverse the connections and record your observations after 5 and 10 minutes.

6. Follow your teacher's instructions for proper disposal of the materials.

Data Record

Table 46.1 Observations of Electroplating	
Time of Observation	**Condition of Coin**
after 5 minutes of current flow:	
5 minutes after reversal of current flow:	
10 minutes after reversal of current flow:	

Conclusions

1. Write equations for the reactions that occur at the anode and at the cathode during electroplating.

2. What is oxidized in this experiment? At which electrode does oxidation occur?

3. What is reduced in this experiment? At which electrode does reduction take place?

4. To which battery terminal must an object be attached for it to become electroplated?

5. Sketch your electrochemical cell. Show the direction of ion movement and electron flow.

Extensions

1. The dry cell, or battery, used in this experiment is an example of a voltaic cell. Explain the construction of a voltaic cell. Explain how a voltaic cell produces an electric current. What results in a "dead" battery? How does a car battery differ from the battery used in a flashlight?

2. Research how nonmetal objects, such as baby shoes or leaves, are electroplated.

3. Electrolytic cells are used in the manufacture of sodium, magnesium, and aluminum metals. Choose one of these metals and research how it is produced commercially.

Experiment

47 Reactivity of Metals

Text reference:
Chapter 23

Background

The application a metal is used for depends in part on its chemical reactivity. For example, gold, which is commonly used in jewelry, is highly resistant to chemical reactions. Sodium, however, is not used in jewelry because it is so reactive it will explode if it contacts water. The chemistry of the metals is based on their ability to lose electrons. Differences in chemical reactivity between metals depend on the relative ease with which they give up electrons.

You can measure the relative reactivity of two metals by placing a small pure sample of one metal in a solution containing the ions of the other metal. If the small metal sample is more reactive than the metal whose ions are in solution, electrons will move from the solid metal sample into the solution. For example, a piece of iron placed in a solution containing copper(II) ions will corrode while fine copper particles deposit on the iron. However, no reaction occurs when a strip of copper metal is placed in a solution of iron(II) ions.

In this experiment, you will test the reactivities of a variety of metals with different metal ions. You will then use the results of your tests to construct a scale of relative reactivities of the metals.

Goals

- **Measure** the reactivities of a variety of metals.
- **Classify** the metals used into an activity series.

Equipment

safety goggles
8 medium test tubes
1 test-tube rack
2 dropper pipets
8 glass-marking pencils/class
1 tweezers

Materials

solutions, 5% w/v, in dropper bottles, of:

- lead(II) nitrate, $Pb(NO_3)_2$ T
- copper(II) sulfate, $CuSO_4$ T I
- silver nitrate, $AgNO_3$ T I
- zinc chloride, $ZnCl_2$ T
- potassium chloride, KCl
- sodium chloride, NaCl
- magnesium chloride, $MgCl_2$

thin metal strips, approximately 1.0 cm × 0.25 cm, in the quantities noted:

- 8 strips copper, Cu
- 8 strips zinc, Zn
- 8 strips magnesium, Mg F
- steel wool

Safety

- Note the Safety Symbols used here and in the Procedure section. Review safety information on pages 7–10.
- Always wear safety goggles when working in the lab.
- Solutions of lead and copper ions are toxic.
- Silver nitrate is toxic and will stain skin and clothing.
- Magnesium metal is flammable, keep it away from open flames.

Procedure

Copy Table 47.1 into your laboratory notebook. As you perform this experiment, record your observations in this table.

1. Polish metal strips of copper, zinc, and magnesium with steel wool until they are clean and shiny.

2. Using glass-marking pencil, label eight test tubes with the numbers 1–8. Place the tubes in a test-tube rack.

3. To tube 1, add 5 drops of $Pb(NO_3)_2$ solution. To tube 2 add 5 drops of $AgNO_3$ solution. Using tweezers, add one strip of copper metal to each tube. Record your observations.

4. Add 5 drops of solution to each tube as follows: tube 3, $CuSO_4$; tube 4, $Pb(NO_3)_2$; tube 5, $MgCl_2$. Add a strip of zinc metal to each tube. Record your observations.

5. Add 5 drops of solution to each tube as follows: tube 6, $ZnCl_2$; tube 7, NaCl; tube 8, KCl. Add a strip of polished Mg metal to each tube. Record your observations.

6. Follow your teacher's instructions for proper disposal of the materials.

Data Record

Table 47.1 Observations of the Activities of Metals

Tube	Metal ion	Metal	Observations
1			
2			
3			
4			
5			
6			
7			
8			

Conclusions

1. Why is it necessary to polish the metal strips before doing the experiment?

2. Write balanced chemical equations for those reactions that actually occurred.

3. Consult the activity series of metals in your textbook. Then complete the reactions that follow, indicating which would proceed without assistance (spontaneously) and which would require electrical energy.

4. Using your experimental data, list the metals in order of increasing activity. Explain how you arrived at your list.

$2Ag + Sn^{2+} \rightarrow$

$Sn + 2Ag^{+} \rightarrow$

$2Ag + Ni^{2+} \rightarrow$

$Zn + Ni^{2+} \rightarrow$

$Al + 3Ag^{+} \rightarrow$

5. Using the results of question 3, do you think there would be a reaction if strips of copper or zinc were placed in solutions of KCl or NaCl? Explain.

Extension

1. Compare the order of activities of metals with such properties as atomic radii, ionization energies, and electron affinities. Indicate any correlations between group and period trends of these properties and the activities of metals.

Experiment

48 Allotropic Forms of Sulfur

Text reference: Section 23.6

Background

Some elements can have several different structural forms while in the same physical state. These differing forms are called *allotropes.* Environmental conditions, such as temperature and pressure, determine which allotrope will form. Carbon is an element with several allotropic forms. The allotropes of carbon have very different physical properties. A diamond is hard, clear, and shiny. Graphite is black, with a slippery, greasy feel. Buckminsterfullerenes contain 60 carbon atoms arranged in a round molecule resembling a soccer ball. Sulfur is another element with several allotropic forms; unlike carbon, however, these allotropic forms can be easily produced in the lab.

In this experiment, you will examine the allotropes of sulfur.

Goals

- **Observe** the allotropic forms of sulfur.
- **Compare** the gross physical structures of these allotropes.

Equipment

safety goggles
1 50-mL beaker
1 100-mL beaker
1 250-mL beaker
1 ring stand
1 ring support
1 wire gauze
1 gas burner
1 medium test tube
1 test-tube holder
1 watch glass
1 dropper pipet
1 tweezers
2 magnifying glasses or 2 microscopes/class

Materials

vegetable oil [F]
powdered sulfur, S [F] [T]

filter paper circles
paper towels

Safety

- Note the Safety Symbols used here and in the Procedure section. Review safety information on pages 7–10.
- Always wear safety goggles when working in the lab.
- This experiment must be conducted in a well ventilated fume hood. Use a low flame to heat the sulfur. Sulfur is flammable and can be ignited.
- Molten sulfur can cause severe burns.
- Avoid breathing fumes from heated sulfur.
- Individuals with asthma or allergies to sulfur compounds should not be present when this experiment is conducted.

Procedure

This experiment must be done in a fume hood. It is intended to be conducted as a teacher demonstration.

Copy Table 48.1 into your laboratory notebook. As the experiment is performed by your teacher, record your observations and draw sketches in Table 48.1. Note that the instructions in the Procedure are written for the teacher.

Part A. Orthorhombic Sulfur

1. Pour vegetable oil to a depth of about 0.5 cm into a 50-mL beaker.

2. Add a pea-sized sample of sulfur to the oil.

3. Using a gas burner, heat the oil–sulfur mixture over a low flame for a few seconds. **CAUTION:** *Excessive heating may cause the sulfur–oil mixture to ignite, producing toxic fumes.*

4. Using a dropper pipet, place a few drops of the warm oil–sulfur mixture on a watch glass. Put the watch glass and beaker aside. After about 20 minutes, examine the product under a magnifying glass or a microscope. Record your observations and sketch the shapes of any crystals that have formed.

Part B. Monoclinic Sulfur

5. Fold a circle of filter paper into the conical shape used for filtering and place it in a 100-mL beaker for support, as shown in Figure 48.1.

6. Fill a medium test tube about one-third full with powdered sulfur.

7. Heat the test tube over a low flame. **CAUTION:** *Slow heating is recommended.* Continue heating until all the sulfur has melted to an orange-yellow liquid.

8. CAUTION: *Molten sulfur can cause painful burns.* Pour the liquid sulfur rapidly into the filter paper cone. As soon as solidification of the sulfur begins, carefully remove the filter paper from the beaker using tweezers. Place the open filter paper on a watch glass. Examine the product with a magnifying glass or a microscope. Record your observations and sketch any crystals that have formed.

Part C. Plastic Sulfur

9. Add 150 mL of water to a 250-mL beaker. Fill the test tube used in Part B about one-third full with sulfur.

10. Heat the test tube in a burner flame until the sulfur just begins to boil. The sulfur should be dark red at the boiling point. **CAUTION:** *Boiling sulfur is very hot. Its boiling point is 444° C!*

Figure 48.1

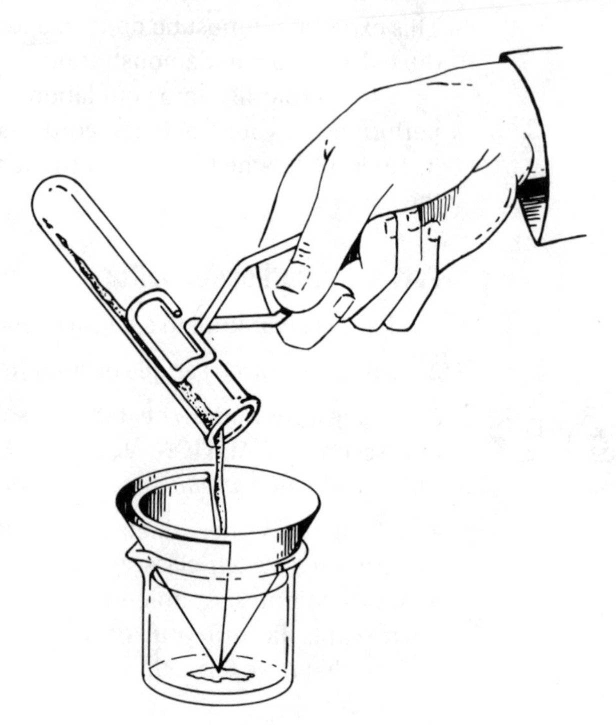

11. Rapidly pour the hot sulfur into the beaker of cold water, as shown in Figure 48.2. When the sulfur is cool, remove it from the water and place it on a paper towel to dry. Examine the dry sulfur, using a magnifying glass or microscope. Record your observations and sketch the form of the sulfur.

12. Your teacher will properly dispose of the materials.

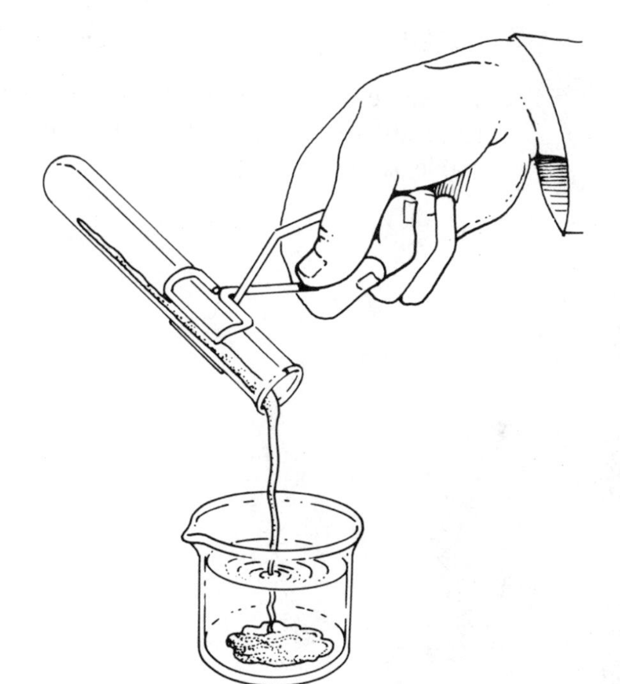

Figure 48.2

Data Record

Table 48.1 Observations of Allotropic Sulfur

Allotrope	Description
orthorhombic sulfur	
monoclinic sulfur	
plastic sulfur	

Conclusions

1. Which allotropic forms of sulfur are crystalline? Compare the structure of any crystals formed.

2. What happened to the plastic sulfur upon standing for a time? What does this suggest about the stabilities of the allotropic forms of sulfur?

Extension

1. Name two allotropic forms of oxygen. Which of these allotropes is less stable? What conditions are necessary for the formation of the less stable oxygen allotrope?

Hydrocarbons: A Structural Study

Text reference: Section 24.1

Background

The physical, chemical, and biological properties of molecules are determined, to a large extent, by their three-dimensional shapes. Molecular substances made up of molecules that pack tightly together often form large, beautiful crystals. Other substances made up of molecules that do not pack together remain liquids even at low temperatures. Many medicinal drugs are effective because their shapes resemble those of molecules in the body. Consequently, an understanding of molecular shape is very important to an understanding of chemistry or biology. Like many people, you may find it easier to work in three dimensions if you use molecular models. By working with models, you can learn to visualize and understand molecular shapes.

In this experiment, you will use ball-and-stick models to study the shapes of hydrocarbon molecules.

Goals

- **Make models** of hydrocarbon molecules.
- **Compare** the three-dimensional models with the structural formulas of chemical compounds.
- **Make models** of structural and geometric isomers.

Equipment

safety goggles
1 ball-and-stick molecular model kit/4 students

Safety

- Note the Safety Symbol used here. Review safety information on pages 7–10.
- Always wear safety goggles when working in the lab.

Procedure

For each molecular model, indicate the molecular and structural formula in your laboratory notebook. Also provide sketches of any structural or geometric isomers, and any different conformations. Refer to Table 49.1 for the color code of the atoms.

Table 49.1 Color Code for Models

Color	Atom Represented
black	carbon
yellow	hydrogen
red	oxygen
blue	nitrogen
green	chlorine
purple	iodine
orange	bromine

Part A. Continuous-Chain and Branch-Chain Alkanes

1. Make a model of methane, CH_4. Are all the angles formed by any two C–H bonds the same?

2. Make a model of ethane, C_2H_6. Can you hold one carbon and its hydrogens in a fixed position and rotate the other carbon and its hydrogens, without breaking the C–C bond?

3. Make a model of propane, C_3H_8. Can this model be rearranged to form a different molecule?

4. Make a model of butane, C_4H_{10}. Can this model be rearranged to form a new molecule that has the same molecular formula but a different structural formula? If so, name the structures. Molecules that have the same molecular formula, but different structural formulas, are called *structural isomers.*

5. Make a model of pentane, C_5H_{12}. Construct as many structural isomers of pentane as you can. For each of these structural isomers, give the name of the structural formula here and draw a sketch in Table 49.2a.

Part B. Cycloalkanes

6. Construct a model of hexane, C_6H_{14}. Manipulate the structure to form a ring. (You will have to remove two hydrogens to join the ring.) This ring structure is cyclohexane.

Manipulate your cyclohexane molecule so that two carbons directly across the ring from each other are above the plane of the other four carbons. This is called the *boat conformation*. Now manipulate the molecule so that one of these carbons is above, and the other below, the plane of the remaining four carbons. This is the *chair conformation*. In Table 49.2a, draw these two conformations.

Is there free rotation about the C–C bond in cyclohexane?

Part C. Alkenes and Geometric Isomers

7. Make a model of ethene, C_2H_4. Can you rotate the carbons about the double bond?

8. Remove one hydrogen from each carbon in ethene and replace it with a chlorine. The name of the resulting compound is 1,2-dichloroethene, $C_2H_2Cl_2$. There are two structures possible for this compound. They are called *geometric isomers*, and are distinguished by the prefix *cis* or the prefix *trans* added to the name. Construct models of both geometric isomers.

9. Make a model of butene, C_4H_8. This compound has two structural isomers. Name these isomers and in Table 49.2, give their molecular and structural formulas.

Are there also geometric ("cis" and "trans") isomers for butene?

Part D. Alkynes

10. Make a model of ethyne, C_2H_2. In the space provided in Table 49.2b, describe the shape of the molecule. Can you rotate the molecule about the triple bond?

Part E. Arenes

11. Make a model of benzene, C_6H_6, using alternating single and double bonds to approximate the aromatic bonds. Do all the atoms in this molecule lie in the same plane?

Can benzene exist in the boat and chair conformations?

Experiment

50 Esters of Carboxylic Acids

Text reference:
Section 25.11

Background

Did you know the aromas of the bananas, strawberries, and other fruits are the result of organic chemistry? Esters account for the distinctive odors of many fruits. Many of these ester compounds have pleasant odors. You can synthesize an ester in the lab by reacting a carboxylic acid with an alcohol. You will need a catalyst to speed up the reaction.

$$\underset{\text{carboxylic acid}}{R\text{—}CO_2H} + \underset{\text{alcohol}}{R'\text{—}OH} \overset{H^+}{\rightleftharpoons} \underset{\text{ester}}{R\text{—}CO_2R'} + \underset{\text{water}}{H_2O}$$

In this experiment, you will react carboxylic acids and alcohols, in the presence of a strong acid catalyst, to form esters.

Goal

- **Create** esters from carboxylic acids and alcohols.

Equipment

safety goggles
5 medium test tubes
1 test-tube rack
1 ring stand
1 ring support
1 250-mL beaker
1 wire gauze
1 gas burner
1 dropper pipet
1 thermometer
1 10-mL graduated cylinder

Materials

methanol, CH_3OH T F
ethanol, C_2H_5OH T F
2-methyl-1-propanol, C_4H_9OH T F
1-pentanol, $C_5H_{11}OH$ T F
glacial ethanoic acid, CH_3COOH T F C
salicylic acid, $C_6H_4OHCOOH$ T
18*M* sulfuric acid, H_2SO_4 T C
ice

1-octanol, $C_8H_{17}OH$ T F

90% methanoic acid, HCOOH T F C

distilled water

Safety

- Note the Safety Symbols used here and in the Procedure section. Review safety information on pages 7–10.
- Always wear safety goggles when working in the lab.
- All acids are corrosive, and several of the acids used in this experiment are concentrated and particularly hazardous.
- Alcohols are flammable liquids. Do not dispense these compounds near an open flame.
- Mix chemicals only according to directions.
- Never *add water to* 18*M* sulfuric acid.
- Never add 18*M* sulfuric acid to any other concentrated acid or to an alcohol.

Procedure

Copy Table 50.1 into your laboratory notebook. As you perform the experiment, record your observations in this table.

1. CAUTION: *The acids used in this experiment are extremely corrosive.* Label five medium test tubes with the numbers 1–5. Put the tubes in a test-tube rack. To each of the tubes, add 1 mL of a carboxylic acid and 1 mL of an alcohol, as listed in Table 50.1. In the case of the solid carboxylic acid, salicylic acid, add 1 g of acid and 1 mL of alcohol to the tube.

2. CAUTION: *Keep containers of alcohols and carboxylic acids away from flames.* Add 3–5 drops of concentrated sulfuric acid to each tube and heat the tubes in a water bath at 60°C for 10–15 minutes.

3. Turn off the burner and remove the test tubes from the hot water bath. Cool the tubes in an ice bath. Add 5 mL of distilled water to each tube. Any ester produced in the reaction will float on the water in the tube. Note the odor of the ester by wafting the fumes toward your nose with your hand. Try to relate each odor to a familiar odor of fruit, flower, or vegetable. Record your observations in Table 50.1.

4. Follow your teacher's instructions for proper disposal of the materials.

Data Record

Test Tube	Carboxylic Acid	Alcohol	Ester Made	Odor
1	formic	2-methyl -1-propanol		
2	acetic	ethanol		
3	acetic	1-pentanol		
4	acetic	1-octanol		
5	salicylic	methanol		

Table 50.1 Results and Conclusions

Conclusions

1. Complete Table 50.1 by naming the esters that were synthesized in the experiment.

2. Write a general equation for the acid-catalyzed formation of an ester from an alcohol and a carboxylic acid.

3. Why was water added to the tube before you were asked to smell it? (**Hint:** What was in the water layer in the test tube?) To answer this question, discuss the relative solubility of acids, alcohols, and esters in water.

4. Why were the reactions kept free of water during heating?

Extensions

1. Write equations for each of the esterification reactions in this experiment. Use structural formulas in the equations and write the name of each compound below its structural formula.

2. In esterification reactions, the products are in chemical equilibrium with the reactants. Suggest several ways of causing the equilibrium to shift in favor of the production of additional ester.

Experiment

51 Preparation of Soap

Text reference: Section 25.14

Background

Have you ever considered that soap is one of society's major defenses against disease? The cleansing power of soap helps rinse away many disease-causing organisms, making your home and school a healthier place than they otherwise would be. Soaps are alkali metal salts of carboxylic acids. They are generally produced by the reaction of metallic hydroxides with animal fats and vegetable oils. The major components of these fats and oils are triglycerides, esters of glycerol, and various fatty acids. Typically, soaps are made by hydrolyzing the ester bonds of triglycerides with solutions of sodium hydroxide. This soap-making reaction is called *saponification* (in Greek *sapon* means soap). The products of the hydrolysis reaction are soap and glycerol.

In this experiment, you will saponify a vegetable oil and examine some properties of your product. You will compare the properties of the soap you make with the properties of a commercial detergent and a commercial hand soap.

Goals

- **Apply** saponification to vegetable oil.
- **Observe** the properties of the soap that is formed.
- **Compare** the properties of the soap formed to the properties of commercial detergents and hand soaps.

Equipment

safety goggles
2 50-mL beakers
2 250-mL beakers
1 10-mL graduated cylinder
1 glass stirring rod
1 wire gauze
3 medium test tubes
3 cork stoppers
1 test-tube rack
1 dropper pipet

4 centigram balances/class
1 gas burner
1 ring stand
1 ring support
1 plastic wash bottle
1 spatula
1 scoopula

Materials

8 glass-marking pencils/class
vegetable oil
paper towels
50%(v/v) ethanol-water mixture
saturated sodium chloride solution, NaCl
sodium hydroxide, NaOH [C]
wide-range indicator solution or wide-range test paper
laundry detergent [I]
hand soap
0.1*M* calcium chloride, $CaCl_2$ [T]
0.1*M* iron(III) chloride, $FeCl_3$ [T] [I]
0.1*M* magnesium chloride, $MgCl_2$ [T]

Safety

- Note the Safety Symbols used here and in the Procedure section. Review safety information on pages 7–10.
- Always wear safety goggles when working in the lab.
- Sodium hydroxide is corrosive and can cause severe burns. Never handle sodium hydroxide pellets with your fingers; use a small beaker and a scoopula. Solid sodium hydroxide will absorb water from the atmosphere; do not leave the container of sodium hydroxide open.
- Keep ethanol and ethanol-water mixtures away from open flames.
- Aqueous iron chloride will stain clothes permanently and is irritating to the skin. Avoid contact with this material.

Procedure

Copy Table 51.1 into your laboratory notebook. As you perform the experiment, record your results in this table.

Part A. Preparation of Soap

1. Pour 5 mL (5.0 g) of vegetable oil into a 250-mL beaker.

2. Measure 15 mL of 50% ethanol-water mixture into a 50-mL beaker. Slowly dissolve 2.5 g of NaOH pellets in ethanol-water mixture.

3. Add 2–3 mL of the NaOH solution to the beaker containing the oil. **CAUTION:** *Keep your face away from the beaker.* Heat the mixture over a *low flame* while stirring. Every few minutes, for about 20 minutes, add a portion of the ethanol-water mixture while continuing to stir. Heat and stir for about 10 more minutes. The oil should be dissolved and a homogeneous solution should be obtained.

4. Add 25 mL of cold water to the hot solution. Using a towel "handle" as shown in Figure 30.1, pour this solution into a 250-mL beaker containing 150 mL of saturated NaCl. Stir this mixture gently and allow it to cool for several minutes.

5. Using a spatula, skim off the top layer of soap and place it in a 50-mL beaker.

Part B. Properties of Soaps and Detergents

6. Place a pea-sized lump of your soap into a test tube. Use a scoopula to put a similar amount of laundry detergent in a second tube and a similar amount of hand soap in a third tube. Add 10 mL of water to each tube, stopper them, and shake the tubes thoroughly. In this step and throughout this experiment, use a test-tube rack as needed.

7. Estimate the pH of the solutions, using wide-range indicator solution or wide-range test paper. Record the results. Pour the contents of the test tubes down the drain. Rinse the test tubes and stoppers with water.

8. Mark three test tubes with the labels "$CaCl_2$", "$FeCl_3$", and "$MgCl_2$," respectively.

9. Prepare a detergent solution by dissolving 0.3 g of detergent in 30 mL of water. Divide this solution equally among the three test tubes. Add solutions to the test tubes as follows:

$CaCl_2$ test tube 1.0 mL (or 20 drops) of 0.1M $CaCl_2$
$FeCl_3$ test tube 1.0 mL of 0.1M $MgCl_2$
$MgCl_2$ test tube 1.0 mL of 0.1M $FeCl_3$

Stopper each tube and shake it to mix. Record your observations. Pour the contents of the test tubes down the drain. Rinse the test tubes and stoppers with water.

10. Repeat step 9, but replace the detergent solution with a hand-soap solution of the same strength. Record your observations.

11. Repeat step 9, but replace the detergent solution with a solution of your soap of the same strength. Record your observations.

12. Follow your teacher's instructions for proper disposal of the materials.

Data Record

Table 51.1 Properties of Soaps and Detergents				
Test Substance	pH of Solution	Effect of Adding $CaCl_2$	$FeCl_3$	$MgCl_2$
your soap				
detergent				
hand soap				

Conclusions

1. Write the reaction for saponification of a typical fat (or oil) with sodium hydroxide. Include structural formulas.

2. How does the pH of the soap solution that you prepared compare with those of the solution of commercial laundry detergent and the solution of hand soap? Which of these products would have the harshest effect on the skin?

3. The metal ions Ca^{2+}, Fe^{3+}, and Mg^{2+} all contribute to the formation of *hard water.* What differences did you observe when the metal ions Ca^{2+}, Fe^{3+}, and Mg^{2+} were added to a soap or a detergent? Do you think that a soap or a detergent would make a better cleansing agent in hard water? Explain.

Experiment

52 Radioactivity and Radiation

Text reference:
Section 26.1

Background

Although radiation is generally considered dangerous to living things, radiation and radioisotopes are very important in the diagnosis and treatment of some diseases. Nevertheless, the penetrating power of some types of radiation and the ionizations they produce in the body are potentially hazardous. When radioactive elements decay, they can emit three types of radiation: alpha (α), beta (β), and gamma (γ). Radiation cannot be seen, but its presence can be detected through the ionizations produced when it interacts with matter.

How can X-ray technicians and other people who work with radioactive materials minimize their exposure to the potentially hazardous effects of radiation? In this experiment you will investigate how to minimize your exposure to radiation from low-level radioactive sources.

Goals

- **Measure** radiation using a Geiger–Müller counter.
- **Infer** how distance, shielding, and time affect the degree of exposure to a radioactive source.

Equipment

safety goggles
1 forceps
1 Geiger–Müller counter
1 ring stand
1 ring support
1 meter stick

Materials

radioactive sources, sealed and kept in shielded container when not in use:

carbon-14, ^{14}C
thallium-204, ^{204}Tl
cesium-137, ^{137}Cs

shielding materials, 10-cm × 10-cm squares, 1 of each of the following:

paper
wood, 3 mm thick
aluminum foil
glass, picture
lead foil
cotton fabric
plastic (film)

Safety

- Note the Safety Symbols used here and in the Procedure section. Review safety information on pages 7–10.
- Always wear safety goggles when working in the lab.
- The amount of radiation from the sources used in this experiment presents a negligible health hazard. Nevertheless, proper handling of radioactive materials should always be practiced.

Procedure

Copy Tables 52.1, 52.2 and 52.3 into your laboratory notebook. Your teacher will describe the Geiger–Müller tube and counter, and will demonstrate proper procedures for handling the sealed radioactive sources. Follow your teacher's directions! As the experiment is performed, record observations in Tables 52.1, 52.2, and 52.3.

Part A. Background Radiation

1. Remove all radioactive material from the region near the Geiger–Müller tube. Measure the detected background radiation in counts per minute (cpm) and record the measurement in Table 52.1.

Part B. Effect of Distance

2. Place the Geiger–Müller tube at one end of the meter stick with a sealed source (preferably a gamma emitter) at the other end as shown in Figure 52.1.

3. Measure the detected radiation in (cpm) at distances between the source and the detector of 4 cm, 2 cm, and 1 cm. Record your measurements in Table 52.1.

Figure 52.1

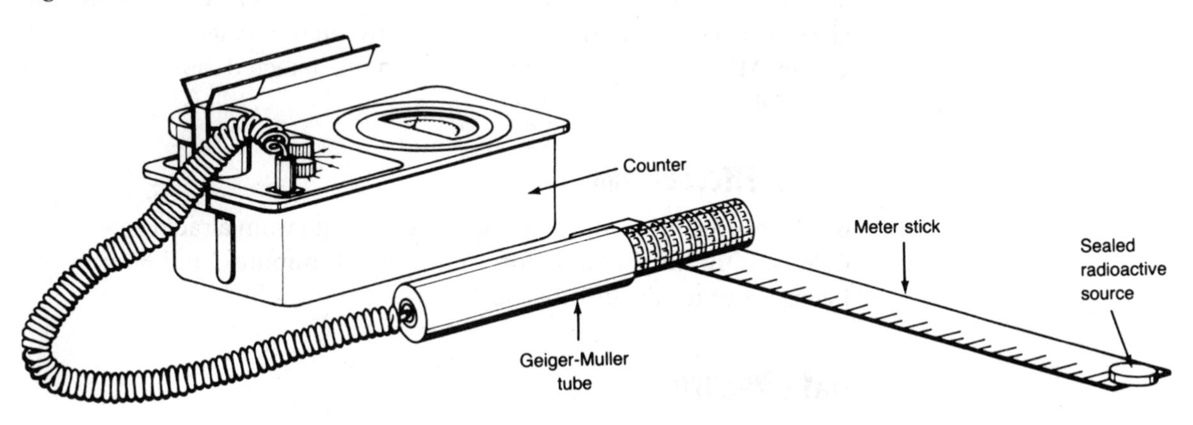

Part C. Effect of Shielding

4. Place a sealed source 5–10 cm below a Geiger–Müller tube as shown in Figure 52.2. Measure the detected radiation and record the measurement in Table 52.2.

Figure 52.2

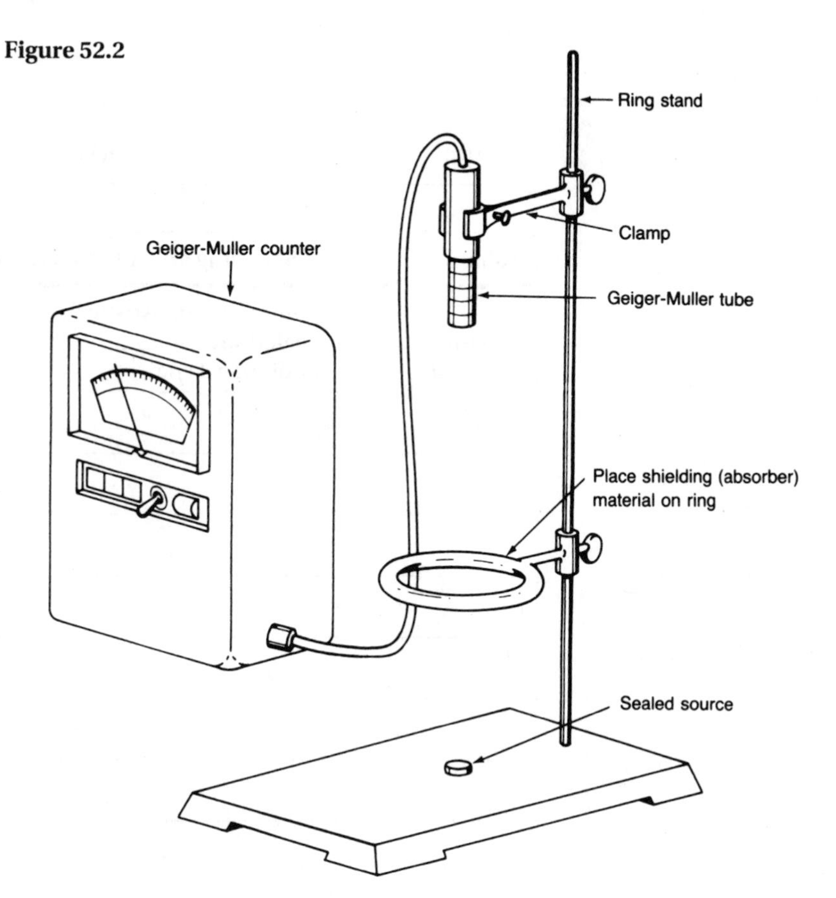

5. Place thin pieces of the various materials (paper, wood, aluminum, glass, lead, cotton fabric, and plastic) between the sealed source and the Geiger–Müller tube. Measure and record the detected radiation for each material.

Part D. Effect of Time

6. Measure and record the counts per minute from a radiation source. Calculate the total counts for 5 minutes, 30 minutes, and 60 minutes. Record your results in Table 52.3.

Data Record

Table 52.1 Effect of Distance on Radiation Intensity

Distance from Source (cm)	Radiation Intensity (cpm)
4	
2	
1	
Source: ______	Background radiation: ______ cpm

Table 52.2 Effect of Shielding on Radiation Intensity

Shielding Material	Radiation Intensity (cpm) Sealed source ______ Radiation Type ______	Radiation Intensity (cpm) Sealed source ______ Radiation Type ______

Table 52.3 Effect of Time on Radiation Exposure (Source: ______)	
Time (min)	**Total Counts**
1	
5	
30	
60	

Data Analysis

Note, **one page of graph paper** is required for your report.

1. What types of radiation—alpha (α), beta (β), or gamma (γ)—can be detected with a Geiger–Müller counter?

2. Graph the radiation intensity (in counts per minute) versus distance (in centimeters from the source). Be certain to identify the type of sealed source the data represents.

3. What did you find to be the best shielding material?

4. When you double the distance from the radiation source, how do the counts per minute change?

5. Is there an advantage in limiting your exposure to a radiation source to the shortest time possible? Explain.

Extensions

1. Describe what is meant by the half-life of a radioisotope.

2. What criteria would be important in selecting a radioisotope for use as a tracer in the body during a medical procedure?

Sample Laboratory Report

Name: Matt Walker **Class:** 2 **Date:** October 5, 1996

Experiment Number and Title: Experiment 4: Mass, Volume, and Density

Purpose: (Give a clear, concise description of exactly what the experiment was intended to demonstrate.)

The purpose of this experiment was to investigate the relationship between mass and volume for a metal and to determine if that relationship can be used as an identifying property of the metal.

Equipment/Materials: (List the equipment and materials that you actually used in the experiment.)

graduated cylinder (25-mL)
metal A
metal B
centigram balance
ruler (cm)

Methods: (Describe all laboratory techniques and types of calculations that you used in the experiment.)

Mass measurements were made by weighing clean, dry samples of metals on a centigram balance. The mass measurements were made to the nearest 0.01 g.

Volume measurements were made by the method of water displacement. A 25-mL graduated cylinder was half-filled with water and the volume recorded. The volume was read at the bottom of the meniscus. Then the metal sample was immersed in the water in the graduated cylinder. The new volume, of the water and the metal sample together, was read and recorded. The volume of the metal sample was determined by subtracting the initial volume of the water from the final volume. The density of each sample was calculated by dividing the mass of the sample by its volume.

Other groups in the class had different-sized samples of the same metals, A and B. Class data was pooled to obtain data points for graphing mass (the independent variable) versus volume (the dependent variable) for each metal. The slope of the line obtained for each metal is equal to mass/volume and represents the density of the metal. The slope was determined according to the formula $y = mx + b$, where x = mass value, y = the volume associated with that mass, m = slope of the line, b = y-intercept of the line.

Procedure: (Describe the major steps of the procedure, exactly as you carried them out. Include here any qualitative observations you made during the experiment.)

We received one sample of metal A and one sample of metal B from the teacher. Metal A was shiny, smooth, and black. Metal B was dull, rough, and tan in color. We cleaned and dried the samples, using tap water and paper towels. Metal B was more difficult to dry than metal. We then weighed each sample on the centigram balance as described above and recorded the masses. We weighed metal A first and metal B second. I did the weighings and Paul recorded the data.

We then made the volume measurements, using the water displacement method described in the Method section. Paul added the samples to the water and I made the initial and final volume readings. We did this first for metal A and then for metal B. After making these measurements, we dried the samples and returned them to the teacher.

Data and Calculations: (Record here any measurements and calculations that you make during the experiment. Make sure to clearly distinguish between the two. Be especially careful to include units for all measurements and all calculations. Pay close attention to significant figures and clearly indicate when you have made a calculation. If possible, present your data in the form of a table and/or graph so that patterns in the data may be more easily recognized.)

Group 1 Data and Calculations		
Quantity	Metal A	Metal B
mass	10.10 g	33.41 g
volume of water alone	12.0 mL	19.7 mL
volume of water and metal	15.8 mL	23.5 mL
volume of metal	3.8 mL (15.8 mL–12.0 mL)	3.8 mL (23.5 mL–19.7 mL)
density of metal	2.7 g/mL (10.10 g/3.8 mL)	88 g/mL (33.41 g/3.8 mL)

Class Data and Calculations						
Lab Group*	Metal A Mass	Metal A Volume	Metal A Density	Metal B Mass	Metal B Volume	Metal B Density
1	10.10 g	3.8 mL	2.7 g/mL	33.41 g	3.8 mL	8.8 g/mL
2	4.31 g	1.7 mL	2.6 g/mL	34.62 g	3.9 mL	8.9 g/mL
3	8.05 g	3.0 mL	2.7 g/mL	27.63 g	3.1 mL	8.9 g/mL
4	9.00 g	3.4 mL	2.6 g/mL	21.00 g	2.4 mL	8.4 g/mL
5	6.25 g	2.5 mL	2.5 g/mL	20.92 g	2.5 mL	8.4 g/mL

*1 = Janet & Paul 2 = Phil & Pat 3 = Ellen & Emily 4 = Dave & Alice 5 = Frank & Bill

Graph of Class Data for Metal A (Remember to plot the independent variable on the *x*-axis, the horizontal axis, and the dependent variable on the *y*-axis, the vertical axis.)

mass (x)	volume (y)
10.10 g	3.8 mL
4.31 g	1.7 mL
8.05 g	3.0 mL
9.00 g	3.4 mL
6.25 g	2.5 mL

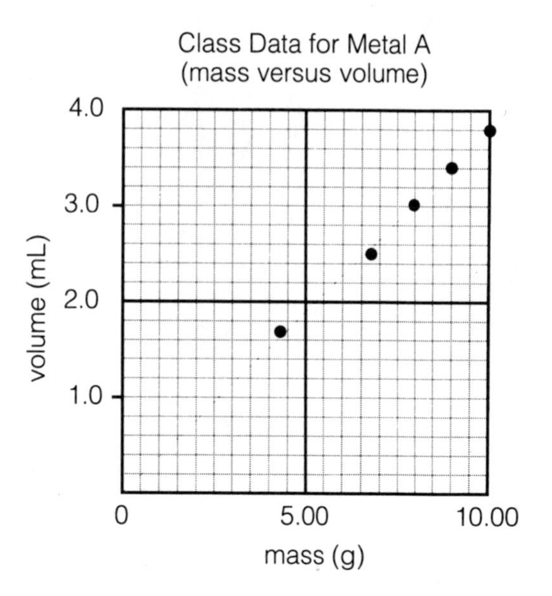

Conclusions: (Record here the answers to all the questions in the Conclusions section of the experiment. Also answer any additional questions that your teacher may ask.)

1. The results of this experiment indicate that the density of a specific substance is a constant. They indicate also that the densities of different substances can be quite different. For these reasons, density should be useful in the identification of substances.

(And similarly for the remainder of the questions posed in the lab manual.)

Table A.1 Symbols of Common Elements

Symbol	Element	Symbol	Element	Symbol	Element
Ag	silver	Cu	copper	O	oxygen
Al	aluminum	F	fluorine	P	phosphorus
As	arsenic	Fe	iron	Pb	lead
Au	gold	H	hydrogen	Pt	platinum
Ba	barium	Hg	mercury	S	sulfur
Bi	bismuth	I	iodine	Sb	antimony
Br	bromine	K	potassium	Sn	tin
C	carbon	Mg	magnesium	Sr	strontium
Ca	calcium	Mn	manganese	Ti	titanium
Cl	chlorine	N	nitrogen	U	uranium
Co	cobalt	Na	sodium	W	tungsten
Cr	chromium	Ni	nickel	Zn	zinc

Table A.2 Symbols of Common Polyatomic Ions

Symbol	Ion	Symbol	Ion	Symbol	Ion
$C_2H_3O_2^-$	ethanoate	$Cr_2O_7^{2-}$	dichromate	NH_4^+	ammonium
ClO^-	hypochlorite	HCO_3^-	hydrogen carbonate (bicarbonate)	NO_3^-	nitrate
ClO_2^-	chlorite			NO_2^-	nitrite
ClO_3^-	chlorate	H_3O^+	hydronium	O_2^{2-}	peroxide
ClO_4^-	perchlorate	HPO_4^{2-}	hydrogen phosphate	OH^-	hydroxide
CN^-	cyanide	HSO_3^-	hydrogen sulfite	PO_4^{3-}	phosphate
CO_3^{2-}	carbonate	HSO_4^-	hydrogen sulfate	SO_3^{2-}	sulfite
CrO_4^{2-}	chromate	MnO_4^-	permanganate	SO_4^{2-}	sulfate

Table A.3 Solubilities of Compounds at 25°C and 101 kPa

	ethanoate	bromide	carbonate	chlorate	chloride	hydroxide	iodide	nitrate	oxide	perchlorate	phosphate	sulfate	sulfide
aluminum	S	S	—	S	S	I	S	S	I	S	I	S	d
ammonium	S	S	S	S	S	S	S	S	—	S	S	S	S
barium	S	S	I	S	S	S	S	S	sS	S	I	I	d
calcium	S	S	I	S	S	S	S	S	sS	S	I	sS	I
copper(II)	S	S	—	S	S	I	S	S	I	S	I	S	I
iron(II)	S	S	I	S	S	I	S	S	I	S	I	S	I
iron(III)	S	S	—	S	S	I	S	S	I	S	I	sS	d
lithium	S	S	sS	S	S	S	S	S	S	S	sS	S	S
magnesium	S	S	I	S	S	I	S	S	I	S	I	S	d
potassium	S	S	S	S	S	S	S	S	S	S	S	S	S
silver	sS	I	I	S	I	—	I	S	I	S	I	sS	I
sodium	S	S	S	S	S	S	S	S	S	S	S	S	S
strontium	S	S	I	S	S	S	S	S	S	S	I	I	I
zinc	S	S	I	S	S	I	S	S	I	S	I	S	I

Key:
- S = soluble
- sS = slightly soluble
- I = insoluble
- d = decomposes in water
- — = no such compound

Table A.4 Some Properties of the Elements

Element	Symbol	Atomic number	Atomic mass	Melting point (°C)	Boiling point (°C)	Density (g/cm^3) (gases at STP)	Major oxidation states
actinium	Ac	89	(227.0482)	1050	3200	10.07	+3
aluminum	Al	13	26.98154	660.37	2467	2.6989	+3
americium	Am	95	243	944	2607	13.67	+3, +4, +5, +6
antimony	Sb	51	121.75	630.74	1950	6.691	−3, +3, +5
argon	Ar	18	39.948	−189.2	−185.7	.0017837	
arsenic	As	33	74.9216	817	613	5.73	−3, +3, +5
astatine	At	85	(210)	302	337	—	
barium	Ba	56	137.33	725	1640	3.5	+2
berkelium	Bk	97	(247)	986	—	14.78	
beryllium	Be	4	9.01218	1278	2970	1.848	+2
bismuth	Bi	83	208.9804	271.3	1560	9.747	+3, +5
boron	B	5	10.81	2079	3675	2.34	+3
bromine	Br	35	79.904	−7.2	58.78	3.12	−1, +1, +5
cadmium	Cd	48	112.41	320.9	765	8.65	+2
calcium	Ca	20	40.08	839	1484	1.55	+2
californium	Cf	98	(251)	900	—	14	
carbon	C	6	12.011	3550	4827	2.267	−4, +2, +4
cerium	Ce	58	140.12	799	3426	6.657	+3, +4
cesium	Cs	55	132.9054	28.40	669.3	1.873	+1
chlorine	Cl	17	35.453	−100.98	−34.6	.003214	−1, +1, +5, +7
chromium	Cr	24	51.996	1857	2672	7.18	+2, +3, +6
cobalt	Co	27	58.9332	1495	2870	8.9	+2, +3
copper	Cu	29	63.546	1083.4	2567	8.96	+1, +2
curium	Cm	96	(247)	1340	—	13.51	+3
dysprosium	Dy	66	162.50	1412	2562	8.550	+3
einsteinium	Es	99	(252)	—	—	—	
erbium	Er	68	167.26	159	2863	9.006	+3
europium	Eu	63	151.96	822	1597	5.243	+2, +3
fermium	Fm	100	(257)	—	—	—	
fluorine	F	9	18.998403	−219.62	−188.54	.001696	−1
francium	Fr	87	(223)	27	667	—	+1
gadolinium	Gd	64	157.25	1313	3266	7.9004	+3
gallium	Ga	31	69.72	29.78	2403	5.904	+3
germanium	Ge	32	72.59	937.4	2830	5.323	+2, +4
gold	Au	79	196.9665	1064.43	3080	19.3	+1, +3
hafnium	Hf	72	178.49	2227	4602	13.31	+4
helium	He	2	4.00260	−272.2	−268.934	.001785	
holmiun	Ho	67	164.9304	1474	2695	8.795	+3
hydrogen	H	1	1.00794	−259.14	−252.87	.00008988	+1
indium	In	49	114.82	156.61	2080	7.31	+1, +3
iodine	I	53	126.9045	113.5	184.35	4.93	−1, +1, +5, +7
iridium	Ir	77	192.22	2410	4130	22.42	+3, +4
iron	Fe	26	55.847	1535	2750	7.874	+2, +3
krypton	Kr	36	83.80	−156.6	−152.30	.003733	
lanthanum	La	57	138.9055	921	3457	6.145	+3
lawrencium	Lr	103	(260)	—	—	—	+3
lead	Pb	82	207.2	327.502	1740	11.35	+2, +4
lithium	Li	3	6.941	180.54	1342	.534	+1
lutetium	Lu	71	174.967	1663	3395	9.840	+3
magnesium	Mg	12	24.305	648.8	1090	1.738	+2
manganese	Mn	25	54.9380	1244	1962	7.32	+2, +3, +4, +7
mendelevium	Md	101	257	—	—	—	+2, +3
mercury	Hg	80	200.59	−38.842	356.58	13.546	+1, +2
molybdenum	Mo	42	95.94	2617	4612	10.22	+6

Table A.4 Some Properties of the Elements (cont.)

Element	Symbol	Atomic number	Atomic mass	Melting point (°C)	Boiling point (°C)	Density (g/cm^3) (gases at STP)	Major oxidation states
neodymium	Nd	60	144.24	1021	3068	6.90	+3
neon	Ne	10	20.179	–248.67	–246.048	.0008999	
neptunium	Np	93	237.0482	640	3902	20.25	+3, +4, +5, +6
nickel	Ni	28	58.69	1453	2732	8.902	+2, +3
niobium	Nb	41	92.9064	2468	4742	8.57	+3, +5
nitrogen	N	7	14.0067	–209.86	–195.8	.0012506	–3, +3, +5
nobelium	No	102	(259)	—	—	—	+2, +3
osmium	Os	76	190.2	3045	5027	22.57	+3, +4
oxygen	O	8	15.9994	–218.4	–182.962	.001429	–2
palladium	Pd	46	106.42	1554	2970	12.02	+2, +4
phosphorus	P	15	30.97376	44.1	280	1.82	–3, +3, +5
platinum	Pt	78	195.08	1772	3827	21.45	+2, +4
plutonium	Pu	94	(244)	641	3232	19.84	+3, +4, +5, +6
polonium	Po	84	(209)	254	962	9.32	+2, +4
potassium	K	19	39.0982	63.25	760	.862	+1
praseodymium	Pr	59	140.9077	931	3512	6.64	+3
promethium	Pm	61	(145)	1168	2460	7.22	+3
protactinium	Pa	91	231.0359	1560	4027	15.37	+4, +5
radium	Ra	88	226.0254	700	1140	5.5	+2
radon	Rn	86	(222)	–71	–61.8	.00973	
rhenium	Re	75	186.207	3180	5627	21.02	+4, +6, +7
rhodium	Rh	45	102.9055	1966	3727	12.41	+3
rubidium	Rb	37	85.4678	38.89	686	1.532	+1
ruthenium	Ru	44	101.07	2310	3900	12.41	+3
samarium	Sm	62	150.36	1077	1791	7.520	+2, +3
scandium	Sc	21	44.9559	1541	2831	2.989	+3
selenium	Se	34	78.96	217	684.9	4.79	–2, +4, +6
silicon	Si	14	28.0855	1410	2355	2.33	–4, +2, +4
silver	Ag	47	107.8682	961.93	2212	10.50	+1
sodium	Na	11	22.98977	97.81	882.9	.971	+1
strontium	Sr	38	87.62	796	1384	2.54	+2
sulfur	S	16	32.06	112.8	444.7	2.07	–2, +4, +6
tantalum	Ta	73	180.9479	2996	5425	16.654	+5
technetium	Tc	43	(98)	2172	4877	11.50	+4, +6, +7
tellurium	Te	52	127.60	449.5	989.8	6.24	–2, +4, +6
terbium	Tb	65	158.9254	1356	3123	8.229	+3
thallium	Tl	81	204.383	303.5	1457	11.85	+1, +3
thorium	Th	90	232.0381	1750	4790	11.72	+4
thulium	Tm	69	168.9342	1545	1947	9.321	+3
tin	Sn	50	118.69	231.968	2270	7.31	+2, +4
titanium	Ti	22	47.88	1660	3287	4.54	+2, +3, +4
tungsten	W	74	183.85	3410	5660	19.3	+6
uranium	U	92	238.0289	1132.3	3818	18.95	+3, +4, +5, +6
vanadium	V	23	50.9415	1890	3380	6.11	+2, +3, +4, +5
xenon	Xe	54	131.29	–111.9	–107.1	.005887	
ytterbium	Yb	70	173.04	819	1194	6.965	+2, +3
yttrium	Y	39	88.9059	1522	3338	4.469	+3
zinc	Zn	30	65.38	419.58	907	7.133	+2
zirconium	Zr	40	91.22	1852	4377	6.506	+4
Element 104	(Rf)	104					
Element 105	(Ha)	105					
Element 106		106					
Element 107		107					
Element 109		109					

Periodic Table of the Elements

1 ← This numbering system is used by the International Union of Pure and Applied Chemistry (IUPAC)

Key: State — (S) 11 — Atomic number; 2-8-1 — Electrons in each energy level; **Na** — Element symbol; Sodium 22.990 — Average atomic mass

State
- (S) Solid
- (L) Liquid
- (G) Gas
- (N) Not found in nature

1 1A	2 2A	3 3B	4 4B	5 5B	6 6B	7 7B	8	9 8B	10	11 1B	12 2B	13 3A	14 4A	15 5A	16 6A	17 7A	18 0
(G) 1 **H** Hydrogen 1.0079 1																	(G) 2 **He** Helium 4.0026 2
(S) 3 **Li** Lithium 6.941 2-1	(S) 4 **Be** Beryllium 9.0122 2-2											(S) 5 **B** Boron 10.81 2-3	(S) 6 **C** Carbon 12.011 2-4	(G) 7 **N** Nitrogen 14.007 2-5	(G) 8 **O** Oxygen 15.999 2-6	(G) 9 **F** Fluorine 18.998 2-7	(G) 10 **Ne** Neon 20.179 2-8
(S) 11 **Na** Sodium 22.990 2-8-1	(S) 12 **Mg** Magnesium 24.305 2-8-2											(S) 13 **Al** Aluminum 26.982 2-8-3	(S) 14 **Si** Silicon 28.086 2-8-4	(S) 15 **P** Phosphorus 30.974 2-8-5	(S) 16 **S** Sulfur 32.06 2-8-6	(G) 17 **Cl** Chlorine 35.453 2-8-7	(G) 18 **Ar** Argon 39.948 2-8-8
(S) 19 **K** Potassium 39.098 2-8-8-1	(S) 20 **Ca** Calcium 40.08 2-8-8-2	(S) 21 **Sc** Scandium 44.956 2-8-9-2	(S) 22 **Ti** Titanium 47.90 2-8-10-2	(S) 23 **V** Vanadium 50.941 2-8-11-2	(S) 24 **Cr** Chromium 51.996 2-8-13-1	(S) 25 **Mn** Manganese 54.938 2-8-13-2	(S) 26 **Fe** Iron 55.847 2-8-14-2	(S) 27 **Co** Cobalt 58.933 2-8-15-2	(S) 28 **Ni** Nickel 58.71 2-8-16-2	(S) 29 **Cu** Copper 63.546 2-8-18-1	(S) 30 **Zn** Zinc 65.38 2-8-18-2	(S) 31 **Ga** Gallium 69.72 2-8-18-3	(S) 32 **Ge** Germanium 72.59 2-8-18-4	(S) 33 **As** Arsenic 74.922 2-8-18-5	(S) 34 **Se** Selenium 78.96 2-8-18-6	(L) 35 **Br** Bromine 79.904 2-8-18-7	(G) 36 **Kr** Krypton 83.80 2-8-18-8
(S) 37 **Rb** Rubidium 85.468 2-8-18-8-1	(S) 38 **Sr** Strontium 87.62 2-8-18-8-2	(S) 39 **Y** Yttrium 88.906 2-8-18-9-2	(S) 40 **Zr** Zirconium 91.22 2-8-18-10-2	(S) 41 **Nb** Niobium 92.906 2-8-18-12-1	(S) 42 **Mo** Molybdenum 95.94 2-8-18-13-1	(N) 43 **Tc** Technetium (97) 2-8-18-14-1	(S) 44 **Ru** Ruthenium 101.07 2-8-18-15-1	(S) 45 **Rh** Rhodium 102.91 2-8-18-16-1	(S) 46 **Pd** Palladium 106.4 2-8-18-18	(S) 47 **Ag** Silver 107.87 2-8-18-18-1	(S) 48 **Cd** Cadmium 112.41 2-8-18-18-2	(S) 49 **In** Indium 114.82 2-8-18-18-3	(S) 50 **Sn** Tin 118.69 2-8-18-18-4	(S) 51 **Sb** Antimony 121.75 2-8-18-18-5	(S) 52 **Te** Tellurium 127.60 2-8-18-18-6	(S) 53 **I** Iodine 126.90 2-8-18-18-7	(G) 54 **Xe** Xenon 131.30 2-8-18-18-8
(S) 55 **Cs** Cesium 132.91 2-8-18-18-8-1	(S) 56 **Ba** Barium 137.33 2-8-18-18-8-2	(S) 71 **Lu** Lutetium 174.97 2-8-18-32-9-2	(S) 72 **Hf** Hafnium 178.49 2-8-18-32-10-2	(S) 73 **Ta** Tantalum 180.95 2-8-18-32-11-2	(S) 74 **W** Tungsten 183.85 2-8-18-32-12-2	(S) 75 **Re** Rhenium 186.21 2-8-18-32-13-2	(S) 76 **Os** Osmium 190.2 2-8-18-32-14-2	(S) 77 **Ir** Iridium 192.22 2-8-18-32-15-2	(S) 78 **Pt** Platinum 195.09 2-8-18-32-17-1	(S) 79 **Au** Gold 196.97 2-8-18-32-18-1	(L) 80 **Hg** Mercury 200.59 2-8-18-32-18-2	(S) 81 **Tl** Thallium 204.37 2-8-18-32-18-3	(S) 82 **Pb** Lead 207.2 2-8-18-32-18-4	(S) 83 **Bi** Bismuth 208.98 2-8-18-32-18-5	(S) 84 **Po** Polonium (209) 2-8-18-32-18-6	(S) 85 **At** Astatine (210) 2-8-18-32-18-7	(G) 86 **Rn** Radon (222) 2-8-18-32-18-8
(S) 87 **Fr** Francium (223) 2-8-18-32-18-8-1	(S) 88 **Ra** Radium 226.03 2-8-18-32-18-8-2	(S) 103 **Lr** Lawrencium (260) 2-8-18-32-32-9-2	(N) 104 **Unq** (261) 2-8-18-32-32-10-2	(N) 105 **Unp** (262) 2-8-18-32-32-11-2	(N) 106 **Unh** (263) 2-8-18-32-32-12-2	(N) 107 **Uns** (264) 2-8-18-32-32-13-2	(N) 108 **Uno** (265) 2-8-18-32-32-14-2	(N) 109 **Une** (266) 2-8-18-32-32-15-2									

Lanthanide Series

(S) 57 **La** Lanthanum 138.91 2-8-18-18-9-2	(S) 58 **Ce** Cerium 140.12 2-8-18-20-8-2	(S) 59 **Pr** Praseodymium 140.91 2-8-18-21-8-2	(S) 60 **Nd** Neodymium 144.24 2-8-18-22-8-2	(N) 61 **Pm** Promethium (145) 2-8-18-23-8-2	(S) 62 **Sm** Samarium 150.4 2-8-18-24-8-2	(S) 63 **Eu** Europium 151.96 2-8-18-25-8-2	(S) 64 **Gd** Gadolinium 157.25 2-8-18-25-9-2	(S) 65 **Tb** Terbium 158.93 2-8-18-27-8-2	(S) 66 **Dy** Dysprosium 162.50 2-8-18-28-8-2	(S) 67 **Ho** Holmium 164.93 2-8-18-29-8-2	(S) 68 **Er** Erbium 167.26 2-8-18-30-8-2	(S) 69 **Tm** Thulium 168.93 2-8-18-31-8-2	(S) 70 **Yb** Ytterbium 173.04 2-8-18-32-8-2

Actinide Series

(S) 89 **Ac** Actinium (227) 2-8-18-32-18-9-2	(S) 90 **Th** Thorium 232.04 2-8-18-32-18-10-2	(S) 91 **Pa** Protactinium 231.04 2-8-18-32-20-9-2	(S) 92 **U** Uranium 238.03 2-8-18-32-21-9-2	(N) 93 **Np** Neptunium 237.05 2-8-18-32-22-9-2	(N) 94 **Pu** Plutonium (244) 2-8-18-32-24-8-2	(N) 95 **Am** Americium (243) 2-8-18-32-25-8-2	(N) 96 **Cm** Curium (247) 2-8-18-32-25-9-2	(N) 97 **Bk** Berkelium (247) 2-8-18-32-27-8-2	(N) 98 **Cf** Californium (251) 2-8-18-32-28-8-2	(N) 99 **Es** Einsteinium (254) 2-8-18-32-29-8-2	(N) 100 **Fm** Fermium (257) 2-8-18-32-30-8-2	(N) 101 **Md** Mendelevium (258) 2-8-18-32-31-8-2	(N) 102 **No** Nobelium (259) 2-8-18-32-32-8-2